Stories of Sports

Stories of Sports

Critical Literacy in Media Production, Consumption, and Dissemination

Edited by Katherin Garland,
Katie Shepherd Dredger, Crystal L. Beach,
and Cathy Leogrande

LEXINGTON BOOKS
Lanham • Boulder • New York • London

Published by Lexington Books
An imprint of The Rowman & Littlefield Publishing Group, Inc.
4501 Forbes Boulevard, Suite 200, Lanham, Maryland 20706
www.rowman.com

6 Tinworth Street, London SE11 5AL, United Kingdom

British Library Cataloguing in Publication Information Available

Library of Congress Cataloging-in-Publication Data

Names: Garland, Katherin, editor. | Dredger, Katie Shepherd, editor. |
    Beach, Crystal L., editor. | Leogrande, Cathy, editor.
Title: Stories of sports : critical literacy in media production, consumption,
    and dissemination / edited by Katherin Garland, Katie Shepherd Dredger,
    Crystal L. Beach and Cathy Leogrande.
Description: Lanham : Lexington Books, [2021] | Includes bibliographical
    references and index.
Identifiers: LCCN 2020057144 (print) | LCCN 2020057145 (ebook) |
    ISBN 9781793622228 (cloth) | ISBN 9781793622235 (epub)
    ISBN 9781793622242 (pbk)
Subjects: LCSH: Mass media and sports—United States. | Sports in popular
    culture—United States. | Sports—Social aspects—United States.
Classification: LCC GV742 .S86 2021 (print) | LCC GV742 (ebook) |
    DDC 306.4/83—dc23
LC record available at https://lccn.loc.gov/2020057144
LC ebook record available at https://lccn.loc.gov/2020057145

Contents

Foreword

I told my mom and dad I wanted to be a collegiate basketball player for Pat Summitt and the University of Tennessee when I was seven years old. In the six years after my declaration, I trained for thousands of hours, played in countless tournaments, represented the United States of America in the 2010 Youth Olympic Games, lost an Amateur Athletic Union (AAU) national championship, won three high school state championships and four AAU state championships, and at sixteen years old, I committed and accepted a full athletic scholarship to the University of Tennessee. I loved the game with my whole heart: I watched it, studied it, and kept up with leagues around the country through various sports media outlets as much as possible.

In my childhood mind, sports media painted an image of what I believed my future would look like at the University of Tennessee even more than my actual visits to campus did. Everything that I watched and read highlighted my future as an athlete: *I'm going to win with humility and lose with my head held high. I'm going to be so tired in class because of practice and traveling, but it will all be worth it. I'll have injuries, and I'll battle back from them. I'll travel the world with my teammates and form the best friendships with them. News articles will be written about my teammates and me and they will tell our stories.* Lucky for me, all of those things came true.

I had an incredible college career and am thankful for every single day during those four years that my seven-year-old dream became a reality. Games were won and lost. I visited almost every state in the country. I traveled the world, the Bahamas, Italy, and Brazil. I finished school with my bachelor's and master's degrees, with honors from both academic programs, so the exhaustion paid off. Injuries occurred and recoveries followed. And, of course, articles were written, and sports news reports were broadcasted. It was a dream come true. I could look back and think, "This is exactly what I imagined it to be," until one article, in 2014, was published: *Fourth-ranked Tennessee has suspended four players for academic reasons. Coach Holly Warlick said two players would miss one game and two would miss two games.*

> Warlick said Wednesday that . . . Andraya Carter would miss one game because (she) did "not live up to our academic standards."
>
> "We don't have a lot of rules," Warlick said. "You can't miss a class. You miss a class, you miss a game. You've got to sit in the first three rows. You can't be late. It's pretty black and white and simple. (Those are) our rules. If those types of rules, you don't abide by them, the consequence is right there." (Four Players Suspended, 2014)

Yes, I was suspended, and I did miss a game. However, I did not miss class. In fact, in the pursuit of two degrees as a college athlete, I never missed a class that wasn't due to travel, sickness, or surgery. This article hurt my heart, but it wasn't actually being suspended that troubled me the most. Don't get me wrong. I was devastated when I got suspended, but I knew I could recover from this minor mishap because as a kid I had read about athletes who were suspended and came back even stronger. I also saw athletes, who let their teams down by breaking team rules, come back as the "hero" in media headlines all the time. This article hurt my heart, mostly, because the reason *why* I was suspended wasn't true. I missed curfew on a Sunday night, but I was in class Monday morning. I wanted clarity. I wanted clarification. I wanted everyone to know I didn't actually miss class because of how much I valued my education.

My coach's words were taken from her interview, context wasn't given by the writer to give clarity to the actual reason for suspension, and a picture of me was painted that wasn't entirely true. The hardest part was I knew so many people would read this article and think it was completely accurate, just like I did as a young athlete aspiring to play in college any time I read or watched anything related to sports media.

My situation was minor. It was something that passed quickly; it was something that I recovered from. However, it's one of the many examples of how sports media can misrepresent reality and change public views of athletes. Growing up, I was *not* a critical consumer of sports stories. I was young and didn't know any better, but I learned that quotes are manipulated to tell a more convincing story from firsthand experience; once my eyes were opened, I recognized it often. Take these misleading headlines, for example:

> "Teammates say Johnny Manziel is a 'nightmare' in practice" (NBC Sports)— Manziel's teammates were praising him for his innate instincts and intangibles.

"Matt Ryan: Kyle Shanahan's Super Bowl calls were too slow" (AJC)—Ryan said outright that he was not discrediting his offensive coordinator.

"Tom Brady says his teammates should put 'politics aside' when it comes to visiting the White House" (USATodaySports)—Brady clearly said, "politics aside" before starting a statement about himself and not his teammates.

"Nick Saban blames USC for heated exchange between Alabama players" (For the Win/USAToday)—Saban explicitly said he was not critical of USC and put the responsibility on his own player.

"Oh, #MACtion: Ref tells Central Michigan cheerleaders not to distract Toledo" (Yahoo!Sports)—Cheerleaders were not being distracting, but instead breaking the rules by chanting snap-counts.

The truth in sports media as one can see, then, is as Oscar Wilde once said, "rarely pure and never simple."

How many people are there that never learn the importance of critical media literacy (CML) in the sports world and consider what they read to be a truth that may not exist? How many people fail to recognize when details are left out or quotes are reconstrued to create controversy for the sake of a "better story"? How many people have had their opinions of the sports world and "the way things should be" shaped by what they've seen on television or read about in articles? The answer is simple—too many.

Sports media has played and will continue to play an incredible role in our society. The widespread appeal of sports across the world has created an influential social institution out of what may have been genuine "fun and games" once upon a time; however, that social institution continues to perpetuate harmful stereotypes. For example, the significant role sports media has played in the reinforcement of stereotypical gender roles is clear:

"Curl power! Girls sweep their way to bronze as Britain equals its best ever Winter Olympics medal tally." (DailyMail)

"Wife of a Bears' lineman wins a bronze medal today in Rio Olympics." (Chicago Tribune)

"'Pebbles Flintstone': Latest Serena Williams outfit divides fans." (Yahoo!Sports)

"'Looks unreal': Tennis world erupts over Serena Williams' US Open outfit." (Yahoo!Sports)

"The female Michael Phelps: Triple-world record holder Katie Ledecky, 19, wins gold in 400m freestyle." (DailyMail)

The reality is that reinforcing stereotypical gender roles by negating female athletes' success with comparisons to men, reporting on their outfits, infantilization, and patronization is not the only way sports media influences our society. Headlines written and the stories that follow can create false narratives, support agendas, cater to privileged populations, manifest issues of equity and inequity, highlight social justice issues, break down or build barriers of intersectionality, and guide or misguide the opinions people have of others and sometimes even of themselves. The many ways sports media can be used, whether intentionally or by accident, as a critical tool in influencing modern society is why it must be dealt with carefully.

All media is created with a purpose. Specific words are chosen to create impact. Certain quotes are left out to support a story. I know this because I've experienced it, and I'm now fortunate enough to work in the sports media industry. I've been a reporter, an in-game analyst, and an in-studio analyst for ESPN, and it's a dream come true after a dream deferred when my playing days ended. I love my job so incredibly much, especially as it allows me to engage with the sport I will always love. Yet, before I even stepped in the industry, I knew I was walking into a world that was complex when I encountered comments like these:

> "You will be amazing on TV—you know the game plus you look great on camera."
> "We need more Black women represented on TV so I'm sure opportunities will be given to you."
> "Be prepared to lose opportunities to White men and women because I've seen it before."
> "Maybe don't cut all of your hair off before your first season on TV. You want to look . . . a certain way and appeal to . . . a particular audience. Once you have a name for yourself then you can change your looks."
> "Maybe choose pants that are a size too big, so they don't look too tight. Heels might not be the best idea either because they just give off a certain impression."
> "Are you going to be an openly gay woman in your career, or do you plan on keeping your relationship private?"

All of the comments, even though they didn't mean to, were reminders of the following: there *aren't* many openly gay women on TV besides the ones that expressed their sexuality after gaining fame; there are *more* White women than women of color; and there are *way more* White men than men of color and women of any race combined. So, is it a good thing that I am a woman of color starting in this field, or do I need to watch my back to make sure I am getting what I deserve? Can I tell stories that I want to tell without seeming biased or missing the "main audience"? Am I really not supposed to wear clothes that are appropriate, comfortable, and that I feel confident in because they might be too distracting for men? Who made these invisible, unwritten rules, and how long have they been around? I'm sure all the statements were told to me with the greatest intentions. Yet, every single comment—whether offhand or serious—came from a place of either experience or perception of the power structures and dynamics that have been in place in the world of sports media.

Nonetheless, we are making progress. We are seeing so much more diversity in every area represented on the TV screens or in print in the world of sports media. We are seeing athletes, analysts, reporters, and hosts be themselves, speak their truths, and stand up for what they genuinely believe. We are seeing a genuine fight for social justice blaze through the sports world, too. We are seeing content producers, writers, directors, and creators take more time to think about the narrative being told and the people being represented. An appreciation for integrity, inclusion, and diversity in the representation of athletes by the creators of sports media has grown over time. CML throughout the consumers of sports media is what has to follow.

Andraya N. Carter
SEC Network/ESPN Women's Basketball Color Analyst
University of Tennessee Women's Basketball Alumnus
MS, Kinesiology; BA, Communication Studies

Introduction

Katie Shepherd Dredger, Crystal L. Beach, Katherin Garland, and Cathy Leogrande

People tell stories in order to examine universal themes of what it is to be human and to better understand the way we shape power and privilege. With this point in mind, schools, and specifically the English language arts classroom, can be a contemporary place where students examine language and culture. While canonical texts may strive to teach readers about leadership and love, and fiction of the likes of Toni Morrison may examine joy in hard places and strength in adversity, students also need to work to make sense of the print they read and the media they watch in their lives. Words shape readers' emotions, and stories in cultural lore that examine realistic characters and authentic events have always been similar to stories that surround one of our nation's pastimes today—sport.

Athletic competitions permeate the fabric of our society. Within this tapestry come the stories of perseverance, thrilling comebacks, and painful losses, and also the larger stories of what is valued, whose stories get told, and why. English language arts classrooms, then, can be vibrant and necessary places where students respond to texts critically, and where the words of today's media can be discussed in safe places where language is relevant. For this reason, each chapter in this collection examines privilege and power in the way that sport is chronicled and consumed, specifically using the lens of critical media literacy (CML).

Garland gives a comprehensive review of CML and critically examines activism of Black athletes and how the media has silenced and subverted their social justice messages. Sheehy's chapter gives examples of the monetization of patriotism in Major League Baseball, and the ways that baseball and its stories have been used to manipulate viewers to conflate country and sport. Rodesiler et al. examine coach-athlete relationships in popular sports-related films. They call for a deeper critical reading of those relationships in order to offer more realistic, responsible, and diverse representation in future films. Fabrizi offers an examination of the mutual responsibility of artists and consumers concerning historical sport representations in popular culture. He encourages a critical examination of texts in order to further develop knowledge, agency, and empowerment for all. McGrail et al. explore the representation of youth with disabilities in the television program, *Friday Night Lights*, including quad rugby played by characters in the show. Scenes are analyzed for sociocultural attitudes, such as personal attributes of the (dis) abled athletes, the stereotypes of disability, and the impact of quad rugby on identity and relationships. Martin provides a critical examination of portrayals of individuals with type 1 diabetes in sports media coverage. She brings a deeply personal perspective as the parent of a young athlete with diabetes and discusses the lack of positive representations and the impact more accurate and empowering counternarratives could have on all members of society, especially youth and families living with this condition. Beach and Caraballo analyze a perspective in which language, action, and perception are seen as inseparable (or "languaging"). When used by sports reporters and commentators, this perspective reflects discourses of corporate, commercial agendas and highlights teams over individual players to attract and maintain fans and sponsors. Beach and Dredger examine ways language has been used to reduce female athletes to fashion symbols and objects of sexual attention. They advocate for using classrooms as places where all students can be encouraged to learn to critically analyze labels and generalizations as a way to dispel myths of sporty girls and tomboys while creating a space where all can see strength in what a body can do instead of serving as an ornament for the visual satisfaction of others. In the final chapter, Leogrande provides details about the three roles most often occupied by women in sports broadcasting in order to question how media messages from these spaces maintain and subvert the dominance of male sports broadcasters. She demonstrates how through the lens of CML, viewers can and should ask why women are seen more (or less) in certain sports and settings, how they compare to male colleagues in similar roles, and how the decisions about these spaces perpetuate dominant power structures.

This book is for secondary classroom teachers, youth coaches, critical media scholars, and for anyone who watches sports media and wonders whose stories are absent, which stories are skewed, and why. The authors ask who is getting paid and with what currency, how diverse audiences may respond, how emotions are manipulated in an audience, and the ways that stories reflect and amplify the best and worst of our societal values, especially concerning sports. All media are biased texts that perpetuate or challenge norms. Teaching consumers ways to critically read the world (Freire & Macedo, 1987), in both media and society, maybe one of the most important calls of our time. The ways in which we tell stories about sport are relevant, engaging, and authentic as we strive to bring the world into the classroom.

REFERENCES

Freire, P., & Macedo, D. (1987). *Literacy: Reading the word and the world.* South Hadley, MA: Bergin & Garvey.

Chapter 1

Using Critical Media Literacy Pedagogy to Analyze Colin Kaepernick's Athletic Activism

Katherin Garland

A BRIEF HISTORY OF BLACK PEOPLE
AND ATHLETIC ACTIVISM

Black athletes have had a history of expressing athletic activism to expose social justice issues. However, Black athletes who engage in athletic activism also have had a history of being reprimanded and blackballed from engaging in sport due to using their voice. Publicized and well-known examples include Muhammad Ali, who refused to fight in the Vietnam War and was subsequently exiled from boxing (Brown, 2018), as well as U.S. Olympians, Tommie Smith and John Carlos, who protested poverty and lynchings by removing their shoes, bowing their heads, and lifting one raised fist during the 1968 medal ceremony in Mexico City (Brown, 2017). Iconic media images have been etched in the American collective conscious as examples of how to use an athletic platform to raise awareness of injustice.

Though the results of basketball players Craig Hodges and Mahmoud Abdul-Rauf's activism were similar to Ali, Smith, and Carlos, in the 1990s, their stories were marginalized in the media. Hodges, who had a history of activism prior to becoming a professional athlete, saw his acquired NBA status as a platform for amplifying the voices of oppressed people. According to Hodges, he was blackballed after attempting to highlight the lack of Black NBA ownership and for providing President Bush with an eight-page letter outlining the conditions of youth in impoverished areas (Squadron, 2019). Conversely, Abdul-Rauf, former Denver Nuggets point guard, converted to Islam mid-season and began protesting the national anthem because he "viewed the American flag as a symbol of oppression and racism" and noted that "standing for the anthem would conflict with his Muslim faith"

(Washington, 2016). Shortly after going on the record with a reporter, Abdul-Rauf was suspended, fined, and suffered decreased playing time. Two years after his contract expired, no NBA team would hire him. Hodges and Abdul-Rauf were players who were at the beginning of their careers and the top of their games, and who after advocating for social justice issues, were ousted not only from their teams but also from the profession.

Decades later when Colin Kaepernick chose to sit, and later kneel during the national anthem, his actions were reminiscent of Ali, Smith, Carlos, Hodges, and Abdul-Rauf; however, media had changed significantly. Whereas journalists and cameramen were the primary ones documenting and reporting media narratives in the 1960s and 1990s, now social media provides sports fans everywhere with the ability to initiate, disseminate, and comment on news stories. The power of social media is exemplified with Kaepernick; his protest during the national anthem went unnoticed for two games, until a San Francisco 49ers fan tweeted an image of him (Coombs, Lambert, Cassilo, & Humphries, 2017).

After the 49ers next game against Green Bay, Kaepernick revealed that he was protesting "a country that oppresses black people and people of color" (Wyche, 2016). His dissent was focused on the police brutality of Black people, which continues to be a long-standing national conversation, but had been intensified by social media, particularly with the deaths of Michael Brown, Philandro Castile, and Alton Sterling. Kaepernick said that his activism was "bigger than football and it would be selfish on my part to look the other way" (Wyche, 2016). He chose to use his National Football League (NFL) privileged platform to raise awareness about a historically disenfranchised race with whom he identifies. When he eventually knelt during the national anthem, he was using his power within one hegemonic structure (football) to protest social injustice of another hegemonic structure (police brutality against unarmed Black people).

In some ways, social media provided a vehicle to both mute and supplant Kaepernick's message with patriotic discourse debates (Martin & McHendry, 2016). In other ways, social media and sports media conversations influenced what has been coined "The Kaepernick Effect" (McNeal, 2017, p. 148), which is the deliberate emulation of Kaepernick's actions of protest that extended into K-12 educational settings. Across the United States, K-12 students and athletes, including a six-year-old, took a knee during the "Pledge of Allegiance" to protest social injustice the same way Kaepernick had (Coleman, 2017; Schering, 2017; Tate, 2017). Students of all ages physically brought the conversation to their schools. However, instead of support, some students were met with consequences. The six-year-old student was criticized for not showing "loyalty and patriotism" (Tate, 2017), and high school football players in Houston were temporarily kicked off their team (Coleman, 2017).

The unique way that social media served as a tool for public discourse during Kaepernick's protest as well as the role this and other media played in engaging K-12 students in social activism warrants analysis. Furthermore, educators can benefit from pedagogy that can support classroom conversations which extend beyond social media discussions. For these reasons, critical media literacy (CML) pedagogy is optimal for this type of academic discourse. Therefore, this chapter differentiates between critical literacy pedagogy and CML pedagogy and demonstrates how attention to CML pedagogy can help to examine the role that traditional and social media played in Kaepernick's athletic activism and can serve as an example of demonstrating how media establish and perpetuate ideology about race, power, and capitalism.

Critical Literacy Pedagogy

Critical literacy pedagogy is rooted in critical theory, which was established by philosophers at the Frankfurt Institute for Social Research. Critical theory is built upon the idea that societal ideologies are not neutral; ideologies always espouse the messages of those who hold power in a society (Funk, Kellner, & Share, 2016; Hanks, 2020). Additionally, biased belief systems are intentionally communicated through specific media, which at the time when critical theory was developed included "film, radio, newspapers" (Funk et al., 2016, p. 4). Central to critical theory is *immanent critique*, an analysis of the ideologies of a society and how that society uses beliefs to advance and maintain control of a population (Critical Social Theory). Theorists used the process of immanent critique to "analyze how popular culture and the new tools of communication technology (e.g., film and radio) perpetuated ideology and social control" (Funk et al., 2016, p. 4).

Critical literacy pedagogy is an extension of critical theory, which positions schools as powerful institutions that use texts to indoctrinate dominant ideologies to students and teachers through passive methods of literacy education (Freire & Macedo, 1987). Critical literacy requires teachers and students to become actively engaged in their own literacy and is defined as "the capacity to analyse, critique and transform social, cultural, and political texts and contexts" (Freire, 1970 as cited by Luke, 2019, p. 354). In working with Brazilian citizens, Freire legitimized critical literacy as a method to liberate people in oppressed communities by teaching them to "read the word" as a way to "read the world" (Freire & Macedo, 1987). Critical literacy is based on the idea of teachers guiding students in critically analyzing relevant texts in new and different ways, so that students will develop "critical consciousness" that will shape and awaken new perspectives for understanding how to use texts in their personal lives (Freire, 1998, p. 36).

Critical literacy pedagogy is intended to lead students to action, or *praxis*, a sense of empowerment and confidence in students' abilities to change the social conditions of their communities (Freire, 1998). One way to encourage praxis is to embed critical literacy in students' academic and out-of-school literacy practices, where they are expected to not only critically analyze the role texts play in teaching about and controlling society but also produce texts that are transformative in some way (Funk et al., 2016; Hetrick et al., 2020; Vasquez, Janks, & Comber, 2019). Contemporary scholars advocate for using critical literacy with K-12 and postsecondary students (Funk et al., 2016; Hetrick et al., 2020; Kelly & Brower, 2017; Vasquez et al., 2019). Vasquez et al. suggest that when educators center texts important in students' lives and ask them to analyze them in relation to how messages perpetuate dominant beliefs, then it will support them in "making sense of sociopolitical aspects of life" and educate "them to become transformative meaning makers" (p. 307).

CML AND CML PEDAGOGY

By the 1980s, critical theorists included diverse scholars, such as women and people of color; consequently, they "urged that the concept of ideology be expanded to include representations of gender, race, and sexuality because media representations included sexist, racist and heterosexist (homophobic) images and narratives that reproduce ideologies of patriarchal, racist, and heterosexist domination" (Funk et al., 2016, p. 7). Subsequently, scholarship began to examine ways that educators could center media analysis focused on sociocultural issues with K-12 students (Alvermann, Moon, & Hagood, 1999; Morrell, 2004). Alvermann et al. were the first to use the term *critical media literacy* to describe creating intentional lessons that use popular culture texts relevant to students' lives to develop their critical consciousness. Specifically, findings from Alvermann's case study showed that eighth-grade students began to view female artists they valued as women whose CD covers embodied negative gender stereotypes. Likewise, Morrell's (2004) qualitative research, which was also centered on shaping students' critical views of texts, illustrated how pairing culturally relevant films with canonical novels helped students develop new perspectives about social justice issues and deepened understandings of their own social and cultural worlds.

While Alvermann et al.'s (1999) and Morrell's (2004) research studies were seminal in illustrating CML in academic settings, Kellner and Share (2007b) were the first to formally conceptualize CML and to foreground critical theory and critical literacy pedagogy in its definition:

Critical media literacy is an educational response that expands the notion of literacy to include different forms of mass communication, popular culture, and new technologies. It deepens the potential of literacy education to critically analyze relationships between media and audiences, information, and power. Along with this mainstream analysis, alternative media production empowers students to create their own messages that can challenge media texts and narratives. (p. 60)

In other words, CML begins with the premise that media are biased texts created to perpetuate societal ideologies. Similar to critical theory, with CML, it is necessary to analyze and evaluate media as a way to understand the meanings embedded in media texts. Like critical literacy pedagogy, it is imperative to teach students how to recognize the influence media has in teaching and maintaining views about social and cultural issues and to provide them with opportunities for producing their own meaningful media messages.

CML pedagogy is explicit instruction that can help students develop CML. Because the media teach about and influence society and culture, Kellner and Share (2005; 2007a; 2007b) have said that educators have a responsibility to teach K-12 students how to recognize and resist implicit media instruction. According to them, "critical media literacy involves cultivating skills in analysing media codes and conventions, abilities to criticize stereotypes, dominant values, and ideologies, and competencies to interpret the multiple meanings and messages generated by media texts" (Kellner & Share, 2005, p. 372). Thoman (1993) was one of the first to provide a framework called Five Core Concepts of Media Literacy that K-12 teachers could use as CML pedagogy in schools. Kellner and Share (2005) posited that Thoman's Five Core Concepts of Media Literacy was a structure that could support students' emerging critical media literacies.

The Five Core Concepts of Media Literacy were based on Thoman's (1993) suggestions for how to teach about media and have been summarized and shared for K-12 teachers' use in varied formats (Five Key Questions of Media Literacy, 2005; Jolls & Wilson, 2014; Kellner & Share, 2005). Thoman's addition to the framework, Five Key Questions, was created to better facilitate students' application of media analysis and evaluation (Jolls & Wilson, 2014). Together, the core concepts and questions help students to understand aspects of media, such as authorship, format, audience, content, and purpose, and to "navigate . . . media culture" (Five Key Questions of Media Literacy, 2005).

The Five Core Concepts of Media Literacy and the Five Key Questions are as follows:

1. Principle of Nontransparency: All media messages are "constructed." *Who created this message?*

2. Codes and Conventions: Media messages are constructed using a creative language with its own rules. *What creative techniques are used to attract my attention?*
3. Audience Decoding: Different people experience the same media message differently. *How might different people understand this message differently from me?*
4. Content and Messages: Media have embedded values and points of view. *What lifestyles, values, and points of view are represented in, or omitted from, this message?*
5. Motivation: Media are organized to gain profit and/or power. *Why is this message being sent?*

Funk et al. (2016) shared a modified version of the Center for Media Literacy's Five Core Concepts of Media Literacy and the Five Key Questions "with the goal of aligning these ideas from cultural studies with critical pedagogy" (p. 7). Funk et al.'s adaptations include six foci and questions that are more intentional and forthright in leading teachers and students toward the type of immanent critique with which critical theory began. In particular, concepts 4 and 5 address how purposeful media are in perpetuating biased ideology and concept 6 is concentrated on the idea that media are not neutral. Funk et al.'s concepts and questions provide teachers with CML pedagogy that can be used in formal school settings to support students' CML (table 1.1).

ADDITIONAL COMPONENTS OF CML PEDAGOGY

The CML Questions and Concepts (Funk et al., 2016) provide foundational ideas to guide teachers who want to use CML pedagogy; however, educators should also consider these three suggestions: (a) recognize and use media that reflect students' social and cultural worlds (Kesler, 2019; McArthur, 2019), (b) introduce mentor texts (Fabrizi & Ford, 2014; Heppeler & Manderino, 2018; McArthur, 2019), and (c) produce counternarratives as examples of transformative pedagogy (Funk et al., 2016; Kelly & Brower, 2017; Kesler, 2019; Saunders et al., 2017; Share, Mamikonyan, & Lopez, 2019; Vasquez et al., 2019).

Media, including popular culture, is seen as a pervasive and steady text in many adolescents' lives; therefore, educators should consider using media that are engaging and relevant to students. Studies showed that with the rise of digital technology, youth ages eight to eighteen, no matter their race or socioeconomic status, engage with screen media at higher rates each year (Rideout, Foehr, & Roberts, 2010; Roberts, Foehr, & Rideout, 2005; Roberts, Foehr, Rideout, & Brodie, 1999). Anderson and Jiang's (2018) findings

Table 1.1   Critical Media Literacy Questions and Concepts

Critical Media Literacy Concepts	*Critical Media Literacy Questions*
1. *Social Constructivism*: All information is co-constructed by individuals and/or groups of people who make choices within social contexts.	1. Who are all the possible people who made choices that helped create this text?
2. *Languages/Semiotics*: Each medium has its own language with specific grammar and semantics.	2. How was this text constructed and delivered/accessed?
3. *Audience/Positionality*: Individuals and groups understand media messages similarly and/or differently depending on multiple contextual factors.	3. How could this text be understood differently?
4. *Politics of Representation*: Media messages and the medium through which they travel always have a bias and support and/or challenge dominant hierarchies of power, privilege, and pleasure.	4. What values, points of view, and ideologies are represented or missing from this text or influenced by the medium?
5. *Production / Institutions*: All media texts have a purpose (often commercial or governmental) that is shaped by the creators and/or systems within which they operate.	5. Why was this text created and/or shared?
6. *Social Justice*: Media culture is a terrain of struggle that perpetuates or challenges positive and/or negative ideas about people, groups, and issues; it is never neutral.	6. Whom does this text advantage and/or disadvantage?

support former trend predictions and confirmed that "95% of teens now report they have a smartphone or access to one" and "45% of teens now say they are online on a near-consistent basis" (para. 2), primarily using social media sites, such as Snapchat, YouTube, and Instagram. Data (Matsa & Shearer, 2018) also indicate that 75 percent of "Snapchat's news consumers are ages 18–29" and "the majority of news consumers on Instagram are 'nonwhite'" (Demographics section, para.1). Statistically speaking, youth, who are contemporary K-12 students, are engaging with media in multiple formats regardless of their demographic.

Literacy scholars who study CML pedagogy practices have acknowledged data that report on youth's increased use of traditional and social media and have found that media can be used in a variety of socially and culturally relevant ways to support students' CML development. For example, Elmore and Coleman (2019) demonstrated how teaching middle school language arts students to critically read political memes often shared through social media can help them to better differentiate between positive and negative messaging. Fabrizi and Ford's (2014) research showed the importance of asking students to analyze multiple forms of media (e.g., song, film, and news article) as a way to question an artist's responsibility in conveying messages as fact. The Advanced Placement U.S. History students in Heppeler and Manderino's (2018) investigation evaluated how music and production influence a documentary's message; furthermore, these students learned to use documentary to develop historical arguments.

Another important aspect of CML pedagogy is introducing students to mentor texts. Traditionally, mentor texts are "pieces of literature that you—both teacher and student—can return to and reread for many different purposes. They are texts to be studied and imitated" (National Writing Project, 2013). Mentor texts are used to highlight textual characteristics and to exemplify specific genres and styles of writing. Studies focused on CML pedagogy have illustrated how several types of texts, including media, can also serve as mentor texts, depending on the academic activity. Students in Heppeler and Manderino's (2018) study viewed *13th*, a documentary about racial inequality, to understand how media include primary sources to produce historical arguments. Fabrizi and Ford (2014) asked students to read articles from famed sports journalists to typify the way athletes are portrayed in media. The students in McArthur's (2019) research used mentor texts, such as music videos, television, and film clips, to analyze sociohistorical stereotypes of Black women. In each of these studies, mentor texts are useful for demonstrating a pattern of how the media represent ideas about people prior to asking students to respond to ideology.

CML pedagogy is also intended to be transformative (Funk et al., 2016; Kellner & Share, 2007b). As a facet of critical literacy pedagogy, students are expected to use the CML they've developed to be social change agents (Freire, 1998; Vasquez et al., 2019). Therefore, a third and integral part of CML pedagogy is producing and sharing stories that counter mainstream ideology (Funk et al., 2016; Kesler, 2019). Providing students with the space, tools, and language for using their voice to effect change in their lives is essential for showing them how to counteract media messages (Funk et al., 2016; Kesler, 2019).

It is typical for counternarratives to be created and shared within a classroom. For example, after students conducted an historical analysis of how Black women have been negatively stereotyped in media, they wrote personal narratives to create positive stories about their own Black, female identities (McArthur, 2019). However, if counternarratives are intended to be texts that impact students' communities, they should be shared publicly. An early example of creating text for public influence is when students interviewed members of their communities and created digital narratives similar to radio documentaries to share with their local school board (Callahan, 2002). A more recent account of counternarrative demonstrated how teachers and students used Twitter, Tumblr, and Facebook to critically analyze and disagree with an invited guest speaker's message and intent (Saunders et al., 2017). With the use of hashtags and tagging, the conversation between the students, teachers, and guest speaker grew to be global. An international dialogue taught students how to engage in an authentic, responsible conversation in real time. Sharing counternarratives in public spaces is imperative because that is where different ideas can be presented and discussed to provoke thought.

COLIN KAEPERNICK'S ATHLETIC ACTIVISM AND CML PEDAGOGY

To analyze the role that traditional and social media played in Colin Kaepernick's athletic activism, the remainder of this chapter uses CML pedagogy based on Funk et al.'s (2016) CML Questions and Concepts and integrates the importance of mentor texts and counternarratives. Using CML pedagogy offers a perspective for understanding Kaepernick's social justice stance, the role media play in shifting and perpetuating specific messages away from his activism, and in what ways these actions demonstrate how media influence dominant sociocultural messages.

Social Constructivism

All information is co-constructed by individuals and/or groups of people who make choices within social contexts (Funk et al., 2016, p. 7). Social constructivism is considered foundational for understanding that media producers are co-constructing messages with other people. The question "Who are all the possible people who made choices that helped create this text?" requires students to question and investigate who is responsible for producing specific media. One way to highlight the idea of how media are socially constructed is to compare similar messages created about the same topic. In this case, comparing online sports websites, like nfl.com and espn.com, seems appropriate because they have similar objectives to report sports-related news.

Colin Kaepernick was first noticed protesting the national anthem during an August 26, 2016, preseason game; nfl.com and espn.com reported the story on August 27 and August 28, respectively (Wagoner & Associated Press, 2016; Wyche, 2016). Asking the question "Who are all the possible people who made choices that helped create this text?" may initially lead to superficial answers directed to each byline: Steve Wyche wrote the nfl.c om story and Nick Wagoner and the Associated Press created the espn.com one. However, answers shouldn't stop there. Students should be encouraged to research both sites as well as each journalist's background. For example, who owns each website and what is each company's motivation? Although nfl.com and espn.com may seem one in the same, they are owned by different corporations: nfl.com is owned by NFL Network and espn.com is owned by The Walt Disney Company, which yields differing perspectives on how and which facts are reported. Further student investigation should be conducted to begin comparing how each site reported Kaepernick's initial protest, with consideration to each affiliation and core stance on the topic. Students should also understand that writers work in concert with editors to produce a final article; rarely do writers produce material without others reading it prior to publication, which adds another layer to co-construction.

Another way to understand how media is socially constructed is to analyze the public conversation surrounding Kaepernick's protest. Unlike past approaches to athletic activism, Kaepernick's was unique because public conversation began with a football fan's tweet (Coombs, Lambert, Cassilo, & Humphries, 2017) and continued through social media. While the NFL and ESPN reported on Kaepernick's sideline activity, society voiced their opinions through varied memes, which quickly replaced his message of protesting police brutality. One meme implied that Kaepernick made too much money to protest and shifted his message to "refuses to stand for the anthem because he is 'oppressed.'" A second meme compared Kaepernick to a former San Francisco 49er's player, Glen Coffee, who left the NFL for a military career; asking "Who's the real hero?" sought to construct a view of Kaerpernick's social justice stance as antagonistic. Analyzing these or other memes (which can be found using a Google search) in addition to media, such as online sports reports, can serve to provide a holistic perspective of how media is used to co-construct messages.

Languages/Semiotics

Each medium has its own language with specific grammar and semantics (Funk et al., 2016, p. 7). The second concept is intended to teach the idea that not only all media are co-constructed but each one is also produced using specific guidelines. For example, a film uses angles and shots to convey a message, as opposed to a written article, which uses rhetorical strategies. Also, even within the same overarching genre of nonfiction, different types of articles (e.g., editorial, feature, news reports) follow different sets of rules set by industry standards. The question "How was this text constructed and delivered/accessed?" can be used as an opening question to prompt students' thinking; however, analyzing media codes and conventions may require a mini-lesson focused on technical aspects of the media being examined.

Using Wyche's (2016) and Wagoner et al.'s (2016) articles, students should understand that journalistic writing includes four basic parts: angle, introduction, quote, and attribution. Likewise, they should also learn about the rules for internet writing, which oftentimes include using shorter sentences and visual images. After identifying specific conventions, students may notice that the espn.com article includes several ways to attract attention that the nfl.com story does not. For example, there is a sidebar that leads to ESPN editorial links; Kaepernick's rationale for protesting is demonstrated as a block quote in bold letters, with his image next to it; quotes from differing points of view are embedded; and there are screenshots of another NFL player, Justin Pugh's Twitter feed, highlighting his own patriotism and respect for the American flag (Wagoner et al., 2016) (figure 1.1; figure 1.2).

According to Kellner and Share (2005), "a goal of cultivating media literacy is to help students distinguish connotation and denotation" (p. 374). For example, students should spend time examining how an article's images represent and augment literal published words. Follow-up questions, such as "Why would espn.com include additional conventions for their article?" or "How could espn.com's additions impact readers' opinions?", can shape students' perspectives of the differences between explicit and implicit media meanings, and consequently, awareness of how the media can shape ideas and dialogue.

It is equally important to ask the question "How was this text constructed and delivered/accessed?" when discussing language and semiotics used with memes. Memes are typically viewed on social media and in less time than an online article, and as Elmore and Coleman (2019) explained, students benefit from taking the time to read and reread how these types of media messages are created. In the first meme, it's important to notice if words are capitalized,

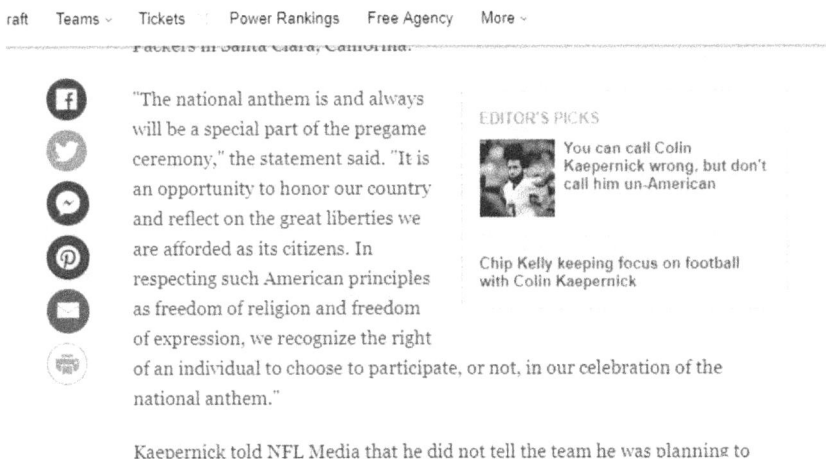

Figure 1.1 Editorial Links from ESPN Article. *Source*: Screenshot taken from Wyche (2016).

> **"I am not going to stand up to show pride in a flag for a country that oppresses black people and people of color. To me, this is bigger than football and it would be selfish on my part to look the other way."**
>
> 49ers quarterback Colin Kaepernick, on his decision to sit during the national anthem

Kaepernick also did not stand for the national anthem during the other preseason games, but he wasn't dressed for those contests because of tightness in his right shoulder.

NFL spokesman Brian McCarthy said Saturday that "players are encouraged but

Figure 1.2   Block Quote from ESPN Article. *Source*: Screenshot taken from Wyche (2016).

what colors are used, and why. To emphasize connotation and denotation (Kellner & Share, 2005), students should question why *oppression* is written with single quotation marks. Similar observations about how words are used to convey messages can be made with the second meme, where the words "stands for oppression" are also in quotation marks.

Follow-up questions centered on language and semiotic analysis can be combined with the idea of social constructivism to provide a recursive process to support and understand how media perpetuate ideology. Together, students should begin to develop an opinion about how ESPN created meaning by juxtaposing a White NFL player's "patriotic" tweets with Kaepernick's quote about *not* standing during the national anthem and how memes further advanced alternate messages through images and texts that convey an opinion.

Audience/Positionality

Individuals and groups understand media messages similarly and/or differently depending on multiple contextual factors (Funk et al., 2016, p. 7). With audience/positionality, students are expected to acknowledge their own and others' media interpretations. Prior to social media, classroom dialogue may have included reflecting on personal interpretations and comparing them with classmates. Currently, social media serve as a repository of data. To answer the question "How could this text be understood differently?" students can either search for other Colin Kaepernick memes or examine a hashtag. They can mimic researchers and collect artifact data from Twitter to conduct a textual analysis of #colinkaepernick. Thematic grouping of data will show that although viewers sometimes observed the same event and heard Kaepernick's rationale for protesting via some form of media, there were varied interpretations of what his athletic activism meant to individuals or groups of people.

Martin and McHendry's (2016) rhetorical analysis of the dialogue centered on Kaepernick's patriotism illustrated three overarching public opinions: (1) Americans have the right to not stand during patriotic events; (2) Americans who do not stand for patriotic events are not honoring the flag, country, or military; and (3) Americans have the right to not stand during patriotic events, but I wouldn't do that. However, many responses are racially divided, with some Black people and other people of color agreeing with the first and third statements and some White Americans subscribing to the second point of view (Boyce, 2017). Part of the objective of CML is to examine how "different subject positions, like gender, race, class, or sexuality will also produce different readings" (Kellner & Share, 2005, p. 376). To highlight the cultural differences that may be found in social media comments, students can conduct an historical media analysis of the conversations that have surrounded other Black activist athletes, such as Jack Johnson or Muhammad Ali (Boyce, 2017). Noting these reactions may provide an understanding of how patterns of media conversation have influenced American culture throughout history and impacted each athlete's activism and role in sports.

Politics of Representation

Media messages and the medium through which they travel always have a bias and support and/or challenge dominant hierarchies of power, privilege, and pleasure (Funk et al., 2016, p. 7). The fourth concept and its associated question, "What values, points of view, and ideologies are represented or missing from this text or influenced by the medium?," is designed to highlight the media's biased messages, which are always based on specific perspectives. An historical examination of the consequences that Black athletes have faced when they choose to use their voice as a platform is necessary to recognize a long-standing bias against Black people who take part in athletic activism. To underscore the politics of representation, mentor texts, such as articles or documentaries that describe the circumstances surrounding Black athletic activists, during different time periods, and within different sports, can be used to scaffold a sociohistorical interpretation of the consequence that athletes, who identify as Black, face when they become activists.

Next, students can return to Kaepernick's protest of the national anthem versus how his actions were discussed online. A textual analysis of Wyche's (2016) NFL article exemplifies the ways that media perpetuate values. In this article, the NFL seems to distance itself from Kaepernick's message. In the first paragraph, Wyche writes that the former quarterback "has willingly immersed himself into controversy." By the fourth paragraph Wyche reports the 49ers statement that "the national anthem is and always will be a special part of the pre-game ceremony" and that "in respecting such American principles as freedom of religion and freedom of expression, we recognize the right of an individual to choose and participate, or not, in our celebration of the national anthem." The article continues with a quote from the 49ers coach reiterating Kaepernick's right as a citizen to do what he wants. Asking students to carefully reread Wyche's article may support them in noticing these details and formulating an opinion about nfl.com's message and subsequent values. What is the NFL saying about Kaepernick and his protest? What message about the NFL does nfl.com want the reader to conclude? These questions can help students reveal structures of control and power within society and how media frame messages to perpetuate that control.

Production/Institutions

All media texts have a purpose (often commercial or governmental) that is shaped by the creators and/or systems within which they operate (Funk et al., 2016, p. 7). The fifth concept is intended to create student awareness that show media control and power. A conversation centered on current media monopolization can create this type of cognizance. Having students read an article, like Vinton's (2016) "These 15 billionaires own America's news media companies" and pairing it with Ritholtz's (2012) infographics that reveal which television, news, radio, and movies six media companies own can pique their interests and reveal the extent of how American viewership is regulated and by whom. However, to add depth to this concept and to support students' connections for what media motivation means for content and messaging, they should be encouraged to examine media ownership and how it is aligned with specific messages.

As previously mentioned, nfl.com is owned by NFL Network, which is owned by the NFL and is a part of NFL Media. Ownership is oftentimes tied to media content and messaging. When a company owns a network, for example, they are able to monitor what is viewed and heard, thus controlling an overall message. More student research can reveal how ownership and media content are inextricably linked. According to cbssports.com (Dubin, 2015), "the Department of Defense has paid 14 different NFL teams a total of $5.4 million over the last four years in exchange for patriotic displays at games" (para. 1). Events included "military flyovers, flag unfurlings, emotional color guard ceremonies, enlistment campaigns . . . and national anthem performances" (Schmitz, 2017, para. 6). Although the 49ers are not reported as receiving money for such endeavors, students should be asked to reevaluate how language and semiotics (concept 2) are linked to content and messages, which many times reflect ownership. What is Wyche's message and how is it aligned with the NFL's values? How can media ownership influence media content and subsequently shape society's cultural values?

Social Justice

Media culture is a terrain of struggle that perpetuates or challenges positive and/or negative ideas about people, groups, and issues; it is never neutral (Funk et al., 2016, p. 8). The premise of the final concept is to emphasize that media are never neutral. Even if the message is positive, there is media bias which advances ideology. The question "Whom does this text advantage or disadvantage?" encourages students to comprehensively reflect on media messages. To examine how media implicitly and explicitly convey messages about ideas, people, and issues to advance an agenda, students should research two newly created NFL-related social justice organizations, Players Coalition and Inspire Change, and view and analyze a Players Coalition advertisement within the context of Kaepernick's 2016 advocacy against police brutality of unarmed Black people.

In 2019 (three years after Kaepernick's protest), the NFL "announced the launch of the *Inspire Change* platform, showcasing the collaborative efforts of players, owners and the league to create positive change in communities across the country" (NFL Launches Inspire, 2019). Inspire Change has three goals: (a) education and economic advancement, (b) police and community relations, and (c) criminal justice reform. The NFL website encourages readers to visit the Inspire Change website for more information about their social justice grants and goals and to use the hashtag "#InspireChange."

January 2020, Anquan Boldin (a former 49ers player) tweeted an advertisement centered on his experiences with police brutality. The video uses re-created scenes from the night Boldin's cousin was shot by a plainclothes police officer and video from his family's news press. During the commercial, Boldin explains that he cofounded the Players Coalition (an organization that works with Inspire Change) to "focus on police-community relations," among other social justice issues. In the advertisement, Boldin also says, "There are some things that are bigger than football" (Boldin, 2020), a quote similar to one Kaepernick used when he went on record and said his activism was "bigger than football" (Wyche, 2016). The commercial was re-aired a month later during Super Bowl LIV.

Prior to asking "Whom does this text advantage or disadvantage?," students should consider what implicit and explicit messages the advertisement conveys about the NFL, NFL players, protesting, social justice issues, police brutality, and Colin Kaepernick. Further analysis should include interpretations of how the preceding five critical media concepts are interrelated and create a message about specific ideas, people, or issues. For example, who are all the possible people who created the Players Coalition video? Who wrote Boldin's voice-over? How are music, video, images, and voice-overs used to create a message about Black people who are murdered by police? Why did Boldin's voice-over partially quote Kaepernick but not assign attribution? What is the NFL's agenda? Why was this video created and shared by Boldin via Twitter or by the NFL during the Super Bowl? What message is the NFL sending about how NFL players can support social justice issues? After in-depth analysis of the Players Coalition video, then students can determine who the text advantages or disadvantages.

Table 1.2 provides an outline of sample questions to ask students as they become more critically media literate.

Producing Counternarratives

Counternarratives are student-produced texts that offer alternative perspectives of a person, issue, or idea. With CML pedagogy, multiple types of texts, such as media, should be an option for students to produce. To begin, teachers should help students determine what person, issue, or idea they are countering. For example, student athletes may want to offer a narrative for athletic activism as a citizen's right and as a form of peaceful protest. Others may want to produce a positive response to Kaepernick's activism, thus countering social media stories that were propagated. Because CML pedagogy is not a top-down approach, it is also important to listen to and support students' independently developed ideas.

Once students have a plan, it is integral to work with them to select an appropriate text. Will the student athlete share a written opinion via the school's blog or online newspaper? Perhaps that same student will create statement T-shirts that their teammates can wear on game day. If students are creating counternarratives of social media messages, carefully creating a meme with a social justice message and sharing it via Snapchat, Instagram, or Twitter may be appropriate. No matter the concept, students should be offered the opportunity to use their voice and the CML they've acquired to change their communities, on- and offline.

CONCLUSION

Colin Kaepernick's social justice protest is an ideal issue for students to critically analyze because it set a precedence for Black athletic activism. A

Table 1.2 Sample Questions for Kaepernick Analysis Based on Critical Media Literacy Questions and Concepts

Critical Media Literacy Concepts	Critical Media Literacy Questions	Sample Questions for Kaepernick Analysis
1. *Social Constructivism*: All information is co-constructed by individuals and/or groups of people who make choices within social contexts.	Who are all the possible people who made choices that helped create this text?	Who created the nfl.com and espn.com sites? What is each site's message? How did memes co-construct ideas about Kaepernick's protest?
2. *Languages/Semiotics*: Each medium has its own language with specific grammar and semantics.	How was this text constructed and delivered/accessed?	What rules for internet writing are used? Why would espn.com include additional conventions? What are the rules for meme production? How are images and words used connotatively?
3. *Audience/Positionality*: Individuals and groups understand media messages similarly and/or differently depending on multiple contextual factors.	How could this text be understood differently?	How have different groups of people responded with #colinkaepernick? How do these responses differ culturally (e.g., race, gender, region)? How have memes shown divided responses to Kaepernick's message?
4. *Politics of Representation*: Media messages and the medium through which they travel always have a bias and support and/or challenge dominant hierarchies of power, privilege, and pleasure.	What values, points of view, and ideologies are represented or missing from this text or influenced by the medium?	What message about the NFL does nfl.com want the reader to conclude? What messages about patriotism, kneeling during the national anthem, does media want to reflect? What has been the consequence (historically) for Black athletes who use their platform to advocate for social justice issues?
5. *Production/Institutions*: All media texts have a purpose (often commercial or governmental) that is shaped by the creators and/or systems within which they operate.	Why was this text created and/or shared?	What are the six media companies? What media do the six media companies own? Who owns Players Coalition? Who owns Inspire Change? Why was the Players Coalition video created and shared?
6. *Social Justice*: Media culture is a terrain of struggle that perpetuates or challenges positive and/or negative ideas about people, groups, and issues; it is never neutral.	Whom does this text advantage and/or disadvantage?	Who benefits or doesn't benefit from this text?

football fan tweeting Kaepernick's protest and prompting reporters to add it to the news cycle, which caused society to share opinions via social media, added a new dimension to how news is reported and shaped. When the ubiquity of youths' engagement with smartphones and media is added, then the need for a pedagogy that questions media intentions is warranted. The theory and sample questions provided here are intended to support students in developing an awareness of how the media initiate and frame sociocultural views and to foster students' CML as they become active participants in media engagement and society at large.

REFERENCES

Alvermann, D. E., Moon, J. S., & Hagood, M. C. (1999). *Popular Culture in the Classroom: Teaching and Researching Critical Media Literacy.* New York, NY: Routledge.

Anderson, M., & Jiang, J. (2018). Teens, social media & technology 2018. *Pew Research Center, 31,* 2018.

Boldin, A. (2020, January 19). There are some things just bigger than football. *#InspireChange* [Twitter moment]. Retrieved from https://twitter.com/Anqua nBoldin/status/1218996416019697665.

Boyce, T. (2017). Putting learning into practice: Integrating social media, crowd learning, and #ColinKaepernick in an introductory African American history class. *Radical Teacher, 109*(1), 21–28.

Brown, D. L. (2017). They didn't #taketheknee: The Black power protest salute that shook the world in 1968. *The Washington Post.* Retrieved from https://www.was hingtonpost.com/news/retropolis/wp/2017/09/24/they-didnt-takeaknee-the-black -power-protest-salute-that-shook-the-world-in-1968/?utm_term=.41533b567ec4.

Brown, D. L. (2018, June 16). "Shoot them for what?" How Muhammad Ali won his greatest fight. *The Washington Post.* Retrieved from: https://www.washingtonpos t.com/news/retropolis/wp/2018/06/15/shoot-them-for-what-how-muhammad-ali -won-his-greatest-fight/?noredirect=on&utm_term=.af363abb6c82.

Callahan, M. (2002). Intertextual composition: The power of the digital pen. *English Education, 35*(1), 46–65.

Coleman, A. (2017, September 30). Local high school football players kicked off team after protest during anthem. *Houston Chronicle.* Retrieved from https://www .chron.com/sports/highschool/article/High-school-football-kicked-off-team-anthe m-kneel-12242713.php.

Coombs, D. S., Lambert, C. A., Cassilo, D., & Humphries, Z. (2017, March). Kap takes a knee: A media framing analysis of Colin Kaepernick's anthem protest. *20th International Public Relations Research Conference,* 48–62. Retrieved from: https ://www.instituteforpr.org//wp-content/uploads/IPRRC20-proceedings_Final.pdf.

Dubin, J. (2015, May 11). US defense department paid 14 NFL teams $5.4M to honor soldiers. *CBS Sports.* Retrieved from https://www.cbssports.com/nfl/news/us-de fense-department-paid-14-nfl-teams-54m-to-honor-soldiers/.

Fabrizi, M. A., & Ford, R. D. (2014). Sports stories and critical media literacy. *English Journal*, *104*, 42–47.

Fatal Force. (2020, January 20). *The Washington Post*. Retrieved from https://www .washingtonpost.com/graphics/national/police-shootings-2016/.

Five Key Questions of Media Literacy. (2005). Retrieved from: http://www.medialit. org/sites/default/files/14B_CCKQPoster+5essays.pdf.

Freire, P. (1998). *Pedagogy of Freedom*. Lanham, MD: Rowman & Littlefield.

Freire, P., & Macedo, D. (2005). *Literacy: Reading the Word and the World*. Routledge.

Funk, S., Kellner, D., & Share, J. (2016). Critical media literacy as transformative pedagogy. In M. N. Yildiz & J. Keengwe (Eds.), *Handbook of Research on Media Literacy in the Digital Age* (pp. 1–30). Hershey, PA: IGI Global.

Hanks, J. C., (2020). Critical social theory. *Encyclopedia of Science, Technology, and Ethics*. Retrieved from https://www.encyclopedia.com/science/encyclopedias-alma nacs-transcripts-and-maps/critical-social-theory.

Has a Ten Million Dollars Net Worth [Digital Image]. (2016). Retrieved from https ://www.memesmonkey.com/topic/colin+kaepernick+national+anthem#&gid=1&p id=2.

Heppeler, J., & Manderino, M. (2018). Critical media literacy in the disciplines: Using 13th to support historical argumentation. *Journal of Adolescent & Adult Literacy*, *61*(5), 567–571.

Hetrick, C., Wilson, C. M., Reece, E., & Hanna, M. O. (2020). Organizing for urban education in the new public square: Using social media to advance critical literacy and activism. *The Urban Review*, *52*(1), 26–46.

Jolls, T., & Wilson, C. (2014). The core concepts: Fundamental to media literacy yesterday, today and tomorrow. *Journal of Media Literacy Education*, *6*(2), 68–78.

Kellner, D., & Share, J. (2005). Toward critical media literacy: Core concepts, debates, organizations, and policy. *Discourse: Studies in the Cultural Politics of Education*, *26*(3), 369–386.

Kellner, D., & Share, J. (2007a). Critical media literacy, democracy, and the reconstruction of education. In D. Macedo & S. R. Steinberg (Eds.), *Media Literacy: A Reader* (pp. 3–23). New York, NY: Peter Lang.

Kellner, D., & Share, J. (2007b). Critical media literacy is not an option. *Learning inquiry*, *1*(1), 59–69.

Kelly, C., & Brower, C. (2017). Making meaning through media: Scaffolding academic and critical media literacy with texts about schooling. *Journal of Adolescent & Adult Literacy*, *60*(6), 655–666.

Kesler, T. (2019). Critical pedagogy. In R. Hobbs & P. Mihailidis (Eds.), *The International Encyclopedia of Media Literacy* (pp. 1–10). Hoboken, NJ: Wiley-Blackwell.

Luke, A. (2019). Regrounding critical literacy: Representation, facts and reality. In D. E. Alvermann, N. J. Unrau, M. Sailors, & R. B. Ruddell (Eds.), *Theoretical Models and Processes of Literacy* (7th ed., pp. 349–361). New York, NY: Routledge.

Martin, S., & McHendry, G. F., Jr. (2016). Kaepernick's stand: Patriotism, protest, and professional sports. *Journal of Contemporary Rhetoric*, *6*(3/4), 88–98.

Matsa, K. E., & Shearer, E. (2018, September 10). News use across social media platforms 2018 *Pew Research Center: Journalism and Media*. Retrieved from: https://www.journalism.org/2018/09/10/news-use-across-social-media-platforms-2018/.

McArthur, S. A. (2019). Centering student identities in critical media literacy instruction. *Journal of Adolescent & Adult Literacy, 62*(6), 686–689.

McNeal, L. R. (2017). From hoodies to kneeling during the national anthem: The Colin Kaepernick effect and its implications for K-12 sports. *Louisiana Law Review, 78*, 145–198. Retrieved from https://digitalcommons.law.lsu.edu/lalrev/vol78/iss1/8.

Morrell, E. (2004). *Linking Literacy and Popular Culture: Finding Connections for Lifelong Learning*. Norwood, MA: Christopher Gordon-Publishers, Inc.

NFL Launches Inspire Change Social Justice Platform. (2019, January 11). Retrieved from https://operations.nfl.com/updates/football-ops/nfl-launches-inspire-change-social-justice-platform/.

National Writing Project. (2013, March 28). Reading, writing, and mentor texts: Imagining possibilities. [Audio podcast]. Retrieved from https://archive.nwp.org/cs/public/print/resource/4090.

Rideout, V. J., Foehr, U. G., & Roberts, D. F. (2010). *Generation M2 media in the lives of 8– to 18–year-olds: A Kaiser Family Foundation study*. Retrieved from http://kff.org/other/event/generation-m2-media-in-the-lives-of/.

Ritholtz, B. (2012, July 16). Media consolidation: The illusion of choice. *The Big Picture*. Retrieved from https://ritholtz.com/2012/07/media-consolidation-the-illusion-of-choice-2/.

Roberts, D. F., Foehr, U. G., & Rideout, V. J. (2005). *Generation M media in the lives of 8-18 year-olds: A Kaiser Family Foundation study*. Retrieved from http://kff.org/other/event/generation-m-media-in-the-lives-of/.

Roberts, D. F., Foehr, U. G., Rideout, V. J., & Brodie, M. (1999). *Kids & Media at the New Millennium*. Menlo Park, CA: Kaiser Family Foundation.

Saunders, J. M., Ash, G. E., Salazar, I., Pruitt, R., Wallach, D., Breed, E., . . . Szachacz, A. (2017). "We're already somebody": High school students practicing critical media literacy IRL (in real life). *Journal of Adolescent & Adult Literacy, 60*(5), 515–526.

Schering, S. (2017, September 29). Oak Park River Forest players, band members kneel during anthem. *Chicago Tribune*. Retrieved from https://www.chicagotribune.com/suburbs/oak-park/news/ct-oak-park-football-anthem-protest-tl-1005-20170929-story.html.

Schmitz, M. (2017, September 25). How the NFL sold patriotism to the U.S. military for millions. *Think Progress*. Retrieved from https://thinkprogress.org/nfl-dod-national-anthem-6f682cebc7cd/.

Share, J., Mamikonyan, T., & Lopez, E. (2019). Critical media literacy in teacher education, theory, and practice. *Oxford Research Encyclopedia of Education*. Retrieved from https://oxfordre.com/education/view/10.1093/acrefore/9780190264093.001.0001/acrefore-9780190264093-e-1404.

Squadron, A. (2019, April 11). Former Chicago Bull Craig Hodges tells his story, opens up about NBA activism. *Slam*. Retrieved from https://www.slamonline.com /nba/craig-hodges-story/.

Tate, A. S. (2017, October 9). Children taking a knee to protest in school: What are their rights? *Today*. Retrieved from https://www.today.com/parents/children-t aking-knee-school-what-are-their-rights-t117028.

Thoman, E. (1993). Skills and strategies for media education. *Center for Media Literacy*. Retrieved from http://www.medialit.org/reading-room/skills-strategies-med ia-education.

Vasquez, V. M., Janks, H., & Comber, B. (2019). Critical literacy as a way of being and doing. *Language Arts*, *96*(5), 300–311.

Vinton, K. (2016, June 1). These 15 billionaires own America's news media companies. *Forbes*. Retrieved from https://www.forbes.com/sites/katevinton/2016/06/01/ these-15-billionaires-own-americas-news-media-companies/#5d6815e8660a.

Wagoner, A., & Associated Press. (2016, August 27). Colin Kaepernick protests anthem over treatment of minorities. *ESPN*. Retrieved from http://www.espn.com/ nfl/story/_/id/17401815/colin-kaepernick-san-francisco-49ers-sits-national-anthe m-prior-preseason-game.

Washington, J. (2016, September 1). Still no anthem, still no regrets for Mahmoud Abdul-Rauf. *The Undefeated*. Retrieved from https://theundefeated.com/features/ abdul-rauf-doesnt-regret-sitting-out-national-anthem/.

Who's the Real Hero? [Digital Image]. (2016) Retrieved from https://www.mem esmonkey.com/topic/colin+kaepernick+national+anthem#&gid=1&pid=3.

Wyche, S. (2016). Colin Kaepernick explains why he sat during national anthem. *NFL*. Retrieved from http://www.nfl.com/news/story/0ap3000000691077/article/ colin-kaepernick-explains-why-he-sat-during-national-anthem.

Chapter 2

Selling Patriotism On and Off the Field

Media Connections between Baseball, the Military, and the Government

Brian Sheehy

Baseball is called the national pastime and it has always been closely tied to American history. Baseball-related media materials that portrayed a connection with government policy have been prominent since the Civil War. One of the first political cartoons depicting baseball was a Currier and Ives print entitled "The national game: Three 'outs' and one 'run'" (Mauer, 1860). In this print, the 1860 presidential campaign is portrayed as a baseball game in which Lincoln stands at home plate after defeating John Bell, Stephen A. Douglas, and John C. Breckinridge. Since that time, this symbiotic relationship between baseball, government, and media has worked to present a particular view of America. Over the years, the game was used to promote a picture of what an ideal American maybe. While fans may not notice these subtle messages, critical media literacy (CML) skills help examine ways in which the production and dissemination of sports communication are controlled and constructed to present and maintain dominant ideologies. Specific aspects of apparently neutral images, sounds, and merchandise carry deeper, and sometimes troubling, messages. These media constructions may be seen as objective, yet they carry the weight of social norms and values that foster business and government agendas. This chapter will focus on the way baseball and the government have joined together to foster a narrow definition of patriotism during World War I, World War II, and post 9/11. Examples illustrate how baseball-related media texts are constructed to shape beliefs and behaviors with regard to political ideologies, especially in times of war and political unrest.

CML: A FRAMEWORK FOR INQUIRY

Media is more ubiquitous than ever, especially in relation to sports. Network and cable television channels, talk radio, and social networking are a few formats through which baseball is readily accessible to all individuals. While other media may carry more overt messages, sports-related media can appear impartial and merely entertainment focused. Some claim that sports are and should be apolitical (Fry, 2019; Hsu, 2018; Syrios, 2017). Others recognize that this has never been the case and it is time to "puncture the apolitical facade that hangs over sports like an expensive hermetically sealed dome that hovers over professional sports" (Rosenberg, 2016). Through CML pedagogy, educators can help students become active agents who can question the sports media messages they consume daily (Fabrizi & Ford, 2014; Fortuna, 2015).

CML is more than a series of skills designed to help students deconstruct the components of media. It is a practical pedagogy that can help expose the deeper messages within items and events in order for consumers to thoughtfully consider what they are seeing and hearing, how it makes them feel, and how it shapes their beliefs and behaviors (Alvermann & Hagood, 2000; Harshman, 2017; Redmond, 2012). CML educators guide students to unveil the underlying myths and recognize "the role media play in maintaining hegemony and oppression" (Kellner & Share, 2019, p. 12). Insight and recognition is only the first step; the goal is to challenge the dominant narratives, expose their limitations, and create alternatives. For too long, sports have purported to be a safe haven, posing as a form of entertainment free from the influence of politics. CML provides a theoretical framework to create "socially active and thoughtful citizens" (Feliciano Ortiz, 2012, p. 61).

Baseball is ripe for examination using CML. It is comprised of many popular culture texts, including the game itself, the play-by-play and interviews, highlights on sports studio shows, news coverage, and advertisements. These texts have the power to persuade and "reinforce taken for granted beliefs and behaviors" (Seelow, 2018, p. 8). Throughout American history, baseball has been part of the fabric of the country. Media and baseball worked together to present a wholesome view of America summed up in the jingle "baseball, hot dogs, apple pie and Chevrolet" (Rummel, 2016). Using CML to review historical, as well as contemporary images and events, students can discover that "it is at the level of apparently innocent description that the most profound choices are being made" (Morganthaler, 2010). By studying the ideology underpinning media messages, audiences learn to recognize embedded values that often reproduce the biases and ideologies of the producers as well as those who finance the productions. It is not just a game. Fans must recognize that "from traditional governmental politics to politics of identity and economy, sport cannot, and should not, be separated from the ideological work that it does" (Feliciano Ortiz, 2012, p. 26). What is accepted as "normal" is the result of ideas which have been "produced and disseminated through a dominant frame of thought, expressed in powerful master narratives" (Kellner & Share, 2019, p. 17). Messages can take the form of everything from a song to a T-shirt and still have power to influence. All of these messages can be analyzed using CML concepts and questions.

Baseball is a sport and an industry that is media rich. Broadcasts, print materials, and rituals at the ballpark present a unique challenge with regard to CML. CML can be used to effectively analyze materials from baseball's past, such as posters, newspapers and magazines, songbooks, programs, postcards, and a variety of other media. These media constructions may be seemingly objective, dismissed as the way things were and part of the traditions of the game. Using CML, students can detect the ways the government used baseball, a willing partner, to construct a powerful and particular notion of patriotism beginning with World War I and continuing to the present (Elias, 2010). A fan who bought a scorecard at the game may not have noticed the red, white, and blue cover with Uncle Sam at bat and messages inside encouraging him or her to donate blood and buy war bonds (Boston Red Sox, 1944; Chicago White Sox, 1945). Media carry strong messages about social norms and values. Media have the power "to educate, when people critically reflect on the messages they are getting through the media, and to 'miseducate,' when viewers are passive consumers who don't think much about the images and messages that they are receiving" (Tisdell, 2008, p. 49). Factors such as the format and place in which the messages appear, and availability or limited access add to the meaning. Although it may be challenging to learn to decipher the complex images and sounds of baseball, from language in play-by-play to merchandise sold and music played at the game, it is necessary. Messages produced in baseball almost all portray and support dominant American ideology. The game offers signs that have become iconic messages about the way things are and the way things ought to be (Seelow, 2018).

Media literacy educators designed a number of concepts and questions by which to analyze media messages. Debate continues around the focus and uses of these questions to develop critical thinking and provide students with skills through inquiry (Gainer, 2007, 2010; Hobbs, 1998; Hobbs & Jensen, 2009; Jolls & Wilson, 2014; Scheibe, 2009; Scheibe & Rogow, 2011; Silverblatt, 2014). While these approaches are helpful in teaching students to see beneath messages, "they fall short of offering the examination of power and the inherent inequities that exist in the media" (Ligocki, 2017, p. 6). Several scholars describe the limits of these approaches and the need instead for CML (Buckingham, 2003; Funk, Kellner, & Share, 2005, 2016). This comprehensive framework and method extend beyond analysis to teach how to use media as instruments of democratic participation and change (Kellner & Share, 2019).

In the following sections, two concepts from CML will be used to analyze messages in and around the game of baseball as they relate to government, the military, and messages about patriotism. First, *politics of representation* recognizes that all media messages and the medium through which they are presented have bias. This point of view may support or challenge dominant hierarchies of privilege, power, and pleasure. Questions that help reveal politics of representation include: What values, points of view, and ideologies are represented and embedded in the message? Which ones are missing? Why were they omitted? A second concept, *production/institutions* examines how the individual or system that creates the media message shapes its purpose. In baseball, this is generally governmental or commercial. Questions can help uncover purposeful choices about cost, material, and more. CML provides the kinds of questions that can explore this concept (Feliciano Ortiz, 2012; Kellner & Share, 2019; Scheibe & Rogow, 2008). Why was this text created? Who provided the financial backing? How was it constructed? How does the medium aid in accomplishing the goal? How was the message disseminated? These questions are related to the examples that follow baseball media during times of war. These examples provide opportunities to question the ideologies behind the media and the ways the production elements and dissemination shaped the idea of American patriotism.

In current times when visual and digital messages and sound bites comprise the majority of information transmitted and absorbed, learning to examine and question these messages is more important than ever. To ignore the power of media in sports to persuade and convince, especially around issues such as war, is foolish: "When media is seen as merely transparent windows, the messages become naturalized. . . . Our dependency on media surrenders our active participation and civic duties to question, challenge, and correct social injustices" (Kellner & Share, 2007, p. 65). This chapter will show how baseball as a business and the government joined forces beginning during World War I, and how this partnership continues today to promote and define national ideals and values such as civic duty and patriotism.

IDEOLOGY AND THE POLITICS OF REPRESENTATION

Baseball has been a game that claims to personify the American spirit and values. The game is associated with national identity (White, 2015). It provides myths and legends that support the persona of the United States as a patriotic country that is united by the sport of baseball. There is an economic side to this as well, and citizens spend money to attend games and buy merchandise that allows them to feel connected to the country and each other (Rudd & Most, 2009). The ideas of baseball as a metaphor for democracy and citizenship began with Albert Spalding in the late nineteenth century and were perpetuated by media (Elias, 2010; White, 2015; Zeller, 2006). Spalding touted baseball as similar to war in civilizing—meaning Americanizing—other countries and spreading national qualities such as courage, determination, and pluck (Briley, 2010; Foster, 1917; Golub, 2010). The beginning of professional teams coincided so that at the beginning of the twentieth century, business and politics were already intertwined with the game (Tygel, 2000; Zingg, 1986). William Howard Taft was the first president to throw out the first pitch at a game, publicly connecting baseball and the nation. When global conflicts began, baseball became a tool by which images and events were carefully constructed to present a distinct perspective on what it meant to be a patriotic American (Crissley, 2016a, 2016b, 2016c; White, 2015; Voight, 1976).

The Great War: To Play or Not?

World War I was the first military conflict on a global scale. Although the first shots of World War I were fired in Europe in 1914, the United States managed to remain neutral until April 6, 1917, a few days before the 1917 baseball season was scheduled to begin. Team owners attempted to keep players out of the armed services by promoting baseball as an essential industry. Some players were drafted, and others enlisted. Players who remained took part in public displays of support for the war at games, such as military-type drills with bats. These were prominently featured on front pages of newspapers all over the country (Leeke, 2013). Owners donated to the war effort, raised money at games through bond rallies, and sent baseball gear to the soldiers overseas (Leeke, 2017). Owners also tried to make the case through carefully crafted media messages that baseball was keeping American spirits high and sustaining support for the cause (Barnes, Belmonte, & Barnes, 2019; Hensler, 2013). The singing of the national anthem at games began during this time, further cementing a connection between the game and patriotism (Benjamin, 2018; Roberts & Smith, 2020a). When a government order to "work or fight" threatened this, owners reached a compromise that allowed a shortened 1918 season and a World Series that ended just before the cease-fire (Babwin, 2017; Desjardin, 2018; Kelly, n.d.).

One example of this push to continue playing was combining the image of Uncle Sam with baseball. The famous "I Want You" recruiting poster was created by James Montgomery Flagg in 1917, and over four million posters were printed by 1918 (Andrews, 2017). The image was a powerful one, with strong features that seemed to symbolize "the power of patriotism"

(Kennedy, n.d.). In 1917, The Publicity Committee, Citizens Preparedness Association commissioned a poster entitled "Get in the Game with Uncle Sam," in which Uncle Sam is holding a baseball bat waiting for the pitch that is war (Leyendecker, 1917). The cover of *Frank Leslie's Illustrated Weekly Newspaper* showed Uncle Sam dressed in army khakis swinging a bat at a "ball" that has a Pickelhaube helmet and Kaiser Wilhelm II's mustache (Forsythe, 1918). A political cartoon showed Uncle Sam sitting on a base that says "France" while a confused Kaiser Wilhelm looks on wearing skull and crossbones on his baseball uniform (Sykes, 1917, p. 10). All of these images connect Uncle Sam, a masculine and strong symbol of America, with winning the war effort and beating back the enemy. Representation of American identity in this powerful man dressed in red, white, and blue and using a bat as a weapon reminded citizens that like Uncle Sam, their loved ones were fighting for freedom and democracy. Individuals dressed as Uncle Sam were used at games to sell war bonds along with players (Leeke, 2017). By using baseball imagery, the war was a game to be won (Gems, 2011). Citizens responded emotionally, almost like being a fan at a competitive game.

Newspapers and magazines also spread patriotic messages through stories and images. At the ballpark, Babe Ruth and his teammates, wearing full baseball uniforms, substituted bats for rifles and conducted military maneuvers under the instruction of a drill sergeant before the game. Photos of such events linked baseball skills to the country's war effort ("Baseball," 1918; Roberts & Smith, 2020b). Officers like Major General Leonard Wood threw out the first pitch at the Polo Grounds in New York and said, "The game maintains mental balance, instills patriotism, and arouses manly instincts, which were necessary if the nation was to stand up for its rights" ("Army Recognizes," 1917, p. 4). These images and reports of patriotism were intended to show the general public how supportive and necessary baseball was to the war effort. However, using CML would be a method to question the motives and perspective used. There were business reasons for these displays. The owners based their decision to have players conduct military drills on keeping people and profits coming. These quasi-military displays and stories allowed Major League Baseball (MLB) to capitalize on the positive press. Patriotism was a charade that allowed commerce to continue while fans waved flags and sang the national anthem for the first time at sporting events (Jenkins, 2013; Wakefield, 1997; Wood, 2014). These media texts were used to build financial and moral support for the war from the masses in a way that they could relate to and understand. Analysis of these images and reports brings to light the perspectives of money and power. Brute force and winning, on the battlefield and at the ballpark, became synonymous with patriotism.

World War II: Patriot Games

On December 7, 1941, America was thrust into World War II after the attack on the naval base at Pearl Harbor. The attack on American soil made this war much more personal. Baseball images represented the American way of life, and they were used to remind citizens of exactly what was at stake. When the war began, baseball owners pleaded with President Franklin Roosevelt to allow MLB to begin spring training in anticipation of the 1942 season. Roosevelt gave the owners and fans what they wanted. He called for the continuation of baseball as worthwhile for the country (Bazer & Culbertson, 2002; Cox, n.d.). A cartoon entitled "Let's go all you American players and fans!" depicted President Roosevelt standing in front of an American flag, yelling "Play Ball," and throwing out the "first pitch" (Coyne, 1942a). On the ball is written "1942 season" and two lines of players seem ready to "serve their country" by playing baseball. Baseball images were widely used to justify the sacrifices necessary to protect a country that defined itself by a bat and a ball and a grassy field of competition. Publications had come a long way since the last war. Photographs and other images grabbed readers' attention and made their point with captions and headlines. Baseball terminology was interchangeable with the war. One soldier wrote, "We'll bat the Japs and Germans for home runs. The score is against us now, but our side hasn't been at bat yet" (Brands, 1942, p. 2). Papers like *The Sporting News* blurred lines between objective national news and sports reporting.

As before, the fictional Uncle Sam was used to represent American strength and ability to win. Unlike the last war, many players enlisted in the armed services, so the question of players as slackers who avoided service to keep playing the game was no longer an issue. Images of enlisted players, especially those who were well known, were prominent in newspapers and magazines (Anton & Nowlin, 2008; Gilbert, 1992). In December 1941, an image of Detroit Tigers superstar Hank Greenberg in his baseball uniform was featured in *The Sporting News* ("Hank Greenberg," 1941). Greenberg had already served in the army, but reenlisted after the attacks, acknowledging that this most likely meant the end of his playing career. A cartoon showed the faces of thirteen major league players and the names of twenty-eight more who had enlisted and were serving (Coyne, 1942b). Pictures of famous players who enlisted were shown in ways that reminded their fans they had not abandoned the game but were putting their careers on hold for a greater duty. Images were carefully chosen as part of a calculated strategy that portrayed baseball and its players as helping the country while keeping the business of baseball in positive light (Bullock, 2000). Coverage of players who were overseas fighting extended to include African American players in the Negro Leagues. The cover of the *Negro Baseball Pictorial Yearbook*

(1944) showed two images of pitcher Ernest "Spoon" Carter on the cover, one of him in full military uniform preparing to throw a grenade and one in his Homestead Grays uniform with baseball in hand. CML questions help consider how and why these men were chosen for publicity. They were shown as heroes for enlisting because they had been star players. Which players were selected for these photos and where they were placed was strategic and was meant to bring the most recognition, and therefore, the most unquestioning support (Klima, 2015). Baseball was the essence of America and players and fans both were doing their part. Anyone who didn't support both the game and the war was deemed unpatriotic and cowardly (Pryce, 2010). MLB and the government used these texts to sell civic duty as the only choice.

Baseball Heals America after 9/11

Although there were other global conflicts after World War II, baseball did not respond with the same efforts (Briley, 2003). That changed on Tuesday, September 11, 2001, when two planes were hijacked by terrorists and flown into the twin towers of the World Trade Center in New York City. Two other planes were also hijacked and crashed into the Pentagon and a field in Shanksville, Pennsylvania. The United States was plunged into an immediate period of uncertainty and confusion. Sports and baseball in particular struggled to figure out their place in such a situation since it occurred during the end of the season and beginning of postseason playoffs. Baseball commissioner Bud Selig decided to stop baseball games for six days while America regrouped. Players on both New York teams, the Yankees and Mets, assisted with recovery efforts and struggled to come to grips with how the sport fits into the tragedy (Brown, 2004; Roberts & Smith, 2020a). When baseball resumed, many MLB teams supported New York City by wearing NYPD and FDNY hats. Every action was magnified because of continuous media coverage. Rather than newspapers and magazine, television and digital platforms became vehicles for dissemination. A signature event was when President George W. Bush threw out the first pitch of Game 3 of the World Series. The president's appearance at Yankee Stadium changed baseball and the mood of the country (Butterworth, 2005a, 2005b). That pitch became mythical and an opening salvo in the war on terrorism.

At ballparks, there was a return to overt public displays of patriotism and connection to the military. Unlike previous conflicts, the wars in Iraq and Afghanistan did not claim the lives or careers of professional baseball players. Baseball used small gestures and big ceremonies to support the country's unity. Immediately after the attacks, signs of patriotism were highly visible across ballparks (Gabel, 2008). Teams unveiled flags that covered whole swarths of outfield grass in pregame ceremonies. At Fenway Park, the Green

Monster was draped in red, white, and blue. Ceremonies and events linked to the war on terrorism became commonplace at games. In countless stadiums across the country, navy jets conducted flyovers, families of the victims of the attacks threw out first pitches, and service men and women in full uniform presented flags at the opening of the game (Gems, 2011). The media were supportive and more than happy to join forces and portray images and ceremonies across various platforms. Signs of patriotism and signs of strength became almost required at games.

Patriotism as Support of the Military?

As time passed, two trends occurred. First, MLB escalated the frequency and degree of these tributes which once removed from the attacks were blatantly pro-military (Astore, 2011; Kilgore, 2015). Second, not all Americans shared the same sense of support for all foreign policy actions. What began as national healing through the nation's pastime began to define patriotism as support for armed conflict such as Operation Desert Storm. Once at the ballpark, fans could not help but accept and participate in these activities. Not to do so was seen as an outward show of disrespect for the country rather than the armed forces (Bacevich, 2011; Flores-Rodríguez, 2011). Like the media messages during the two world wars, these forms of mutually beneficial propaganda were intended to portray pride in America. The difference is that these patriotic images were and are disseminated in twenty-four-hour news cycles and through a variety of formats and technology (Fox, 2009; Lukas, 2019). In the ever-changing media landscape, displays of flags and patriotism in baseball are shared on social media and retweeted thousands of times. Millions of eyes see patriotic images of the flag and consciously or subconsciously become indoctrinated that as a baseball fan, one must support these patriotic messages.

The images, material, and rituals reinforce that baseball and patriotism go hand in hand, and the only form of patriotism is acceptance and agreement with government policies (Hawkman & Van Horn, 2019). It is easy for fans who do not deconstruct images and sound or question the purpose behind them to miss connections. Using CML questions to deconstruct these images uncovers a troubling emphasis on the military (Stark, 2010). These displays and images seem to say one is only a patriot if one supports the war (Bryant, 2018). As George W. Bush famously stated nine days after the attacks, "Either you are with us or you are with the terrorists" (Bush, 2006). The idea that "we are all on the same team" blends beautifully with baseball and does not allow for questioning or dissension. Since the 9/11 attacks, media messages have become more widespread and more value laden. Owners and politicians have recognized that baseball is a perfect sport by which to promote the dominant ideology of American strength through military action and a concept of patriotism that does not allow for differing points of view.

PRODUCTION OF MEDIA

Baseball has always included merchandise that allows fans to demonstrate their love of the game, players, or teams. Another way that baseball and the government worked to disseminate messages of patriotism in times of war was to produce items that served a dual purpose. Many items appeared in media stories and enhanced the connection between the game and the war. Each period of war had its own unique media texts that were supplemental to traditional newspaper headlines, photos, and stories. Examination of the variety of ways selected messages were placed in the hands of diehard fans and as well as those who did not necessarily follow the game can reveal ways the government used the power of baseball, through players and fans, to spread the concept of civic duty and to help subtly define what it meant to be a "true American."

World War I: Posters, Songs, and More

During World War I, baseball terminology and familiar imagery were used to draw a parallel between military and playing baseball. A 1918 recruiting poster read, "That Arm—Your Country Needs It," and featured a soldier in uniform winding up to pitch a round object, either a grenade or a baseball (Preissig, 1918). Music was also used to spread patriotic messages (Mosher, 2006). The song "The Great Baseball War Song—Batter Up! Uncle Sam is at the Plate" (Barnes et al., 2019; Tighe & Von Tilzer, 1918) was sung at stadiums. The sheet music cover showed Uncle Sam in a batting stance with soldiers cheering in the stands, and included the words, "Put Sammy to hit and let him do his bit and watch him hit the cover off the ball." The cover for the song "Bobby the Bomber" depicts a soldier in a pitching windup looking to throw a grenade at the opposing trench (McCarron & Morgan, 1919). A poem by famed sportswriter Grantland Rice in the *New York Tribune* celebrated Boston Braves catcher Hank Gowdy who slipped away after playing a series against the Cincinnati Reds to become the first player to enlist (Leeke, 2013; Tener, 1918). Sports writers such as Rice were more than reporters; they created and cultivated images of athletes as heroic or mythological figures. "Old Lank Hank" become a symbol of it means to be a "true American" through the poetry of Rice. Outfield walls across major league ballparks were covered with ads encouraging fans to do their civic duty and support the war effort by buying Liberty Loan bonds (Leeke,

2017). From songs to fundraising games, MLB sought new ways to use their public platform and support the war effort. Owners invested in production of diverse products and venues to ensure their patriotic message permeated all areas of America.

World War II: Patriotism at the Game

During World War II, fans at the game were bombarded with patriotic messages. Harry M. Stevens founded a company that brought food concessions to stadiums, along with printed programs and scorecards (Francis, n.d.). Many of the scorecards and programs sold at games were red, white, and blue and portrayed American flags and other images supportive of the war. The 1943 Yankees program had a batter after hitting a ball in a blue globe with an eagle on top whose wings made a V shape for victory (New York Yankees, 1943). The program for the 1942 World Series between the New York Yankees and St. Louis Cardinals featured a drawing reminiscent of Normal Rockwell's covers and showed a woman in a military uniform sitting at a booth selling war bonds and stamps. There is a child wearing a baseball hat with a bat and glove tucked under his arm purchasing a war stamp to put in his booklet (Baker, 2013). The 1944 Chicago Cubs official program depicts a Liberty dollar coin with the slogan "For Victory Buy Bonds" (Chicago Cubs, 1944). The 1945 Chicago White Sox player roster pamphlet, scorecard, and program encouraged citizens to "Back the Attack: Buy More War Bonds" (Chicago White Sox, 1945). Covers of the 1944 game programs for the New York Yankees and other teams showed two large bolts of radio transmissions sent to groups of soldiers and sailors listening to the game (New York Yankees, 1944). Images, such as these with their patriotic colors, symbols, and emotional appeals, ensured that everyone at the game could not help but understand that baseball was integral to the war effort.

Marketing America through Baseball

Advertisements became another format to connect baseball and patriotism. A 1943 advertisement for Timm Aircraft showed all the Allies on a baseball diamond turning a triple play against Mussolini, Hitler, and Hirohito with Uncle Sam at third base to make the key play ("A Triple Play," 1943). Other ads reflected businesses eager to grow profits and look good by connecting themselves to baseball and the war (Obermeyer, 2010, 2013). As in the first war, Wilson Sports equipment ran advertisements in magazines and supported the troops by providing frontline troops with equipment. Their full-page ad did not even show the company name or equipment. Instead it showed a batter and a catcher in the foreground and soldiers, artillery, and a tank in the background. In it they articulate the way in which the game helped condition American men for the war:

> It has built the sinews, nerves, and courage of so many of our men! It has taught the laws of team play to our nation, for a war in which only team play can win! . . . Hirohito and Hitler, both, will know before the "ninth inning" what those swelling roars of protest from the stands meant in America for nearly a century . . . And so a salute to Baseball, the great American game that has taught team-work and the will to win to millions of our boys and loyalty to millions of our people. Here's to Baseball. ("Play On," 1942, n.p.)

The money spent on this advertisement was an investment in more than sales of bats, balls, and gloves. Parents and other adults reading the publication will be reminded that baseball represents the best American values that need to be protected, defended, passed on, and spread around the world.

The idea of bringing baseball wherever American service men and women went was shown in other print media. A *Saturday Evening Post* cover image entitled "Island Game" (Dohanos, 1945) showed a native in a tropical setting wearing catcher's equipment while an American serviceman holding a bat argues a call. In the background other Marines work on a plane. The note about the cover explains that the artist, Steven Dohanos, depicted a baseball game in the South Pacific League between the Marine Air Corps team and the "Bougainville Native Nine." Dohanos received details from two friends who were home on leave before returning to the war and later fighting at Iwo Jima. They described how the American servicemen taught the native population to play the game and how they had become "Americanized." Baseball, along with American values, went wherever troops were sent (Elias, 2010). Spreading values also meant new markets. Globalization of the game through the war continued in a Louisville Slugger advertisement that showed news headlines about baseball being played in North Africa, South Pacific, and Europe ("Headlines," 1944). The ad closes with the phrase "Louisville Slugger Bats, First Wherever Baseball in Played." Marketing and American ideals combined through baseball (Elias, 2010; Obermeyer, 2013, Wood, 2014). These images are shorthand for American values of democracy and fair play. CML helps decipher the underlying values of masculinity, strength, teamwork, and superiority. By this time, baseball had become ingrained into the concept of what it means to be American.

Messages were produced by those who wished to emphasize that the American way of life was better than that of any other nation. Ads played on emotions. Commercials and print ads began to depict the "perfect" (middle-class) life that would grow after the war and include a deluge of materialism and consumption (Wood, 2014). CML analysis makes it clear that these messages benefited MLB, the government, and now corporations, who linked products to both entities. MLB found new products during World War II to spread American values and culture along with a bat and a ball.

Post 9/11: Show Your Support at the Game (or Marketing Militarism along with Team?)

After 9/11, merchandise that represented solidarity with New York such as the NYPD and FDNY baseball caps was abundant. Uniform patches, special Military Day programs, clothing with flags, and other items with team logos or player names create an indistinct separation between fandom and patriotism. Two examples illustrate this: First, the financial backing of government or corporations had been exposed, leaving questions of how and why MLB selects specific tokens of patriotism. Recent stories detailed the financial deals and unseen connections behind patriotic displays (Bacevich, 2011, Kruzel, 2007). In a "pay-for-patriotism" scandal, it was revealed that the government had paid teams to promote patriotic and pro-military initiatives for propaganda and recruitment purposes. Hidden corporate and government funding for events to improve image and boost sales have been called opportunism and "performative patriotism" at the ballpark (Calcaterra, 2017). For example, at the 2014 World Series, American flags were provided to every fan by Bank of America, the Official Bank of MLB (Calcaterra, 2014). Second, official team merchandise had become militarized. The San Diego Padres introduced the tradition of wearing camouflage-style jersey tops for games in 2000. Since then, all teams have different military and patriotic versions of their uniforms. Jim Caple (2012) humorously criticized these: "Are the Padres honoring the military or playing paintball? I'm sorry, but I don't think it makes me a member of the Taliban to point out you can salute our servicemen without wearing an ugly jersey" (para. 7). Caple's comments drew angry responses on social media from military leaders to housewives. There was no room for disagreement, and no one questioned the profits made by sales of these jerseys (Center, 2012; Jenkins, 2013). Astore (2011) noted the militarization beneath the media messages, by saying, "War is not a sport; it's not entertainment; it's not fun. . . . We've created a dangerous dynamic in this country: one in which sporting events are exploited to sell military service for some while providing cheap grace for all" (paras 6-7). In the years since the 9/11 attacks, media messages have become more widespread and more value laden. Owners and politicians have recognized that baseball is a perfect vehicle by which to promote the dominant ideology of American strength through military action and a concept of patriotism that does not allow for differing points of view (Bryant, 2013; Giamatti, 2015; Hawkman & Van Horn, 2019). CML questions expose the source of financial backing for these events comes from corporations and unknowing taxpayers. Millions are spent on seemingly innocent items and events that are quietly crafted to create a pervasive and narrow perception of patriotism and to discourage dissent (Bacevich, 2011; Boldt, 2018; Calcaterra, 2017; Fry, 2019, Gems, 2011).

CONCLUSION

Sports can be a unifying force in times of chaos and uncertainty. Throughout history, baseball helped bring a sense of hope, resiliency, and normalcy in times of crises. However, blurred lines between baseball and government can result in media coverage that ignores questions of what values, points of view, and ideologies are represented, and which are missing from these patriotic texts (Briley, 2003; Calcaterra, 2017, Kilgore, 2015). When what it means to be a "true American" is defined by coverage of events at baseball games, the power of the media to shape perceptions and beliefs can be overwhelming. Both the government and sports have formed a symbiotic relationship to support each other. This marriage has developed and changed over the years, but the connection is inextricably linked through media. Media messages must be examined using CML questions to support a more informed citizenry who can challenge the messages and the messengers.

Baseball, more than any other sport, is intertwined with American values. With spring training, a long season, and playoffs, the sports' place in American culture is pervasive and so are its media messages. Those messages require CML skills to ensure that audiences, especially young people, become more than media consumers and read these messages for what they are: carefully constructed, purposeful, and often one-sided. What may appear to be human interest stories, product giveaways, and fun moments at the ballpark oftentimes embody hidden meanings. Through covert and overt gestures and images, baseball, the U.S. government, and media have united the country during times of conflict. However, newspapers stories, photos of World War I, and ceremonial first pitches by service men and women have also shaped American beliefs and values. CML questions help to expose implicit messages that are delivered through media messaging presented at baseball games. Careful analysis and examination of media texts that connect baseball to patriotism can support a shift from media consumer to critical thinker.

REFERENCES

Alvermann, D., & Hagood, M. C. (2000). Critical media literacy: Research, theory, and practice in "new times." *Journal of Educational Research, 93*(2), 193–205.

Andrews, T. M. (2017, April 3). The Uncle Sam "I Want YOU" poster is 100 years old. Almost everything about it was borrowed. *Washington Post*. Retrieved from https://www.washingtonpost.com/news/morning-mix/wp/2017/04/03/the-uncle-sam-i-want-you-poster-is-100-years-old-almost-everything-about-it-was-borrowed/.

Anton, T., & Nowlin, B. (Eds.). (2008). *When Baseball Went to War*. Chicago, IL: Triumph Books.

Army Recognizes Baseball's Part. (1917, April 19). *The Sporting News*. p. 4.

Astore, W. (2011, July 28). The militarization of sports - And the sportiness of military service. *Huffington Post*. Retrieved from https://www.huffpost.com/entry/the-militarization-of-sports_b_912004.

A triple play - Against the Axis. (1943). *Flying Magazine*, p. 227.

Babwin, D. (2017, July 3). 1918 World Series key in US love affair with national anthem. *AP News*. Retrieved from https://apnews.com/b99832adbe974cbf8bdfbacd7e01d52b.

Bacevich, A. J. (2011, July 28). Playing ball with the Pentagon. *The Nation*. Retrieved from https://www.thenation.com/article/playing-ball-pentagons.

Baker, J. (2013, October 22). The 10 greatest World Series program covers. *SBNation*. Retrieved from https://www.sbnation.com/platform/amp/2013/10/22/4864712/greatest-world-series-programs-covers.

Barnes, A. F., Belmonte, P. L., & Barnes, S. O. (2019). *Play Ball!: Doughboys and Baseball during the Great War*. Atglen, PA: Schiffer Publishing.

Bazer, G., & Culbertson, S. (2002). When FDR said "Play Ball": President called baseball a wartime morale booster. *Prologue Magazine*, *34*(1). Retrieved from https://www.archives.gov/publications/prologue/2002/spring/greenlight.html.

Benjamin, C. (2018, September 5). Baseball in 1918: Inside the birth of the national anthem in sports, women's teams and Negro leagues. *CBS Sports*. Retrieved from https://www.cbssports.com/mlb/news/baseball-in-1918-inside-the-birth-of-the-national- anthem-in-sports-womens-teams-and-negro-leagues/.

Boston Red Sox. (1944). *Official Score Card*. New York, NY: Harry M. Stevens Publisher.

Brands, E. G. (1942, April 16). "'Keep 'em playing,' men in service chorus to query: 'Should game go on during war?'" *The Sporting News*, p. 2.

Briley, R. (2003). *Class at Bat, Gender on Deck and Race in the Hole: A Line-up of Essays on Twentieth Century Culture and America's Game*. Jefferson, NC: McFarland.

Briley, R. (2010). *The Politics of Baseball: Essays on the Pastime and Power at Home and Abroad*. Jefferson, NC: McFarland.

Boldt, G. (Ed.). (2018). Am I patriotic? Learning and teaching the complexities of patriotism here and now. *Occasional Paper Series, 2018*(40). Retrieved from https://educate.bankstreet.edu/occasional-paper-series/vol2018/iss40/14.

Brown, R. S. (2004). Sport and healing America. *Society*, *42*(1), 37–41.

Bryant, H. (2013, July 3). Sports and patriotism. *ESPN*. Retrieved from https://www.espn.com/espn/story/_/id/9449554/sports-patriotism.

Bryant, H. (2018, July 20). Veterans speak out against the militarization of sports. *Only A Game*. Retrieved from https://www.wbur.org/onlyagame/2018/07/20/military-sports-astore-francona.

Buckingham, D. (2003). *Media Education: Literacy, Learning and Contemporary Culture*. Cambridge, UK: Polity Books.

Bullock, S. (2000). Playing for their nation: The American military and baseball during World War II. *Journal of Sport History*, 27(1), 67–89.

Bush, G. W. (2006, September 6). President Bush's Speech on Terrorism. *New York Times*. Retrieved from https://www.nytimes.com/2006/09/06/washington/06bush_transcript.html.

Butterworth, M. (2005a). George W. Bush as the "man in the arena": Baseball, public memory, and the rhetorical redemption of a president. *Rhetoric and Public Affairs*, 22(1), 1–31.

Butterworth, M. (2005b). Ritual in the "Church of Baseball": Suppressing the discourse of democracy after 9/11. *Communication and Critical/Cultural Studies*, 2(2), 107–129.

Calcaterra, C. (2014, October 28). A veteran says enough is enough when it comes to tributes for the soldiers. *NBC Sports*. Retrieved from https://mlb.nbcsports.com/2014/10/28/a-veteran-says-enough-is-enough-when-it-comes-to-tributes-for-the-soldiers/.

Calcaterra, C. (2017, April 16). A few words on baseball, giant American flags and patriotism. *NBC Sports*. Retrieved from https://mlb.nbcsports.com/2017/04/16/a-few-words-on-baseball-giant-american-flags-and-patriotism/.

Caple, J. (2012, February 29). There are great unis and awful unis. Retrieved from https://www.espn.com/mlb/story/_/id/7629005/ranking-uniforms-worst-best.

Center, B. (2012, March 5). Fans, Padres react to camouflage criticism. *The Morning Call*. Retrieved from https://www.mcall.com/sdut-fans-padres-react-espns-camouflage-criticism-2012mar05-story.html.

Chicago Cubs. (1944). *Official Score Card*. New York, NY: Harry M. Stevens Publishers.

Chicago White Sox. (1945). *Official Score Card*. New York, NY: Harry M. Stevens Publishers.

Cox, M. (n.d.). "Keep baseball going." *National Baseball Hall of Fame and Museum*. Retrieved from https://baseballhall.org/discover-more/stories/short-stops/keep-baseball-going.

Coyne, B. (1942a, April 16). Let's go, all you American players, and fans! [Cartoon]. *The Sporting News*, p. 1.

Coyne, B. (1942b, May 6). The game's own victory regiment - With recruits coming. *The Sporting News*, p. 1.

Crissley, H. E. (2016a, May 9). Baseball and the Armed service (Part One). *Our Games*. Retrieved from https://ourgame.mlblogs.com/baseball-and-the-armed-services-d61bd35af5a3#.1ms077gzn.

Crissley, H. E. (2016b, May 9). Baseball and the Armed service (Part Two). *Our Games*. Retrieved from https://ourgame.mlblogs.com/baseball-and-the-armed-services-part-two-9d7bcb7b51c7.

Crissley, H. E. (2016c, May 9). Baseball and the Armed service (Part Three). *Our Games*. Retrieved from https://ourgame.mlblogs.com/baseball-and-the-armed-services-part-three-1276ec524c89.

Desjardin, S. (2018). *September 1918: War, plague, and the World Series*. Washington, DC: Regnery History.

Dohanos, S. (1945). Island game. [Illustration]. *Saturday Evening Post, 217*(43).

Elias, R. (2010). *The Empire Strikes Out: How Baseball Sold U.S. Foreign Policy and Promoted the American Way Abroad*. New York, NY: New Press.

Fabrizi, M. A., & Ford, R. D. (2014). Sports stories and critical media literacy. *English Journal* 104(1), 42–47.

Feliciano Ortiz, R. J. (2012). Watching the games: Critical media literacy and students' abilities to identify and critique the politics of sports. Unpublished doctoral dissertation. Western University, Canada. Retrieved from https://ir.lib.uwo.ca/etd/441.

Flores-Rodríguez, A. G. (2011). Baseball, 9/11, and dissent: The Carlos Delgado controversy. *OAH Magazine of History, 25*(3), 55–56.

Forsythe, C. (1918, April 27). The great American game. [Illustration]. *Leslie's Illustrated Weekly Newspaper*.

Fortuna, C. (2015). Digital media literacy in a sports, popular culture, and literature course. *Journal of Media Literacy Education, 6*(3), 81–89.

Foster, J. B. (Ed.). (1917). Baseball around the world. In J. B. Foster (Ed.), *Spaulding Official Baseball Guide* (pp. 225–226). New York, NY: American Sports Publishing Company.

Fox, R. (2009). Beyond the game: The imagery of Major League Baseball. *Journal of Sports & Recreation Research Education, 3*(1), 1–11.

Francis, B. (n.d.). Harry M. Stevens created the modern ballpark experience. *National Baseball Hall of Fame and Museum*. Retrieved from https://baseballhall.org/discover/harry-stevens-created-modern-ballpark-experience.

Fry, M. (2019, July 28). Sports media are no longer apolitical. Should they stay that way? *Washington Examiner*. Retrieved from https://www.washingtonexaminer.com/opinion/sports-media-are-no-longer-apolitical-should-they-stay-that-way.

Funk, S., Kellner, D., & Share, J. (2016). Critical media literacy as transformative pedagogy. In M. N. Yildiz & J. Keengwe (Eds.), *Handbook of Research on Media Literacy in the Digital Age* (pp. 1–30). Hershey, PA: IGI Global Publishers.

Gabel, P. (2008). Patriotism at the ballpark. *Tikkun, 23*(4), 30–31.

Gainer, J. (2007). Social critique and pleasure: Critical media literacy with popular culture texts. *Language Arts, 85*(2), 106–114.

Gainer, J. (2010). Critical media literacy in middle school: Exploring the politics of representation. *Journal of Adolescent & Adult Literacy, 53*(5), 364–373.

Gems, G. R. (2011). Baseball, invented tradition, and nationalistic spirit. In S. Wagg (ed.), *Myths and Milestones in the History of Sport* (pp. 106–121). London, UK: Palgrave Macmillan.

Giamatti, A. B. (2015, July 10). Why baseball matters—Still. *George W. Bush Institute*. Retrieved from https://www.bushcenter.org/essays/baseball/

Gilbert, B. (1992). *They also Served: Baseball and the Home Front, 1941-1945*. New York, NY: Crown Publishers.

Golub, A. (2010, June 29). Baseball: Wartime tool then and now. *Forbes*. Retrieved from https://www.forbes.com/sites/booked/2010/06/29/baseball-wartime-tool-then-and-now/#5d3cfc8f5dbb.

Hank Greenberg, back to colors, becomes the Hank Gowdy of '41 (1941, December 18). *The Sporting News*, p. 1.

Harshman, J. (2017). Developing globally minded, critical media literacy skills. *Journal of Social Studies Education Research, 8*(1), 69–92.

Hawkman, A. M., & Van Horn, S. E. (2019). What does it mean to be patriotic? Policing patriotism in sports and social studies education. *The Social Studies, 110*(2), 105–121.

Headlines that thrill Americans around the world. (1944, May 4). *The Sporting News*. p. 25.

Hensler, P. (2013). "Patriotic industry": Baseball's reluctant sacrifice in World War I. *Nine: A Journal of Baseball History and Culture, 21*(2), 98–106.

Hobbs, R. (1998). The seven great debates in the media literacy movement. *Journal of Communication, 48*(1), 16–32.

Hobbs, R., & Jensen, A. (2009). The past, present, and future of media literacy education. *Journal of Media Literacy Education, 1*, 1–11.

Hsu, H. (2018, September 24). Should we keep politics out of sports? *New Yorker*. Retrieved from https://www.newyorker.com/magazine/2018/09/24/should-we -keep-politics-out-of-sports.

Jenkins, T. (2013). The militarization of American professional sports: How the sports–war intertext influences athletic ritual and sports media. *Journal of Sport and Social Issues, 37*(3), 245–260.

Jolls, T., & Wilson, C. (2014). The core concepts: Fundamental to media literacy yesterday, today and tomorrow. *Journal of Media Literacy Education, 6*(2), 68–78.

Kelly, M. (n.d.). "On account of war." *National Baseball Hall of Fame and Museum*. Retrieved from https://baseballhall.org/discover-more/stories/short-stops/1918-w orld-war-i-baseball.

Kellner, D., & Share, J. (2005). Toward critical media literacy: Core concepts, debates, organizations, and policy. *Discourse: Studies in the Cultural Politics of Education, 26*(3), 369–386.

Kellner, D., & Share, J. (2007). Critical media literacy is not an option. *Learning Inquiry, 1*, 59–69.

Kellner, D., & Share, J. (2019). *The Critical Media Literacy Guide: Engaging Media and Transforming Education*. Boston, MA: Brill/Sense.

Kennedy, P. (n.d.). "I Want YOU!" – The story of James Montgomery Flagg's iconic poster. *Illustration Chronicles*. Retrieved from https://illustrationchron icles.com/I-Want-YOU-The-Story-of-James-Montgomery-Flagg-s-Iconic-Post er.

Kilgore, A. (2015, May 23). Military tributes at baseball games: True honors or hollow gestures? *Washington Post*. Retrieved from https://www.washingtonpost.com /sports/nationals/military-tributes-at-baseball-games-true-honors-or-hollow-gest ures/2015/05/23/3dc36364-0154-11e5-833c-a2de05b6b2a4_story.html.

Klima, J. (2015). *The Game Must Go On: Hank Greenberg, Pete Gray, and the Great Days of Baseball on the Home Front in WWII*. New York, NY: Thomas Dunne Books.

Kruzel, J. (2007). Major Leaguers Tour Pentagon. *Armed Service Press Service*. Retrieved from https://archive.defense.gov/news/newsarticle.aspx?id=46880.

Leeke, J. (2013). *Ballplayers in the Great War: Newspaper Accounts of Major Leaguers in World War I Military Service*. Jefferson, NC: McFarland.

Leeke, J. (2017). *From the Dugouts to the Trenches: Baseball during the Great War*. Lincoln, NE: University of Nebraska Press.

Leyendecker, J. C. (1917). Get in the Game With Uncle Sam. [Poster]. *The Strong National Museum of Play*. Retrieved from https://www.museumofplay.org/blog/play-stuff/2010/01/batter-up-uncle-sam.

Ligocki, D. (2017, February). *So What IS Critical Media Literacy? The Differences between Media Literacy and Critical Media Literacy*. Paper presented at the meeting of International Critical Media Literacy, Savannah, GA. Retrieved from https://www.researchgate.net/publication/322578492_So_what_IS_critical_media_literacy_The_differences_between_media_literacy_and_critical_media_literacy.

Lukas, P. (2019, April 23). The man who brought "God Bless America" to MLB ballparks. *UniWatch*. Retrieved from https://uni-watch.com/2019/04/23/exclusive-the-man-who-brought-god-bless-america-to-mlb-ballparks/.

Mauer, L. (1860). Two 'outs' and one 'run' [Illustration]. Retrieved from https://www.loc.gov/pictures/resource/ppmsca.09311/.

McCarron, C. R., & Morgan, C. (1918). Bobby the bomber. [Notated Music]. Retrieved from https://www.loc.gov/item/2013567787/

Morganthaler, D. (2010). Voices of media Literacy: International pioneers speak: Len Masterman. [Interview Transcript]. *Center for Media Literacy*. Retrieved from https://www.medialit.org/reading-room/voices-media-literacy-international-pioneers-speak-len-masterman-interview-transcript.

Mosher, S. (2006). Songs sung red, white, and blue: Music, sports, and the rhetoric of patriotism. In S. S. Prettyman & B. Lampman (Eds.), *Learning Culture through Sports: Exploring the Role of Sports in Society* (pp. 151–167). Lanham, MD: Rowman & Littlefield.

Negro Baseball Pictorial Yearbook. (1944). [Photograph]. Retrieved from https://www.si.edu/newsdesk/photos/negro-baseball-pictorial-yearbook.

New York Yankees. (1943). *Official Score Card*. New York, NY: Harry M. Stevens Publishers.

New York Yankees. (1944). *Official Score Card*. New York, NY: Harry M. Stevens Publishers.

Obermeyer, J. (2010). War games: The business of Major League Baseball during World War II. *Nine: A Journal of Baseball History and Culture, 19*(1), 1–27.

Obermeyer, J. (2013). *Baseball and the bottom line in World War II: Gunning for profits on the home front*. Jefferson, NC: McFarland.

Play on, fight on, America! (1942, August 27). *The Sporting News*, p. 18.

Preissig, V. (1918). That arm - your country needs it. [Poster]. Retrieved from https://www.loc.gov/resource/cph.3g10320/.

Pryce, B. (2010). More than a game: Baseball diplomacy in World War II and the Cold War 1941-1958. In R. Briley (Ed.), *The Politics of Baseball: Essays on the Pastime and Power at Home and Abroad* (pp. 141–156). Jefferson, NC: McFarland.

Redmond, T. (2012). The pedagogy of critical enjoyment: Teaching and reaching the hearts and minds of adolescent learners through media literacy education. *Journal of Media Literacy Education, 4*(2), 106–120.

Roberts, R., & Smith, J. (2020a, March 26). On what should have been Opening Day, American needs baseball more than ever. *Washington Post*. Retrieved from https://www.washingtonpost.com/outlook/2020/03/26/what-should-have-been-opening-day-america-needs-baseball-more-than-ever/.

Roberts, R., & Smith, J. (2020b). *War Fever: Boston, Baseball, and America in the Shadow of the Great War.* New York, NY: Basic Books.

Rosenberg, A. (2016, September 13). We tell ourselves sports are politically neutral. That's a lie. *Washington Post*. Redrived from https://www.washingtonpost.com/news/act-four/wp/2016/09/13/we-tell-ourselves-sports-are-politically-neutral-thats-a-lie/.

Rudd, R., & Most, M. (2009). Patriot's games? Images of American nationalism in baseball films. In W. M. Simons (Ed.), *The Cooperstown Symposium on Baseball and American Culture, 2007-2008* (pp. 92–105). Jefferson, NC: McFarland.

Rummel, S. (2016, June 30). As American as 'baseball, hot dogs, apple pie and Chevrolet.' *Tri-County Times*. Retrieved from www.tctimes.com/as-american-as-baseball-hot-dogs-apple-pie-and-chevrolet/article_dd7083ea-3efe-11e6-8531-43492d385b75.html.

Scheibe, C. (2009). Sounds great, but I don't have time! Helping teachers meet their goals and needs with media literacy education. *Journal of Media Literacy Education, 1*, 68–71.

Scheibe, C., & Rogow, F. (2008). *12 Basic Ways to Integrate Media Literacy and Critical Thinking into Any Curriculum.* Ithaca, NY: Ithaca College.

Scheibe, C., & Rogow, F. (2011). *The Teacher's Guide to Media Literacy: Critical Thinking in a Multimedia World.* Thousand Oaks, CA: Corwin.

Seelow, D. D. (2018). *The Rhetorical Power of Popular Culture* (3rd ed.). Thousand Oaks, CA: Sage.

Syrios, A. (2017, December 14). The political case for sports to be apolitical. *Medium*. Retrieved from https://medium.com/@rios9000/the-policital-case-for-sports-to-be-apolitical-a48a389ae80.

Silverblatt, A. (2014). *Media Literacy: Keys to Interpreting Media Messages* (4th ed.). New York, NY: Praeger.

Stark, S. (2010, September 30). Drill and kill: How Americans link war and sports. *The Atlantic*. Retrieved from https://www.theatlantic.com/entertainment/archive/2010/09/drill-and-kill-how-americans-link-war-and-sports/63832/.

Sykes, C. H. (1917, June 28). Safe on second. [Cartoon]. *Evening Ledger*, p. 10.

Tener, J. (1918, March). Hank Gowdy, the man who blazed the trail: Why organized baseball should unite to honor the first Major League player to enlist. *Baseball Magazine*, pp. 401–402.

Tighe, H., & Von Tilzer, H. (1918). *The Great base ball war song: Batter up—Uncle Sam is at the plate. [Notated Music].* New York, NY: Harry Von Tilzer Music Publishing Company.

Tisdell, E. (2008). Critical media literacy and transformative learning: Drawing on pop culture and entertainment media in teaching for diversity in adult higher education. *Journal of Transformative Education, 6*(1), 48–67.

Tygel, J. (2000). *Past Time: Baseball as History.* Oxford, UK: Oxford University Press.

Voight, D. Q. (1976). *America through baseball.* Lanham, MD: Rowman & Littlefield.

Wakefield, W. E. (1997). *Playing to Win: Sport and the American Military, 1898-1945.* Albany, NY: State University of New York Press.

White, K. R. (2015, April). Baseball and the American character: Exploring the influence of the national pastime on the origins of contemporary American identity. Proceedings of the National Conference On Undergraduate Research (NCUR), Eastern Washington University, Cheney, WA. Retrieved from https://www.ncurproceedings.org/ojs/index.php/NCUR2015/article/view/1515.

Wood, M. (2014). One hundred percent Americanism: Material culture and nationalism, then and now. *International Journal of Historical Archaeology, 18*(2), 272–283.

Zeller, T. W. (2006). *Ambassadors in Pinstripes: The Spalding World Baseball Tour and the Birth of the American Empire.* Lanham, MD: Rowman & Littlefield.

Zingg, P. J. (1986). Diamond in the rough: Baseball and the study of American sports history. *The History Teacher, 19*(3), 385–403.

Chapter 3

Relationships between Youth-Sports Coaches and Athletes

Messages from the "Best" Sports-Related Films

Luke Rodesiler, Mark A. Lewis, and Alan Brown

Many popular sports-related movies are remembered fondly for the words and actions of the coaches they feature. For instance, most anyone who has seen *A League of Their Own* (Abbott, Greenhut, & Marshall, 1992) can recall an exasperated Jimmy Dugan imploring, "There's no crying in baseball!" And who could forget Knute Rockne's ". . . win just one for the Gipper" speech in *Knute Rockne—All American* (Fellows, Wallis, & Bacon, 1940)? In fact, both lines are recognized among the "100 Greatest Movie Quotes of All Time" by the American Film Institute (2005). Coaches depicted in feature films are so influential that real-world coaches have even tried employing their big-screen brethren's strategies. For example, former Los Angeles Rams defensive line coach John Teerlinck, desperate to simulate the pursuit of Detroit Lions running back Barry Sanders, once took a page from the peculiar training regimen Mickey Goldmill drew up for Rocky Balboa in *Rocky II* (Winkler, Chartoff, & Stallone, 1979): he brought a chicken to practice for players to chase (King, 1991). Undoubtedly, coaches in popular movies have long entertained and inspired with their memorable meltdowns, moving speeches, and unconventional approaches.

When it comes to organized youth sports and the relationships coaches have with teenage athletes, portrayals of coaches in popular movies have shaped the public imagination. In Hollywood, youth-sports coaches and teenage athletes have become iconic for their unique, contrasting characteristics. Audiences revere the team-unifying Herman Boone and revile the merciless John Kreese; they cheer the game-saving Julius Campbell and jeer the leg-sweeping Johnny Lawrence. Such characters resonate because audiences tend

49

to want their sports figures to be either heroes or villains. Yet, it seems this sports-viewing phenomenon too often relies upon stereotypical representations of coaches and athletes, which limits the possibilities for the roles and relationships available to them, both fictional and lived. Therefore, this chapter presents an examination of youth-sports coaches and the teenage athletes they serve in celebrated sports-related movies to better understand how cinematic representations of coach-athlete relationships reify and disrupt the roles available to coaches and athletes who participate in organized youth sports.

CRITICAL MEDIA LITERACY (CML)

This investigation into the portrayal of youth-sports coaches and athletes in popular movies is rooted in the scholarship of CML. Specifically, this study is grounded by Kellner and Share's (2019) explanation of six conceptual understandings about CML.

First, all media messages are constructed in social contexts. In those contexts, decisions are made about who and what to include or exclude and how to frame reality. For example, the making of movies and other moving images is driven by intentional choices about casting, shots, framing, angles, camera movement, lighting, sound, and more. Those decisions, which are not made in a vacuum, shape the final product, position the audience in particular ways, and influence how audience members will interpret the text.

Second, each medium uses unique grammar and semantics to communicate messages to the audience. For instance, the grammar of film requires directors to consider how to frame each shot. Directors must consider what they intend to communicate because different shots serve different purposes. As Golden (2001) noted, a long shot—when the subject or object on the screen is shown from a distance—can establish a scene's setting, and it gives viewers leeway regarding where they focus their attention. In contrast, a close shot, when a subject or object takes up most of the screen, forces viewers to see only what the director intended and nothing more (Golden, 2001). Often used for emphasis, a close shot might focus viewers' attention on the determination evident in an athlete's hardened facial expression, the intensity of the moment communicated via a coach's white-knuckled grip on her clipboard, or the sense of defeat conveyed by a towel falling to the mat. No matter the medium, creators use specific grammar and languages to achieve desired effects.

Third, consumers interpret media messages disparately based on their personal backgrounds. Various contextual factors, including education, class, gender, race, sexuality, and lived experiences, may inform how consumers read and interpret media messages. For example, media consumers may be what Janks (2018) calls "ideal readers" (p. 96), those who read *with* the text, accepting the text's positioning and making meaning in line with the dominant ideology. Or, alternatively, education and experiences might lead consumers to be "critical readers" (p. 96), those who read *against* the text, interrogating the text's positioning and questioning who benefits and who suffers as a result. Because contextual factors influence how media messages are read and received, a critical reading of any text ought to include a question like, "How could this text be understood differently?" (Kellner & Share, 2019, p. 8).

Fourth, media messages reflect the politics of representation, supporting and/or challenging social-cultural-political agendas. Media producers are "actively involved in processes of *constructing* or *representing* 'reality' rather than simply transmitting or reflecting it" (Emphasis in original) (Masterman, 1992, p. 20). That is, as Buckingham (2003) explained, media "don't just present reality, they *re*-present it" (p. 57, emphasis added). These media representations either promote or resist established hierarchies of power and privilege and may advance or upend stereotypical depictions. With the power of representation in mind, questions like the following can support the critical reading of media messages: "What information or perspective is left out of this message? Is this an accurate and credible representation? How does this reflect the perspective or bias of the creator?" (Hobbs, 2011, p. 69). An emphasis on media representing reality is particularly relevant to this study, which involved examining cinematic representations of relationships between youth-sports coaches and teenage athletes.

Fifth, media messages are created purposefully, often for profit and/or power. This understanding supports critically examining media messages using questions like "Who created this message?" and "Why was this text created and/or shared?" (Kellner & Share, 2019, p. 8). Answers to those questions can help media consumers identify economic and/or political interests, recognize biases, and discern underlying agendas that shaped a text's construction.

Sixth, media messages are not neutral. Critical literacy scholars have often made this contention. For example, Janks, Dixon, Ferreira, Granville, and Newfield (2014) explained this idea by arguing that all texts are *partial* in that they only convey part of the story and because they reflect the perspective of the person who constructed the text. Likewise, Vasquez, Janks, and Comber (2019) argued that texts are not neutral because they are positioned by their creators and they work to position their audience. Essentially, media messages are created by someone who holds some perspective and, therefore, are not neutral.

These conceptual understandings of CML—and the politics of representation in particular—frame this study examining how coach-athlete relationships in organized youth sports are portrayed in celebrated sports-related films. Further, this study was intended to explore how Hollywood's representations of coach-athlete relationships inform the roles available to youth-sports coaches and athletes within the public imagination because, as Banks (2000) asserted, "The representation of people and groups in the media is a cogent factor that influences children's perceptions, attitudes and values" (p. xii). Given the powerful influence of media, it is worth exploring the messages about youth coaches and athletes that are distributed widely in movies lauded by media outlets.

DEFINED EXPECTATIONS OF COACHES WITHIN THE PROFESSION

The manifestation of coach-athlete relationships is partially the result of the occupational realities of athletic coaches, which include a process of professional and organizational socialization into the diverse roles related to athletic coaching (Brown, 2012; Brown & Sieben, 2013). This socialization process may affect how coaches perceive their roles and orientations and, ultimately, how they view their own professional identities in relation to their athletes (Brown & Wilson, in press).

Particularly, the National Standards for Sport Coaches (SHAPE America, 2018) provide coaches with a list of core responsibilities and competencies for supporting youth athletes. These forty-two standards fall under seven specific categories and offer important context for understanding the roles of coaches and identifying portrayals of coach-athlete relationships in popular sports-related films. These seven categories suggest coaching effectiveness when coaches undertake the following:

1. *Set vision, goals, and standards for sport programs.* This category advises coaches to define an athlete-centered coaching philosophy and vision for the program that emphasizes long-term athlete development.
2. *Engage in and support ethical practices.* This category advises coaches not only to model ethical behavior and abide by codes of conduct but also to teach and reinforce these ethical responsibilities to their players.
3. *Build relationships.* This category advises coaches to build positive relationships with athletes and other stakeholders by developing sociocultural competencies appropriate for a diverse group of athletes and using effective and professional interpersonal and communication skills. These skills include active listening, negotiating, maintaining self-control, resolving conflicts, and providing constructive feedback.
4. *Develop a safe sport environment.* This category advises coaches to use their power in a responsible manner to create a safe and respectful

learning environment that reduces the potential for abuse, harassment, and bullying. Ensuring the health and safety of athletes entails monitoring environmental conditions and nutritional practices as well as instituting proper training and performance procedures. Also important is for coaches to recognize and mitigate conditions that may lead to physical, psychological, and emotional injury.

5. *Create a positive and inclusive sport environment.* This category advises coaches to create a welcoming, inclusive, and collaborative environment that emphasizes team well-being by focusing on learning and development while encouraging athletes to keep winning in perspective and accept personal responsibility for their actions.

6. *Conduct practices and prepare for competition.* This category advises coaches to plan, teach, assess, and adapt their athletic practices while making sure to incorporate developmentally appropriate, evidence-based strategies for physical and mental skills training, instruction, and assessment. Within this category, coaches should also use sound motivational techniques and teach important life skills that not only connect with but also reach beyond the sports context.

7. *Strive for continuous improvement.* This category advises coaches to engage in self-reflection and professional development to help them evaluate and improve their own practices as well as their team's performances while building a culture of continual improvement.

These seven categories can serve as a barometer for how stakeholders come to understand and build coach-athlete relationships, and they have also proven useful for comparing real-world expectations of coaches with portrayals of youth-sports coaches in the movies.

METHODS OF INQUIRY

To identify sports-related films for analysis, the authors compiled multiple "best sports movies of all time" lists from media outlets focused on various aspects of popular culture, including *Sports Illustrated* (SI Staff, 2007), *Entertainment Weekly* (EW Staff, 2015), *Rolling Stone* (Phipps et al., 2015), *Men's Health* (Lutz & St. Clair, 2019), and *Vulture* (Grierson & Leitch, 2019). Then, the authors scoured these lists for films that meet two criteria. First, the film includes a coach character with a significant role in the story, rather than an ancillary character that is not featured in multiple scenes. Second, the story depicts a relationship between a coach of organized youth sports and a teen-age athlete. Additionally, the authors sought to include diverse representation within the final filmography, including parity in identity markers such as race and gender, as well as sports beyond those frequently depicted in Hollywood movies, namely football, basketball, and baseball.

The authors reviewed the lists and eliminated movies that clearly did not meet both criteria, which left nine films. Of these, only two featured female athletes—*The Bad News Bears* (Jaffe & Ritchie, 1976) and *Bend It like Beckham* (Nayare & Chadha, 2002). However, the former focuses on a Little League team, so the athletes were not yet teenagers, and the latter focuses on a women's club soccer team, so it did not focus on youth sports. Therefore, seven films meet both criteria and comprise the final filmography. Unfortunately, all but one of these seven films focus on football and basketball stories, and they all feature male coaches and athletes. These characteristics create a limitation for this analysis. Table 3.1 outlines the coach characters, a brief synopsis of each film, and the "best of" list(s) on which each was named.

The authors analyzed the selected films by applying a heuristic of five distinct coach-athlete relationships (Rodesiler & Lewis, 2019) generated through the analysis of relationships between coaches and youth athletes depicted in award-winning young adult literature. This heuristic identifies five different coach-athlete relationships. Three positive relationships include coach-athlete, mentor-protégé, and counselor-client. Coaches focus on supporting the athletic prowess of the athletes on their teams. Mentors use their life knowledge and experience to advise athletes outside the arena. Counselors intimately advise athletes through emotional hardships. There are also two negative relationships—victor-victim and master-puppet. Victors prioritize winning over everything else, including the well-being of their athletes, and masters use athletes for their own personal gain.

To answer the research question examining how cinematic representations of coach-athlete relationships reify and disrupt the possible roles available to coaches and athletes, the authors followed Saldaña's (2016) process for coding qualitative data. The authors coded *The Karate Kid* independently before meeting to discuss initial codes and generate consensus on the coding definitions. Particularly, each author realized the need to identify subcodes for the five primary codes to identify nuance in how these fictional coaches might embody their coaching roles. For example, Mr. Miyagi was coded as a coach, but in some scenes he serves as a teacher and in others he serves as a tactician. The authors then coded the other six films independently before meeting again to discuss the coach-athlete relationships in each film. At that point, various subcodes for the five types of relationships were discussed, some were collapsed, and the remaining ones were used to further define the five primary codes. Based on these identified representations and informed by Kellner and Share's (2019) conceptual understandings of CML, with a particular emphasis on the politics of representation, the authors drew conclusions about how these sports-related films define coaches, teenage athletes, and sport within society.

Table 3.1   Selected Filmography. Rodesiler, Lewis, and Brown (2020).

Film	Coach Characters	Synopsis	"Best of" Lists
The Blind Side (Netter, Kosove, Johnson, & Hancock, 2009)	Bert Cotton	With an assist from Coach Cotton, Michael Oher enrolls in a private high school and joins the football team. A parent at the school, Leigh Anne Tuohy, quickly learns that Oher is homeless and welcomes him into her home. She becomes a central person in Oher's life, helping him become a better football player and student.	*Entertainment Weekly*
Coach Carter (Gale, Robbins, Tollin, & Carter, 2005)	Ken Carter, Ray White	Coach Carter is recruited by Ray White to take over as basketball coach at Richmond High, an inner-city school with significant social and academic problems. Carter is intent on using basketball to motivate his players not only to become winners on the court but also to become winners in life.	*Entertainment Weekly*
Friday Night Lights (Grazer & Berg, 2004)	Gary Gaines	Gary Gaines coaches football at Permian High in rural Texas. The community thrives off of the football team, and winning a state championship is everyone's ultimate goal. Gaines must navigate pressures from the town to win and support his players.	*Entertainment Weekly* *Men's Health* *Rolling Stone*
He Got Game (Kilik & Lee, 1998)	Cincotta	Jesus Shuttlesworth is a highly recruited basketball player from Coney Island, Brooklyn. Everyone is pressuring him to make a decision on where to play college basketball, including the governor, his incarcerated father, and his coach, Cincotta.	*Vulture*
Hoosiers (De Haven, Pizzo, & Anspaugh, 1986)	Norman Dale, Wilbur Flatch	In Indiana, basketball means everything. Norman Dale has been ostracized from coaching due to some serious mistakes he made with his players but gets a second chance at Hickory High. Under pressure from community members, he works to remain an effective coach and to support his struggling assistant, Wilbur Flatch.	*Men's Health* *Rolling Stone* *Sports Illustrated* *Vulture*

(Continued)

Table 3.1   Selected Filmography. Rodesiler, Lewis, and Brown (2020).   (Continued)

Film	Coach Characters	Synopsis	"Best of" Lists
The Karate Kid (Weintraub & Avildsen, 1984)	Mr. Miyagi John Kreese	Daniel LaRusso has recently moved to California and struggles fitting in at his new high school, where he is bullied by members of the local karate dojo led by John Kreese. Mr. Miyagi, a local handyman, agrees to teach LaRusso karate and prepare him to face his bullies on the mat.	*Vulture*
Remember the Titans (Bruckheimer, Oman, & Yakin, 2000)	Herman Boone Bill Yoast	In the early 1970s, Williams High in Virginia is forced to integrate and Herman Boone, an African American, is hired to coach the football team. His hiring means the current coach, Bill Yoast, is demoted to assistant. Reluctantly thrown together, they attempt to unite the Black and White players on the team in order to win.	*Entertainment Weekly Men's Health Rolling Stone*

DIVERGENT CHARACTERIZATIONS OF HOLLYWOOD'S COACH-ATHLETE RELATIONSHIPS

Through analysis of the representation of youth-sports coaches in popular movies it was determined that coach characters are generally depicted as having nuanced relationships with teenage athletes. The coaches examined are shown filling multiple roles and taking varied approaches to carrying out those roles with the teenage athletes under their tutelage. Largely, coaches in the films examined have positive relationships with teenage athletes. These include (a) coach-athlete, (b) mentor-protégé, and to a lesser extent, (c) counselor-client relationships. Still, some coaches depicted do not have athletes' best interests in mind. Instead, they foster (d) victor-victim and (e) master-puppet relationships.

Coaches Coach, Players Play: The Coach-Athlete Relationship

The coach-athlete relationship reflects instances where the coach is focused on supporting an athlete's development in the arena and positioning them for success in competition. Coaches in the movies analyzed are depicted filling various roles to achieve their aims: (a) teacher, (b) tactician, (c) authoritarian, and (d) disciplinarian.

Teacher

Coach-as-teacher is a nuanced role. At various times, teachers are "instructors" who educate athletes in the fundamentals of their sport, "motivators" who encourage and inspire, and "critics" who find fault with the effort and performance of the athletes they serve.

Instructor. Several movies analyzed represent coaches teaching athletes fundamental elements of their sport. Mr. Miyagi in *The Karate Kid* is a prime example. Miyagi's unconventional approach to teaching Daniel LaRusso the fundamentals of karate involves having LaRusso complete chores requiring repeated movements that mirror various defensive actions, building blocks of success in karate. As LaRusso sands the floor, paints the fence, waxes on and waxes off, he builds muscle memory through repetition, which supports the execution of fundamental movements unique to his sport. Miyagi's unorthodox instructional approach proves masterful, for he leads the novice LaRusso to the All Valley Karate Championship.

Other coaches take a more direct approach to teaching fundamentals. In *Hoosiers*, Coach Dale opens the season by running players through ballhandling and defensive drills. As he explains to the Huskers, "I've seen you guys can shoot, but there's more to the game than shooting! There's fundamentals and defense." Likewise, in *Coach Carter*, the film's namesake is so focused on fundamentals and conditioning that, prior to their first game, players are concerned because they did not work on offense during practice. In response, Carter reasons, "We have all season to do that." For the first game, Carter simply instructs players to do as they did in practice: "I want you to run. I want you to run every second that clock is ticking, all game long." Coaches Dale and Carter have success prioritizing fundamentals and conditioning, yet not all coaches see immediate results.

In *The Blind Side*, Michael Oher struggles at football practice with his new team. Despite his size and athleticism, the offensive lineman cannot sustain his blocks. Coach Cotton repeatedly shouts instruction and eventually shows Oher some blocking techniques. However, it is not Cotton's emphasis on hand placement that unlocks Oher's potential. Leigh Anne Tuohy, matriarch of the family caring for Oher, interrupts practice and upstages Cotton. Knowing Oher better than the coach, Tuohy recognizes the value of tapping Oher's protective instincts. She tells Oher, "Tony here is your quarterback, all right? You protect his blind side. When you look at him, you think of me." After Tuohy's talk, Oher pancakes a defender during the next play and drops multiple defenders on each of the ensuing plays, leaving Cotton to wonder aloud, "What'd you say to him?"

Motivator. The motivating words of on-screen coaches are delivered at different times and in different ways. There are encouraging in-game pep talks like in *Remember the Titans*, when Coach Boone talks to backup quarterback Ronnie "Sunshine" Bass about being thrust into a situation for which one is not prepared. There are inspirational half-time speeches like the one Coach Gaines delivers during the state championship game in *Friday Night Lights*, when he defines "perfection" as not being about winning but "being able to look your friends in the eye and know that you didn't let them down." Coaches' efforts to encourage and inspire athletes also show up before the games even begin. For example, Coach Dale recognizes that players from a small rural school might be intimidated by playing the state championship game in cavernous Butler Fieldhouse. So, with the team gathered in the empty arena, Dale provides a tape measure and asks players to read measurements from the free throw line to the backboard and from the rim to the floor. Dale then assures the Huskers, "I think you'll find this is the exact same measurements as our gym back in Hickory," which brings smiles to the players' faces. In these ways and more, most coaches studied are shown employing motivational tactics to maximize athletic performance.

Critic. Not all the messages cinematic coaches deliver are affirming. Just as teachers correct students' misconceptions and inaccuracies, coaches identify and enhance athletes' areas for improvement. For example, while Jaron "Worm" Willis touts the twelve points and eight assists he accumulated against Hercules, his coach is focused on a different set of numbers: five turnovers and four missed free throws. Coach Carter uses those numbers to make a case for improving the team's fundamentals and to justify adding morning practices to their routine. While Carter's criticism in this instance is performance-based, an athlete's effort is not immune from critique either. For example, when Mr. Miyagi teaches LaRusso to throw a punch, the teen's effort and focus come under fire. Showing off his quick feet and fast talking, LaRusso prompts Miyagi to take him to the ground and deliver a stern critique: "I think you dance around too much. I think you talk too much. I think you no concentrate [*sic*] enough. Lots of work to be done. Tournament just around the corner." Many scenes in these films depict coaches providing criticism aimed at improving athletes' effort and performance.

Tactician

In movies and in life, coaches take on the role of a "tactician," strategizing to put athletes in the best position to win. During in-game action, tacticians draw up plays, make adjustments, or otherwise position athletes to secure victory. Coaches in most of the films analyzed are consistently depicted as tacticians. Coach Gaines is representative, for he is portrayed as a tactician on both sides of the ball and experiences mixed results. Late in the state championship game, Gaines draws up a defensive stunt that helps Permian

High successfully make a crucial stop on fourth down, securing one more possession and giving the Panthers a shot to win. Then, on the ensuing drive, Gaines strategizes with the offense, calling for "I-Right Wiggle, 34 Switch-blade." Despite gaining the yards needed for a first down, a flag for holding nullifies the play, which only underscores the importance of coaches teaching fundamentals and not relying on strategy alone.

Authoritarian

The coach-athlete relationship also includes coaches who take on an "authoritarian" role. In this context, an authoritarian is defined as a coach who conveys that his voice is the only one that should be heard. Early in *Hoosiers*, Coach Dale epitomizes the role. When kicking Buddy Walker out of practice for talking instead of listening, Dale barks, "Don't come back until you learn to keep your mouth shut and listen." Then when Rade Butcher challenges the coach's game plan in Hickory's first contest, Dale fires back, "You keep your mouth shut until I tell you to open it, all right?" Once the game ends, Dale reminds players that team membership requires playing under one condition: "What I say when it comes to this basketball team is the law, absolutely and without discussion." Dale eventually softens his stance and welcomes players' voices as the season continues, yet his embrace of the authoritarian role in his initial interactions with the Huskers is unmistakable.

Like Coach Dale, Coach Boone is also depicted as an authoritarian. When introducing himself to the team, he makes a bold proclamation: "This is no democracy. It is a dictatorship. I am the law." As Dale did, Boone establishes his authority by proclaiming himself the law. And like Dale, Boone has no interest in players' opinions or demands. That becomes evident when Gerry Bertier tells Boone to reserve half of the positions on offense and special teams for White players from Hammond High and insists that no Black players are needed on defense. After publicly ridiculing Bertier, Boone delivers a firm message about the team's hierarchy: "Now, you know who your daddy is, don't you? Gerry, if you want to play on this football team, you answer me when I ask you who is your daddy. Who's your daddy, Gerry? Who's your daddy?" After Bertier reluctantly identifies Boone, the coach presses him to acknowledge whose team it is: "And whose team is this? Is this your team, or is this your daddy's team?" Embodying the authoritarian role, Boone makes it clear who is calling the shots.

Disciplinarian

Each coach in the authoritarian role also fills the role of "disciplinarian" on multiple occasions. The disciplinarian role is marked by instances when the coach punishes athletes for their errors. Coaches Boone and Dale are depicted as disciplinarians, yet Coach Carter is most frequently shown in this role, typically assigning players push-ups and suicides as punishment for their errors. For example, Carter doles out 20 suicides when his son arrives late to practice, and he later requires each team member to do 500 push-ups for taunting the opposition. Players who walk out on the team receive harsher punishments. For instance, Carter tells Junior Battle he must complete 1,000 push-ups and 1,000 suicides before he can rejoin the team, yet his harshest punishment is reserved for Timo Cruz, who attempted to punch Carter and proceeded to quit. Carter tells Cruz, "Before you can play on this team . . . you owe me . . . 2,500 push-ups . . . and 1,000 suicides." Though certainly on the extreme end of the spectrum, Cruz's punishment is illustrative of disciplinarian tactics.

Though the words and actions of coaches in disciplinarian and authoritarian roles may seem harsh, the roles are distinct from plainly negative coach-athlete relationships (i.e., victor-victim and master-puppet). When taking on authoritarian and disciplinarian roles, coaches Carter and Dale, for example, are not trying to win at all costs. In fact, they willingly lose games to teach players a lesson: Carter locks the gym, cancels practices, and forfeits games until players' academic performance improves, and Dale finishes the opening game with only four players on the court when Rade Butcher refuses to follow the coach's game plan. Further, these coaches are not manipulating players for personal gain. Rather, they have athletes' best interests in mind, as Carter explains: "I'm trying to teach these boys the discipline that will inform their lives and give them choices."

The Coach as More than a Coach: Mentor-Protégé and Counselor-Client Relationships

Coaches wearing the mantle of mentor or counselor in their relationships with youth athletes support athletes in ways that include teaching them the game but also helping them in life. In the films analyzed, several coaches, including coaches Gaines, Dale, and Yoast, took on mentor or counselor roles, although the mentor role was much more prominent than the counselor role. Three scenes highlighting Coach Boone, Coach Carter, and Mr. Miyagi stand as emblematic examples.

In addition to serving in various coaching roles, Coach Boone dons the mantle of mentor when necessary to build positive relationships with his football players. He protects one particular athlete, Louie Lastik, from himself by discouraging his self-defeating attitude toward academics. During the preseason training camp, Louie claims he will not be going to college because he "ain't a brainiac like Rev," and Boone publicly laughs with Louie and his joke, but privately he tells him, "If you don't go to college, it's not gonna be because you're not qualified, so I want you to bring me your test scores at the end of every week, and we'll go over them together, okay?" In this way, Boone protects Louie from public shame yet remains a mentor encouraging Louie to continue striving as a student. As viewers discover, with Boone's support Louie succeeds in earning a C+ average and plans to attend college by the film's end.

Mr. Miyagi embraces the mentor role with LaRusso as part of their coach-athlete relationship by imparting life wisdom. For example, he wishes LaRusso happy birthday by gifting him a car from his classic collection. Before allowing LaRusso to drive off, however, he asks him if he remembers the "lesson about balance." In this prior lesson, Miyagi explains that learning balance is more important than learning to punch, which is LaRusso's priority. In his pithy way, Miyagi explains that if fighters have balance then their karate will be good, but if they lose balance then they "better pack up and go home." Now, Miyagi wants LaRusso to see the connection between balance in karate and balance in life: "Whole life have a balance, everything be better [*sic*]. Understand?" LaRusso internalizes that lesson as he thinks about and performs in the film's closing karate tournament.

Although Coach Carter primarily uses his position as coach to instruct and discipline athletes, he also mentors them toward becoming better students. Yet in one particularly intense scene, he also takes on the role of counselor. Timo Cruz, who had twice quit the basketball team, leans on the coach during his darkest moment—witnessing the murder of his cousin, Renny. After futilely attempting to save Renny, Cruz heads to his coach's house and bangs on his door. When Carter answers, Cruz, covered in blood, repeatedly expresses his desire to return to the team. Carter initially just wants him to come inside, presumably to calm him down, but Cruz screams, "You don't understand. I wanna come back on the team. [. . .] Whatever you want me to do, I'll do it, okay?" Cruz is probably referring to Carter's previous disciplinarian tactics, but instead his coach responds, "I got you. Come on. Come on, you're back with us now." His assurances to Cruz—"I got you" and that he is "back with us now"—reveal his desire for Cruz to believe that he will take care of him, to counsel him, as he grieves over his cousin.

Win at All Costs: The Victor-Victim Relationship

A victor is defined as prioritizing winning over all else, including the well-being of athletes, the victims. Coach Dale provides a pertinent example of a victor when describing his lifetime suspension from the NCAA for physically assaulting a player:

> You know, in the ten years that I coached, I never met anybody who wanted to win as badly as I did. I'd do anything I had to do to increase my advantage.

Anybody who tried to block the pursuit of that advantage, I'd just . . . push
'em out of the way. Didn't matter who they were or what they were doing. (De
Haven et al., 1986)

One of the hallmarks of being a victor is imparting or allowing physical or
psychological injury for the sake of winning. Coach Gaines looks the other
way on multiple occasions. In one serious example, Gaines meets with Boo-
bie Miles and his uncle, L. V., after the star player tears his ACL. Knowing
Miles has a serious injury, Gaines asks if he has visited the hospital in nearby
Midland. L. V. lies to Gaines about the extent of the injury. Gaines appears to
recognize the lie but ultimately accepts the explanation that a local clinic indicated there was no ACL tear. Soon after, a desperate Gaines inserts Miles into
a game, and the player aggravates his injury as a result, ending his season. In
another example, when receiver Don Billingsley's father, Charles, confronts
his son after fumbling during practice, the confrontation turns physical, with
the father throwing the son to the ground, yet Gaines chooses not to intervene
or address the father despite the physical (and potentially psychological) consequences. Presumably, Gaines recognizes that Don holding onto the football
will be imperative to winning, which is his priority.

One of the most extreme cases of psychological abuse involves John
Kreese, sensei of the Cobra Kai dojo, in *The Karate Kid*. Kreese regularly
tells his disciples that fear, pain, and defeat do not exist, while encouraging
them to show "no mercy" to their opponents, whom he considers their ene-
mies. Kreese believes in winning at all costs, even if it comes at the expense
of his own competitors. For example, during the karate tournament, he per-
suades one of his athletes, Bobby Brown, to hurt LaRusso, to intentionally put
him "out of commission," despite the act warranting Brown's disqualifica-
tion. Injuring LaRusso increased the odds of Johnny Lawrence, Kreese's top
athlete, winning the tournament.

I'm Gonna Get Mine: The Master-Puppet Relationship

A master is defined as a coach who uses one or more athletes for personal gain.
Coach Cotton provides an example of this coach type. After persuading school
administrators to accept Michael Oher into Wingate Christian School despite
a lowly 0.6 GPA, he later admits to doing so primarily for football reasons.
In fact, just after Oher's admission, Cotton tells Oher's soon-to-be adoptive
father, Sean Tuohy, "This kid's gonna make us all famous." Unbeknownst to
Oher, Cotton eventually parlays the player's success into a job at the University
of Mississippi, the same place Michael Oher will play college football, which
initiates an NCAA investigation. As is common in master-puppet relationships,
Cotton uses Oher's football prowess to advance his own interests.

Coach Cincotta in *He Got Game* shows tendencies of a master as someone who is gaming the system by pressuring protagonist Jesus Shuttlesworth to make up his mind about where to play college basketball. Late in the film, Cincotta offers Shuttlesworth $10,000—what he calls "a little package to help [Shuttlesworth] make [his college] decision" in return for "a little bit of information." When Shuttlesworth declines the money, Cincotta admits to pushing his player into obvious rules violations, including raising his algebra grade and providing money to help him and his sister move out of their uncle's house. Although never explicitly stated, Cincotta's status as a basketball coach stands to benefit from Shuttlesworth selecting a prestigious university, and there is also a presumption that the coach may be receiving compensation for pushing the star toward a particular school. In the end, Cincotta reads a prepared statement from Shuttlesworth, revealing his decision to attend Big State University; Cincotta pumps his fists exuberantly after reading the announcement.

CRITICALLY EXAMINING HOLLYWOOD'S MESSAGES IN SPORTS-RELATED FILMS

The analysis of coach-athlete relationships portrayed in these seven films highlights several messages Hollywood seems to be conveying to the viewing audience. These films communicate ideas about the positioning of coaches and athletes, the roles coaches serve, and the purpose of organized youth sports. They also expose problems of representation and the power of profit in popular entertainment. A CML lens exposes many of these messages as highly problematic, at best, and severely damaging, at worst, to the inter-relationship possibilities the public can imagine between coaches and youth athletes.

Coaches Wield Power

In five of the seven films analyzed, coaches are positioned as dominant in the coach-athlete binary. Obviously, the harm involved within a coach-dominant binary is starkly represented in the character of Sensei Kreese and implicit in the character of Coach Cincotta, but such representations of the coach can be even more harmful when presented subtly in sports-related films. As described previously, even coaches identified as playing positive roles in their relationships with athletes often embraced authoritarian and disciplinarian stances, indicating they had the power in the relationship and could deny athletes entrance into their sport. This power position is further established when athletes, having left of their own volition or not, must ask forgiveness and/or pay penance to return to the team. This phenomenon is evident with Coach Dale and Whit Butcher, as well as with Coach Carter and Timo Cruz. Due to media's influence on how the public understands people serving in defined roles (Kellner & Share, 2019), the audience could internalize the message that it is acceptable for coaches, as long as they have good intentions, to use their positions of power to dominate the bodies and lives of teenage athletes. This message pushes against Standard 12 of the National Standards for Sport Coaches (SHAPE America, 2018), which advises coaches to "treat athletes and all program personnel with respect . . . [and to] use their personal and official power in a responsible manner."

Athletes Need "Molding"

It is quite common to hear the phrase the "molding of men" in media characterizations of what high school coaches (should) do. Most of the coaches in these films portray that perspective. This perspective stems partially from a view of adolescent-athletes as incomplete and needing to become adults (Lewis & Rodesiler, 2018), and partially from the commonly perceived, often media-driven, view that team sports always work toward building productive character. This viewpoint is even observed in Standard 28 of the National Standards for Sport Coaches (SHAPE America, 2018), which encourages coaches to "create intentional strategies to develop life skills and promote their transfer to other life domains." Coaches Boone, Yoast, Gaines, and Carter clearly embody the coach as someone who is responsible for completing their athletes by filling gaps in their lives, either through helping them build productive interpersonal relationships or by remaining focused on their responsibilities as students earning an education. While shrouded in the ultimate positive outcomes of the coach sculpting adolescents into well-rounded, socially productive men (for instance, it would be difficult to argue that Coaches Boone and Yoast's work toward ending interracial strife among players was not a productive endeavor), the implication is that these youth would not be able to achieve such ends on their own. These coaches are presented by Hollywood as saviors of misguided youth, which, when viewed uncritically, can greatly influence the public's imagination of lived coach-athlete relationships.

Sports Are for Men

Any consideration of youth-sports coaches and athletes depicted in celebrated movies would be incomplete without addressing glaring patterns regarding the gender of those characters. In the movies studied, only men are depicted in the role of coach, and only teenage boys are painted as youth athletes. No movies centering female coaches or teenage girls competing in organized youth sports cracked the "best of" lists that drove the selection process, hence their absence in this study. Perhaps the quality of movies centering teenage girls and their coaches—movies like *Gracie* (Shue, Shue, Shue, & Guggenheim, 2007) or *The Mighty Macs* (Chambers, 2009)—is debatable, but the exceptionality of such films in popular culture is undeniable. Considering the politics of representation (Kellner & Share, 2019), the relative absence of female athletes and coaches in movies about youth sports supports a culture where women—coaches and athletes—are sidelined in favor of men taking center court.

Nearly 3.4 million girls participated in organized high school athletics during the 2018–2019 school year (National Federation of State High School Associations, 2019), yet girls looking for inspiration from Hollywood sports stories have limited options—and girls interested in coaching careers have even fewer models available. Recognizing that movies are created for profit, as media often are (Kellner & Share, 2019), the lack of representation may be rooted in assumptions about the limited profit films featuring female athletes and coaches in youth sports would generate—the kind of commercial logic described by sports journalists explaining how they choose what to cover (Knoppers & Elling, 2004). Regardless of its impetus, the scant representation is problematic—especially given Standard 22 of the National Standards for Sport Coaches (SHAPE America, 2018), which advises coaches to "ensure that all athletes have equal opportunity to participate"—because it signals to viewers that sports are not for girls or women, whether they aspire to compete on the court or from the coach's box.

Profit Drives Storytelling

With five of the seven movies analyzed being based on true events—*Coach Carter, Friday Night Lights, Hoosiers, Remember the Titans*, and *The Blind Side*—considerations of representation must also account for how true the depictions are to the lived experiences of those involved. It turns out that the representation of some coaches and athletes in these films are highly disputed. Players from Milan High School's 1954 basketball team, the inspiration for *Hoosiers*, have disputed the depiction of their coach, Marvin Wood, calling Norman Dale "far-removed from our coach" (CBS, 2010). Regarding *The Blind Side*, the real-life Michael Oher has challenged depictions of him not understanding football basics (Hanzus, 2016), and Coach Hugh Freeze, who is represented as Coach Cotton in the film, has questioned his depiction as a bumbling, out-of-touch coach (Braziller, 2014). Likewise, players on the 1999 Richmond High School boys basketball team have contested depictions of the players and coach in *Coach Carter*, alleging false portrayals and embellishments (Ho, 2005). Subjects of sports stories challenging their representations stand as reminders that media "don't just present reality, they re-present it" (Buckingham, 2003, p. 57). Viewers, then, would do well to watch movies based on true events critically, to consider Kellner and Share's (2019) fifth conceptual understanding, and recognize that, like all media, they are constructions of reality created for particular purposes (e.g., profit), and that telling a "better story" may take priority over accurately depicting "real-life" figures and events.

Winning Isn't Everything

The stories told in the movies analyzed for this study also promote particular messages about the outcomes of participation in sport beyond the thrill of victory. The idea that sport participation is not about winning but doing one's best is a message conveyed by Mr. Miyagi and coaches Boone, Dale, and Gaines. Though some movies depict "victor-victim" relationships, where coaches pursue victory to an athlete's detriment, the idea that doing one's best is all that matters in athletic competition is a message relayed again and again across the movies analyzed. It is a message aligned with Standard 21 of the National Standards for Sport Coaches (SHAPE America, 2018), which calls for "emphasizing effort and learning, encouraging athletes to keep winning in perspective." Protagonists failing to win championships in the movies studied (i.e., *Coach Carter* and *Friday Night Lights*) underscores the message that winning is not everything.

The notion that sport is an avenue for success in life is also evident in the movies analyzed. The message is clearly evinced in the words and actions of Coach Carter, who communicates it throughout the movie. In his first team meeting, Carter declares that "winning in here is the key to winning out there." He contends that players developing habits of mind and body that support success on the hardwood will serve them well in life. Then, when appearing before the school board, Carter explains, "I'm trying to teach these boys the discipline that will inform their lives and give them choices." His disciplinarian approach is not just about winning games; it aims to foster discipline and habits of mind that players can use when the games end.

THE CRITICAL CONSUMPTION OF SPORT IN POPULAR MEDIA

The messages communicated by these films have particular implications for school and society, especially since they have been identified as some of the best sports-related films of "all time." These findings underscore the necessity of viewers considering a question Kellner and Share (2019) posed, one that informs a critical reading of all media: "How could this text be understood differently?" (p. 8). Youth-sports coaches play many different roles in relation to teen athletes. How coaches and athletes begin to understand these roles is often influenced by the consumption of texts from popular culture, including sports-related films. With filmmakers presenting stereotypical representations of coaches and athletes, or relying exclusively on prescribed roles commonly affiliated with the canon of popular film, it is incumbent upon viewers to become critical readers (Janks, 2018) actively reading against texts too often dictated by Hollywood filmmakers whose primary motives may include power and profit. What the audience sees on the screen matters, particularly for viewers who are passionate about what they are consuming. As a result, these findings call for a more critical reading of coach-athlete relationships in popular sports-related films. Further still, it is imperative that sports-related movies of the next generation offer a more realistic and responsible representation of the variety and diversity of coach-athlete relationships in youth sports.

REFERENCES

Abbott, E., Greenhut, R. (Producers), & Marshall, P. (Director). (1992). *A League of Their Own* [Motion Picture]. Los Angeles, CA: Columbia Pictures.

American Film Institute. (2005). AFI's 100 years . . . 100 movie quotes: The greatest movie quotes of all time. Retrieved from https://www.afi.com/afis-100-years-100 -movie-quotes/.

Banks, J. A. (2000). Series foreword. In C. E. Cortés, *The Children are Watching: How the Media Teach about Diversity* (pp. xi–xiv). New York, NY: Teachers College Press.

Braziller, Z. (2014, October 24). Portrayed as goof in "The Blind Side," Ole Miss coach Freeze gets the last laugh. *New York Post*. Retrieved from https://nypost. com/2014/10/24/portrayed-as-goof-in-the-blind-side-ole-miss-coach-freeze-gets -the-last-laugh.

Brown, A. (2012). Gender integration of a core content area teacher/athletic coach in the rural southeastern United States. *Sport, Education and Society, 17*(5), 627–646.

Brown, A., & Sieben, N. (2013). The elephant in the classroom: Examining the influence of athletic coaching on secondary preservice teachers. *Teacher Education Quarterly, 40*(3), 107–122.

Brown, A., & Wilson, E. K. (2020). Classroom teaching and athletic coaching: Connecting social positions through interrole symbiosis. *Journal for the Study of Sports and Athletes in Education*. https://doi.org/10.1080/19357397.2020.1840239.

Bruckheimer, J., Oman, C. (Producers), & Yakin, B. (Director). (2000). *Remember the Titans* [Motion Picture]. Burbank, CA: Buena Vista Pictures.

Buckingham, D. (2003). *Media Education: Literacy, Learning, and Contemporary Culture*. Malden, MA: Polity Press.

CBS. (2010, April 3). Real "Hoosiers" better story than the movie's? *CBS News*. Retrieved from https://www.cbsnews.com/news/real-hoosiers-better-story-than-the-movies.

Chambers, T. (Producer & Director). (2009). *The Mighty Macs* [Motion Picture]. Los Angeles, CA: Freestyle Releasing.

De Haven, C., Pizzo, A. (Producers), & Anspaugh, D. (Director). (1986). *Hoosiers* [Motion Picture]. Los Angeles, CA: Orion Pictures.

EW Staff. (2015, November 15). 25 sports movies that score. *Entertainment Weekly*. Retrieved from https://ew.com/gallery/best-sports-movies

Fellows, R., Wallis, H. B. (Producers), & Bacon, L. (Director). (1940). *Knute Rockne—All American* [Motion Picture]. Los Angeles, CA: Warner Bros. Pictures.

Gale, D., Robbins, B., Tollin, M. (Producers), & Carter, T. (Director). (2005). *Coach Carter* [Motion Picture]. Los Angeles, CA: Paramount Pictures.

Golden, J. (2001). *Reading in the Dark: Using Film as a Tool in the English Classroom*. Urbana, IL: National Council of Teachers of English.

Grazer, B. (Producer), & Berg, P. (Director). (2004). *Friday Night Lights* [Motion Picture]. Universal City, CA: Universal Pictures.

Grierson, T., & Leitch, W. (2019, January 31). The 50 best sports movies of all time. *Vulture*. Retrieved from https://www.vulture.com/article/best-sports-movies-ever.html

Hanzus, D. (2016, January 27). Michael Oher at peace with life as "The Blind Side" guy. *NFL*. Retrieved from https://www.nfl.com/news/michael-oher-at-peace-with-life-as-the-blind-side-guy-0ap3000000629087.

Ho, C. (2005, March 17). Remembering a different "Coach Carter." *The Daily Californian*. Retrieved from https://archive.dailycal.org/article.php?id=18062.

Hobbs, R. (2011). *Digital and Media Literacy: Connecting Classroom and Culture*. Thousand Oaks, CA: Corwin.

Jaffe, S. R. (Producer), & Ritchie, M. (Director). (1976). *The Bad News Bears* [Motion Picture]. Los Angeles, CA: Paramount Pictures.

Janks, H. (2018). Texts, identities, and ethics: Critical literacy in a post-truth world. *Journal of Adolescent & Adult Literacy, 62*(1), 95–99.

Janks, H., Dixon, K., Ferreira, A., Granville, S., & Newfield, D. (2014). *Doing Critical Literacy: Texts and Activities for Students and Teachers*. New York, NY: Routledge.

Kellner, D., & Share, J. (2019). *The Critical Media Literacy Guide: Engaging Media and Transforming Education*. Leiden, The Netherlands: Brill Sense.

Kilik, J. (Producer), & Lee, S. (Producer & Director). (1998). *He Got Game* [Motion Picture]. Burbank, CA: Buena Vista Pictures.

King, P. (1991, November 25). The NFL. *Sports Illustrated*. Retrieved from https://www.si.com.

Knoppers, A., & Elling, A. (2004). "We do not engage in promotional journalism": Discursive strategies used by sports journalists to describe the selection process. *International Review for the Sociology of Sport, 39*, 57–73.

Lewis, M. A., & Rodesiler, L. (2018). Between being and becoming: The adolescent-athlete in young adult fiction. In I. P. Renga & C. Benedetti, (Eds.), *Sports and K-12 Education: Insights for Teachers, Coaches, and School Leaders* (pp. 135–150). Lanham, MD: Rowman & Littlefield.

Lutz, E., & St. Clair, J. (2019, October 15). These are the 30 best sports movies ever made. *Men's Health*. Retrieved from https://www.menshealth.com/entertainment/g26343949/best-sports-movies.

Masterman, L. (1992). *Teaching the Media*. New York, NY: Routledge.

National Federation of State High School Associations. (2019). 2018-19 high school athletics participation survey. Retrieved from https://www.nfhs.org/media/102 0412/2018-19_participation _survey.pdf.

Nayare, D. (Producer), & Chadha, G. (Producer & Director). (2002). *Bend it like Beckham* [Motion Picture]. Century City, CA: Fox Searchlight Pictures.

Netter, G., Kosove, A. A., Johnson, B. (Producers), & Hancock, J. L. (Director). (2009). *The Blind Side* [Motion Picture]. Los Angeles, CA: Warner Bros. Pictures.

Phipps, K., Murray, N., Grierson, T., Montgomery, J., Ebiri, B., & Fear, D. (2015, August 10). 30 best sports movies of all time. *Rolling Stone*. Retrieved from https://www.rollingstone .com/movies /movie-lists/30-best-sports-movies-of-all-time-714 67.

Rodesiler, L., & Lewis, M. A. (2019). "I thought coaches were supposed to set an example": Coaches' divergent roles in young adult literature. *The ALAN Review*, *46*(2), 27–39.

Saldaña, J. (2016). *The Coding Manual for Qualitative Researchers* (3rd ed.). Thousand Oaks, CA: SAGE.

SHAPE America. (2018). National standards for sport coaches. Retrieved from https ://www.shapeamerica.org/standards/coaching.

Shue, A., Shue, E., Shue, J. (Producers), & Guggenheim, D. (Producer & Director). (2007). *Gracie* [Motion Picture]. Los Angeles, CA: Picturehouse Entertainment.

SI Staff. (2007, July 26). Best sports movies. *Sports Illustrated*. Retrieved from https ://www.si.com/more-sports/2007/07/27/26best-sports-movies.

Vasquez, V. M., Janks, H., & Comber, B. (2019). Critical literacy as a way of being and doing. *Language Arts*, *96*(5), 300–311.

Weintraub, J. (Producer), & Avildsen, J. G. (Director). (1984). *The Karate Kid* [Motion Picture]. Los Angeles, CA: Delphi II Productions.

Winkler, I., Chartoff, R. (Producers), & Stallone, S. (Director). (1979). *Rocky II* [Motion Picture]. Los Angeles, CA: United Artists.

Chapter 4

Truth be Told

The Mutual Responsibilities of Artists and Consumers

Mark A. Fabrizi

Singer-songwriters, film directors, actors, and writers want to tell a great story, one that consumers will remember long after they have turned off the radio, left the movie theater, or finished the book. They want consumers to engage and reengage with their work, and sometimes this means telling a few "stretchers," as Mark Twain put it, to make real events sound that much better. And the better the story, the larger the audience they are likely to reach and the more commercially viable the product.

While we consumers are sometimes willing to accept superficial changes to historical events in the service of storytelling, we trust the storyteller and often take it for granted that the fundamental reality of the story is true. For this reason, one must engage with the intersection of audio, visual, and print media, examining an artist's sometimes conflicting role between conveying real-life events accurately and telling a compelling story as well as the responsibility of the consumer to question that story critically or merely to accept it. Through a critical engagement with historical adaptations and primary source documents, this chapter will explore what it means to be both socially responsible and commercially viable as an artist, what it takes to be a critical consumer of media in a democracy, and why teachers must encourage the development of critical media literacy (CML) skills in their classrooms.

HISTORY OR NOT?

An examination of the ethical responsibilities of artists who produce socially conscious texts begins with the question of "How far is too far?" as it pertains

71

to their adherence to, or deviation from, factual, verifiable evidence. Many times, in the representations of history within popular culture, the "truth" has been slightly altered for cinematic purposes. Consider the following examples drawn from film adaptations of real-life events:

- The Notre Dame stadium full of fans did not chant Rudy's name as he stormed onto the field to play his only game on the Fighting Irish football squad, unlike the film *Rudy* portrays (Fried, Woods, & Anspaugh, 1993), though a small contingent of friends and relatives in the stands did cheer for him (Jacobi, 2019).
- A contrite Shoeless Joe Jackson, upon leaving the courthouse after being convicted of helping to throw the 1919 World Series of Baseball, can barely meet the eye of a young fan who implores, "Say it ain't so, Joe. Say it ain't so!" It is a moving moment in the film *Eight Men Out* (Pillsbury & Sayles, 1988), but it ain't so: that moment never happened in reality (Goodpaster, 2019).
- On a high school football team's practice field, Leigh Anne Tuohy walked up to her adopted son Michael Oher and told him to protect his team like he was protecting his family. It was an inspiring moment in *The Blind Side* (Kosove, Netter, & Hancock, 2009), one that suggested that the diminutive Leigh Anne was instrumental in helping "Big Mike" learn to play football—except it didn't happen that way as Michael Oher, who had studied football religiously and played the game enthusiastically since he was a child, could tell you (History vs. Hollywood, n.d.).
- During a tense moment in Norman Dale's first season with the Hickory High Huskers in the film *Hoosiers* (De Haven, Pizzo, & Anspaugh, 1986), the basketball coach has to defend himself in a town meeting against an ouster via referendum, but he is ultimately supported unexpectedly by Jimmy Chitwood, the star player. Coach Dale then leads the six-man Huskers team to win the state championship against all odds, squeaking by their opponents at every turn. Except that the season in question was the coach's second, the town supported him fully, and while still underdogs, the *ten*-man team had not only made it to the semifinals in the previous year, but in this, their championship year, they beat seven of their first eight tourney opponents by double digits (Goodpaster, 2020).

Perhaps these alterations to history seem fairly minimal. After all, the changes impact the stories in relatively minor ways, increasing the dramatic tension, heightening our emotional response, and emphasizing thematic development. They are largely innocuous changes undertaken with the artistic license we expect filmmakers to wield (Raab, 1999). They do not change our fundamental understandings of the events portrayed in any significant way, though Michael Oher, by all accounts, was unhappy with his portrayal as a timid football neophyte who learned the game at the hands of his adoptive mother Leigh Anne Tuohy, and he complained that the film negatively impacted the way others perceived him (History vs. Hollywood, n.d.). As consumers of mass media, we recognize that artists (i.e., those who produce or develop creative works, whether written, auditory, tactile, visual, or any combination thereof, such as writers, singer-songwriters, filmmakers, visual artists, composers, etc.) take some liberties when they adapt historical events to their chosen medium, embellishing some events for the sake of their artistic endeavor, though we trust that they will tell a great story or produce an engaging work of art.

But what if, in their efforts to retell a compelling real-life story that will both grip and persuade an audience that a truth is being told, the storyteller does more than stretch the truth? What if facts are cherry-picked, massaged, or even misrepresented in the name of engaging storytelling, and perhaps unwittingly perpetuate stereotypes? To what extent does an artist have a responsibility to the consumer (not to mention the real-life individuals on whose lives these stories are based) to attempt to convey an event truthfully? Does that even matter in the face of a great story? And to what extent are consumers obligated to question the facts of a story, to critically examine its veracity in the interest of truth? Do we tacitly acknowledge that the phrase "based on a true story" puts more emphasis on "story" than it does on "true"? Should we even care to what extent the story is true as long as it is compelling?

Questions such as these entail a much deeper, more complex investigation of what it means to be critically media literate in contemporary society as compared to historical pedagogies addressing media literacy, specifically as such consumer literacy relates to youths in school. Traditionally, media literacy education has been limited to explorations of media as modes of communication or art forms, investigations of the technical aspects of media, discussions of media in relation to audience and/or modality, or a historical overview of the development of media forms (Robertson & Scheidler-Benns, 2016), but this provides only a foundation of knowledge and falls short of the need for students to actively question the messages they receive, rather than passively accept them. A critical examination of media in schools, including the ethical questions raised above, entails the development in students of cognitive skills of analysis and critique beyond the relatively limited understanding of the structure and function of media. In this way, teachers can encourage students to become critical consumers of media, a transformation that is necessary if students are to become thoughtful, engaged participants in a democratic society which is a critical function of schools, according to John Dewey (1916). This critical media pedagogy undergirds the ethical exploration that drives this chapter, including the ethical obligations of the consumer as well as that of the artist.

ARTISTS AS SOCIAL ACTIVISTS

Artists have long been acknowledged as social and political critics, often using their art as a means of activism (Bradley, 2018; Khatchadourian, 1978), even to the point where some scholars consider their art and their activism to be inextricably linked (Diverlus, 2016). As such, artists serve important roles in our society, ones that I have no wish to mitigate, including

> speak[ing] out against what he considers to be evil in his country or the world . . . [and] helping us to know ourselves and the human condition—or to know them better—by tearing off the masks of appearance, illusion, self-deception, or delusion, about ourselves and the world. (Khatchadourian, 1978, pp. 27–28)

These roles cannot be overstated: art can be used as an implicit (sometimes explicit) critique of the status quo, challenging our views of the world. Argument begins with critique of thought, and it is through argument that we come closer to Truth (David, 2016). However, artists have a responsibility to themselves as humans and to the production of their art (Khatchadourian, 1978), art that can be used to comment and critique, to speak truth to power. Through their work, artists can help improve equity in a society by exercising their social responsibility (which involves addressing issues of social justice and equity including, among other things, repression based upon race, ethnicity, language, or religion [Dyck, 2014]) through challenging the status quo or speaking out against oppression and thereby encourage the consumers of their art to engage with those and other social and political issues (Bradley, 2018).

Thus, artists wield enormous influence over their audience (i.e., the consumer), commensurate with the artist's popularity, as well as having a social responsibility to uphold. This suggests that in many ways, artists occupy a privileged position in our society: to be able to speak and to be heard. While there is much discussion of whether and to what extent an artist may exercise their social responsibility (Bradley, 2018; Campbell & Martin, 2006; Diverlus, 2016; Elliott, Silverman, & Bowman, 2016; Gibbons, 2012; Khatchadourian, 1978; Marsh, 2006; Vande Berg, Wenner, & Gronberg, 2004), there is comparatively little discussion on the limitations on artistic freedom, and any discussion of those limitations puts few, if any, restrictions upon the artist. Khatchadourian (1978) notes that "it is society's moral duty to provide the artist with the maximum freedom possible" in which to create, "limited by the right of all other persons, artists and non-artists, to exercise their own freedoms or rights . . . [or to] interfere with the way of life elected by other members of society" (p. 25). This libertarian view maximizes the freedom of the artist who is obligated to actualize themselves artistically, limiting them only to the extent that the creation of their art interferes with another person's freedoms and rights and/or their way of life.

Other limitations address artistic privilege and function more as warnings against causing inadvertent harm against a population or a cause than as restrictions to an artist's actions (Bradley, 2018). This is particularly true of artists who speak for other individuals or who purport to speak for populations they do not inherently represent, such as White artists who embrace the cause of African American oppression, for example, as opposed to artists such as Ai Weiwei who calls out corruption and human rights violations in his own country of China. While this argument may suggest that artists have broad freedom to create, it also raises the question of what parameters, if any, bound the artist ethically, and the following section will explore some of those considerations.

ETHICAL CONSIDERATIONS

While ostensibly free to produce whatever art toward whatever end they wish, artists should be cognizant, if not downright cautious, about speaking on behalf of a cause with which they are not intimately connected. This implies an ethical consideration on the part of the artist: "could" does not always mean "should." If we employ an understanding of *ethics* as "a set of ways of thinking and acting similar to professional codes of conduct" (Gibbons, 2012, p. 258), which implies a self-monitoring and hence self-limiting approach to art, then how are we able to reconcile an ethical approach to artistic creation with Khatchadourian's (1978) libertarian perspective which implies virtually no real limits with respect to an artist's message? If Booth's (1998) assertion that he "can think of no published story that does not exhibit its author's implied judgments about how to live and what to believe about what to live" (p. 353) is to be believed, and if we extend his assertion to embody visual (i.e., film) and auditory (i.e., song) stories, which does not seem unrealistic given the nature of his assertion, then what sort of ethics of artistic creation can we formulate? Perhaps we can work toward developing such an ethics if we examine a potential problem that could result from ill-considered (or even unconsidered) artistic activism.

As noted in the introduction of this chapter, films often dramatize real-life events, and audiences expect (and usually forgive) discrepancies in the adaptations, as long as they increase the film's appeal. The changes implemented by the filmmakers are sometimes cosmetic, as when the Milan Indians became the Hickory Huskers in the film *Hoosiers* (Goodpaster, 2020);

sometimes technical, as when Jim Morris, the aged rookie pitcher, is noted in the epilogue of the film *The Rookie* to have "pitched in the major leagues for two seasons" (Hancock, 2002) when in fact the total was about seven or eight weeks from the end of the 1999 baseball season into the beginning of the next (Merron, n.d.); sometimes dramatic, as when Carroll Shelby bet Henry Ford II his entire business that his friend Ken Miles would win a race and be able to drive at Le Mans in *Ford v Ferrari* (Phelan, 2019); and sometimes they are egregious and defamatory enough to warrant a lawsuit, as when boxer Joey Giardello defeated Rubin "Hurricane" Carter in a unanimous decision, but because he was wrongly portrayed in the film *The Hurricane* (Jewison, 1999) as winning due to racist sentiments by the judges, he subsequently sued Universal Pictures (Neuenschwander, 2009). It is important to note that Carter himself agreed that Giardello deserved the victory and that Giardello ultimately won his lawsuit (Phillips, 2000) since it legally proves that Giardello's depiction in the film was inaccurate and suggests that the scene was intentionally designed to imply that racism, an overarching theme in the film, was a primary motivator for the judges' decision in real life. The deviation from fact in this latter example is one of numerous misrepresentations depicted in the film *The Hurricane* (Jewison, 1999) and in the song "Hurricane" by Bob Dylan (1994), and a more in-depth discussion of both artistic productions will help to illustrate a larger point in this chapter.

This section is not intended to set out an exhaustive case concerning the misrepresentation of the facts in the film *The Hurricane* (Jewison, 1999): that task has been largely accomplished by Mr. Cal Deal, an investigative reporter, who has compiled an extensive database of primary source documents depicting factual evidence that implicate Rubin Carter in the triple-homicide for which he was twice convicted and paint a picture of his character that strongly belies his representation in the film (Deal, n.d.). For this reason, I will select illustrative misrepresentations in both the film and the song "Hurricane" by Bob Dylan (1994) that are particularly egregious and discuss their relevance to the topic of artistic responsibility by interspersing factual evidence from primary documents and source material contemporary to the time period.

Norman Jewison's (1999) Film *The Hurricane*

This film serves as an exemplar for several reasons. First, the subject—a former boxer imprisoned for nearly twenty years on a triple-murder charge due to a racist police detective and a racist system of justice and believed to be innocent—is a particularly compelling human-interest story of social justice. Second, much of the popular culture media has rallied around Carter, especially since the film was released, supporting his conviction as improper and viewing his arrest as racially motivated. In fact, most of the articles surrounding the historical inaccuracies of the film do not address his guilt or innocence, dwelling on relatively superficial elements of the story (Raab, 1999; von Tunzelmann, 2014). Third, the misrepresentations of the characters in the film are particularly egregious—even bordering on downright libelous—with the tarnishing of boxer Joey Giardello's reputation at the beginning of the film being among the least problematic. And finally, the larger story involves fictional representations in both film and music, both of which have helped to sway public opinion in support of Carter, thus clearly illustrating the power of media on the uncritical consumer mind: the fictional accounts exonerated Carter in the court of public opinion, even though the prosecutors' cases convicted him in the courtroom twice, yet his innocence is thoroughly etched in public memory.

Norman Jewison, a Canadian filmmaker who is credited with directing over forty films, made three films that all depict racial prejudice and injustice in particular (*In the Heat of the Night* [1967], *A Soldier's Story* [1984], and *The Hurricane* [1999]), his so-called trilogy of films about race in America (Simon, 2012). The following background information is important since it relates to the reasons Jewison decided to make *The Hurricane*, in addition to its thematic similarity to his other two films. In several interviews (Phillips, 2000; SBS, 2000; Urban Cinefile, n.d.), Jewison remarked that his inspiration for the final film of his trilogy included two books: *The Sixteenth Round* by Rubin Carter (1974) and *Lazarus and the Hurricane* by Chaiton and Swinton (1991), two of the Canadian activists who worked to free Carter from prison. Jewison also noted that these books, as well as Bob Dylan's (1994) song, provided him with source material for the film (SBS, 2000; Urban Cinefile, n.d.). It is important to note that Chaiton and Swinton's book is based upon their experiences freeing Carter as well as Carter's autobiography which had originally inspired them to begin their investigations. Furthermore, Dylan's song is based upon extensive conversations the singer-songwriter had with Carter. This suggests that *virtually all the information upon which the film is based originates from Rubin Carter personally*, not to mention his autobiography, an unvetted text written while he was in jail in an attempt to plead a case for his innocence, a result in which he clearly had a vested interest. Notably, Jewison shares his reflections upon meeting Carter, calling him "totally charismatic" (Urban Cinefile, n.d., para. 11), suggesting that Jewison (and possibly even Dylan and the group of Canadian activists) may have been captivated by Carter's charm and thus easily misled.

Filmmakers often take liberties with historical adaptations and this is tolerated by film audiences, if not expected. However, Jewison himself referenced the importance of historical accuracy in one of the interviews saying that "films are important to this generation. Films are the literature of this generation, so we should be careful of what we put up there" (SBS, 2000). He also speaks to the other half of the adaptation dilemma—entertainment—saying, "You've got to remember, I've got to entertain, too! . . . I've got to make a movie people will want to see" (Urban Cinefile, n.d., para. 25).

The information from these interviews also suggests that (a) Jewison drew from limited source material (i.e., the dubious autobiography of a convicted yet "totally charismatic" felon doing his utmost to secure his release from prison) rather than conducting an in-depth investigation of his topic; (b) he saw in Carter's story an opportunity to add another perspective to his pair of films on race and prejudice; and (c) he was fully aware of his financial responsibilities to the movie studio as well as his ethical responsibilities to his audience, not to mention to his own posterity. At the point he made *The Hurricane*, he had directed and/or produced dozens of highly successful films, so he certainly had the financial means to investigate the story of Hurricane Carter more fully. He made an artistic decision to pursue a story in which he was interested, and despite his avowed recognition of ethical considerations, to dramatize the story further by incorporating additional fictitious elements, not the least of which involved the Giardello fight.

One of the most deplorable fictional elements Jewison incorporated into the film was the character of Detective Sergeant Della Pesca, the racist who hounds Carter throughout the film, attempting to frame him for the triple murder. Della Pesca was based upon Detective Lt. Vincent J. DeSimone, a twenty-six-year veteran of the Passaic, NJ police force who was the lead investigator into the murder. In his obituary, DeSimone was described by a local prosecutor as "a man of enormous courage, implacable determination and unswerving integrity" who would "pray for guidance when a murder investigation brought him to a church" (Gibbons, 1979). DeSimone was quoted as saying, "I would not be able to live with myself if I put a guy in jail for one day, knowing he didn't commit the crime" (Gibbons, 1979), and he was enormously relieved after Carter's second conviction for the triple-homicide which he felt vindicated him. In the film, Della Pesca is portrayed as being relentlessly racist, pursuing Carter doggedly from the time he was eleven years old through both convictions and his eventual release at age fifty in 1986 (DeSimone died in 1979). An on-screen depiction such as this is enormously unfair to a dedicated police officer who devoted his career to serving the public good and had never been accused of harboring racist sentiments.

The myriad discrepancies between the film and historical evidence are too numerous to mention in this space, but they include (a) an inaccurate depiction of Carter's getaway car in the film and omission of the two witnesses who correctly identified the real-life version; (b) omission of Carter's failed lie detector test and his refusal to take other tests, even though passing one of them would have meant his exoneration; (c) omission of the fact that three witnesses who provided alibis for Carter all later recanted, claiming they had been pressured to lie on Carter's behalf by Carter himself or his associates; (d) ignoring the fact that Carter had written a letter to Catherine McGuire which directed her to "remember" specific details about the night of the murder in order to provide him with an alibi (she testified in court that these were fabrications); and (e) omission of evidence of the live ammo found in Carter's vehicle that matched the caliber of two guns used in the attack. The film also misrepresented the racial motivation of the murder, suggesting that it occurred simply because the LaFayette Grill (where the murders took place) did not serve Black patrons. In fact, Rubin Carter's defense team introduced to the jury in 1976 that the murder was a "revenge killing" in retribution for the murder of the stepfather of Eddie Rawls, a friend of Carter and with whom Carter had been speaking on the evening of the night in question (*Carter v. Rafferty*, 1985). All of these misrepresentations suggest that Jewison was neither attempting to be objective in retelling the story nor adhering to ethical standards of research, whether Carter was guilty or not. Instead, he relied upon Carter's autobiography, an unreliable and self-serving book written by a "psychopath," according to a criminal profiler (Brown, 2001), and upon the book written by Chaiton and Swinton (1991), which details their efforts to free Carter from prison.

All of this is not to suggest that racism did not exist in Paterson, NJ, during the time of the murders, since there were documented instances of racial conflict (Rhodin & Murray, 1971), if not overt racism, present within the city. However, in his depiction of the events in the film *The Hurricane*, Jewison seemed to rely more on the word of a twice-convicted felon trying to free himself from prison than on factual evidence offered in newspapers, periodicals, and court transcripts. Furthermore, the Passaic County Prosecutor for the second trial and former civil rights leader (Hirsch, 2000), Burrell Ives Humphreys, discussed his "deliberate decision *not* to seek an all-white jury" in the 1976 retrial of Rubin Carter in his letter to New Jersey governor Brendan Byrne (Emphasis in original) (Humphreys, 1977) in a conscious effort to mitigate any racist tendencies that might be present within the jury.

In presenting his film as being "based on a true story," Jewison misled the public by creating a false narrative of events and impugning the reputations of numerous law enforcement officers, the result of which was to celebrate the cause of a twice-convicted felon who was *never lawfully exonerated for his conviction*, but instead was released, in part, due to the fact that the crime and subsequent "conviction occurred nearly 20 years [earlier], and to retry such . . . does not appear to serve the interests of justice" (*Carter v. Rafferty*, 1985).

Bob Dylan's (1994) Song "Hurricane"

In addition to Carter's autobiography and the Chaiton and Swinton (1991) book, one of the most important impetuses behind Jewison's decision to make *The Hurricane* and a source for material upon which Jewison relied (Phillips, 2000; Urban Cinefile, n.d.) was Bob Dylan's (1994) song "Hurricane," which was released in 1975 with the explicit intention of helping to bring Carter's case to the public eye and ultimately freeing him. Before writing the song, Dylan spent several hours speaking with Carter to uncover the details of the events as Carter himself, *a man who had a vested interest in being seen as a victim of systemic racism,* related them. Although it is certainly possible that Dylan investigated the accusations of racism, examined the then-contemporary evidence, and weighed both sides of the case in his mind before coming to his conclusion and writing the song, the resulting lyrics do not bear out this scenario. "Hurricane" is obviously an impassioned, one-sided, completely subjective, baseless allegation of systemic and overt racism within the Paterson, New Jersey police force, judicial system, and larger community as it pertains to Rubin Carter's crime. As noted above, Paterson, New Jersey, certainly has a troubled history of systemic racism that persists even today (Rumley, 2020; Scott, 2020), which is all the more reason that media portrayals must be as accurate as possible. Inaccurately reported racist encounters, particularly when they involve police, not only call into question the veracity of a resulting exoneration or conviction, but they also feed the flames of racial divisiveness in society and may help to erode public confidence in law enforcement.

Dylan's (1994) portrayal of the events of the night in question as unjust and unlawful is eloquent and forceful, his song lyrics poetic, and its tune memorable. It is by almost any standards an excellent song, which makes his lack of a thorough investigation even less forgivable, particularly when the artistic elements of the film contribute to the persuasiveness of his argument. When seen in the context of Dylan's significant ethos as a voice of social justice issues and a champion of the downtrodden, the obvious lack of objectivity borders on unethical. A short examination of some of the lyrics, compared against documented, factual evidence, will illustrate Dylan's one-sided presentation of the events.

In the second verse of the song, Dylan (1994) formally introduces the boxer by saying, "Here comes the story of the Hurricane" (Dylan, 1994, verse 2), then issues a simple assertion of Carter's innocence unsupported by fact, neither in the song nor in reality, when he refers to Carter as "the man the authorities came to blame / For somethin' that he never done" [*sic*] (Dylan, 1994, verse 2). He ends the verse by attempting to encourage in his audience a sense of sympathy for Carter based upon his status as a sports figure by noting that he was "put in a prison cell but one time he could-a been / The champion of the world" (Dylan, 1994, verse 2).

Although Rubin Carter was ranked as high as third among middleweight fighters in 1964 (BoxRec, 2009), his career was on a decline during the years up to the fatal evening: his record was 7-7-1 during 1965 to 1966, and he was not even ranked among the top ten contenders in 1966 (BoxRec, 2012), which means that it would have been all but impossible for him to fight for the championship. However, Dylan's argument that Carter was on the verge of the ultimate success within the sport of boxing when he was unfairly imprisoned for a crime "he never done" impacts the consumer pathetically, and an uncritical mind could easily be swayed by the frustration such a situation elicits.

A few verses later, Dylan (1994) suggests that Carter was out driving innocently with friends, but they were too far away from the scene of the crime to have been implicated and were completely oblivious to the events at the LaFayette Grill where the shootings took place: "Meanwhile, far away in another part of town / Rubin Carter and a couple of friends are drivin' around" (Dylan, 1994, verse 3). He also identifies Carter as the "number one contender for the middleweight crown" (verse 3), which he never was. Whether this detail was provided by Carter or was simply an artistic embellishment by Dylan is moot: Dylan is attempting again to draw on the sympathies of his audience by exaggerating Carter's boxing reputation to tap into our adulation of sports heroes (Schofield, 2012) who occupy a special place in our hearts.

In the following verse, Dylan (1994) suggests the continual targeting of Black Americans at the hands of police by noting that "a cop pulled him over to the side of the road / Just like the time before and the time before that" (Dylan, 1994, verse 3). He goes on to note that "in Paterson, that's just the way things go" (Dylan, 1994, verse 3), implying a rhetorical, but nonetheless meaningful, shrug of his shoulders, which suggests that little can be done to stop such unfair persecution. He points to racism as an explanation of this treatment, saying, "If you're black, you might as well not show up on the street / 'Less you wanna draw the heat" (Dylan, 1994, verse 3), complaining that Carter and his friends were pulled over solely because they were Black.

While racism in Paterson, New Jersey, during the mid-1960s was certainly prevalent (the bartender of the LaFayette Grill where the murders took place was a known racist), no act of racism by prosecutors in their investigation of Rubin Carter has ever been documented, and the lead prosecutor of the retrial was in fact a civil rights activist (Hirsch, 2000). Further, given the paucity of vehicles traveling on the city streets at 2:45 a.m. on an early Thursday morning, it is not unreasonable that police would have pulled over *any* vehicle they saw after receiving a call involving gunshots. Although racism and police brutality was and continues to be a concern in Paterson (Rumley, 2020), in this particular instance, the facts do not suggest that systemic racism was a factor in Carter's arrest. In fact, police let Carter and his friends go after initially pulling them over, since there were three men in the vehicle, not the two that had been initially reported (Carter had been lying down in the back seat while the vehicle was in motion when it was originally spotted). It was not until later, after receiving a more detailed description of the car by eyewitnesses from the scene—in particular the unusual taillights, the color of the car, and its out-of-state license plates—that police renewed their search for Carter's white car, pulling it over again within thirty minutes (Deal, n.d.). The evidence of the case seems to suggest that the arrest of Carter and his friends had more to do with the similarity of the car to eyewitness reports than to racist police officers.

In the next verse, Dylan (1994) reminds the listener of Carter's fighting prowess by saying that "Rubin could take out a man with just one punch" (Dylan, 1994, verse 8), but this characterization is immediately contrasted with a more philosophical image of Carter when Dylan says, "But he never did like to talk about it all that much" (1994, verse 8). This complex characterization portrays Carter as a man who is able to compartmentalize his boxing, which he sees as his vocation and a distasteful one at that, since he seems to want to avoid discussing it. Dylan drives home the perspective that Carter would prefer to distance himself personally from his job as a boxer: "It's my work, he'd say, and I do it for pay, / And when it's over I'd just as soon be on my way" (Dylan, 1994, verse 8). Dylan emphasizes Carter's peaceful nature by painting an idyllic scene of Carter communing with nature by going "up to some paradise / Where the trout streams flow and the air is nice" (Dylan, 1994, verse 8). This characterization of Carter's private self as a peaceful, nature-loving gentleman contrasts with the public image of his violent boxer self and suggests that a man who values serenity and calm would not be capable of murder.

A person's character is only circumstantial evidence and certainly not proof of a crime, but Dylan is misrepresenting Carter in overstating his serene nature and suggesting that he is not capable of committing such a heinous murder. In fact, the documented reality of Carter's personality is much different than Dylan's fanciful picture. For example, in 1976, Carter, a professional middleweight (between 154 and 160 pounds) boxer, attacked 112-pound Carolyn Kelley, a woman who was working for Carter's release, punching her in the face and kicking her in the back after she fell unconscious to the floor of his hotel room, putting her in traction for a month (Mulshine, 2000).

Furthermore, Dylan's (1994) suggestion that Carter would prefer to "ride a horse along a trail" (Dylan, 1994, verse 8) is sadly ironic when one considers that Carter purchased a riding horse which had gone wild. In one attempt by Carter to "tame" the horse, it bit him as he tried to mount her. According to Carter, "'Before that horse could turn around I whomped her on the side of the head. . . . She went down just like this.' Rubin let himself fall to his knees" (Gross, 1964, p. 76). These documented incidents belie the depiction of the boxer in Dylan's song and suggest that Carter was much more overtly violent and aggressive than the picture painted of him by the renowned singer-songwriter. This is significant when considering the violence of the crime with which he was accused, contrasted against Dylan's portrayal of him as peaceful.

In the final verse, Dylan (1994) refers to Carter as sitting "like Buddha in a ten-foot cell" (verse 11). However, Carter's extensive record of antisocial and criminal behavior suggests that he behaved in a significantly violent manner which continued consistently throughout his life. School records, as quoted in a brief filed in December 1985 by the Passaic County Prosecutor's Office, state that as a youth Carter "'terrorized boys and girls in class so that they were afraid to report him to the teacher.' . . . [The records] show the seeds of violence, threats and retaliation, which is totally consistent with the record that emerges in later years" (*Carter v. Rafferty*, 1985). In a scene from the film, it is suggested that in his youth Carter saved a friend from being molested by a White man, but in reality, Carter was charged with Assault and Robbery after he struck a man over the head with a bottle and stole $55 and his wristwatch. Carter's twenty-one-month military record indicates convictions by court-martial on four occasions, and his subsequent criminal record following his release from the army in 1956 (due to "Unfitness") notes two counts of Robbery and one count of Assault with Intent to Rob, for which he served four years in the New Jersey State Prison. His prison record, in that short time, "unquestionably presents a well-defined picture of consistent, long-standing belligerence, hostility and refusal to adhere to even minimal rules of day-to-day conduct and procedure" (*Carter v. Rafferty*, 1985).

None of these behaviors supports the picture painted by Dylan (1994) of a docile, peace-loving man who was set upon systematically by racist institutions and individuals throughout his life. Instead, Carter's behaviors from the earliest school records illustrate his aggression, hostility, violence, and complete lack of remorse and responsibility for his actions, and he continued to demonstrate consistent antisocial and criminal behavior over many years (*Carter v. Rafferty*, 1985). However, Dylan did not look further for evidence, even newspaper articles contemporary to the time period that would reveal these episodes from Carter's past, nor depict him in any way that would contradict a vision of him as a "Buddha in a ten-foot cell." Instead, Dylan made baseless accusations against law enforcement individuals and the judicial system, positioning Carter as a hero who deserved sympathy and help.

THE RESPONSIBILITY OF ARTISTS AND CONSUMERS

The right of influential artists such as Bob Dylan to create memorable folk songs that champion social justice causes is indisputable, and the right of talented filmmakers such as Norman Jewison to produce movies that illustrate inequity and maltreatment of an individual or group should not be limited. However, such artists have a personal responsibility to their subjects, their audiences, and themselves as honorable individuals to investigate their subjects in a fair and objective manner rather than promote a viewpoint based upon a limited perspective, especially when such popular artists who are known for advocating for social justice causes intentionally promote dubious claims. Such artists, with their wide-ranging and long-lasting influence (at the time of this writing, Dylan's song is forty-five years old), can address issues of social justice and equity substantively and effectively, but they can just as easily impugn the reputations of honest individuals who find themselves vilified in the court of public opinion, while criminals and liars are romanticized as heroes and gain an honored place in the hearts of consumers who often sympathize with the message uncritically. While these and other artists clearly have the right to produce whatever kind of art they see fit (Khatchadourian, 1978), as Passaic-Clifton, NJ, columnist Mike Cleveland (1975) for the *Herald-News* observed, "If we are to believe Dylan and the others when they claim the system has broken down, then we must have from them a commitment to truth" (para. 15). Dylan's song can act as both a frame and filter—a frame through which an audience can view an event and a filter which can influence the way the audience perceives that event—and the clarity of that window can mislead consumers, especially if they do not engage with media using a critical lens.

It is clearly important to increase equity and rectify social injustice in our world, and not automatically presume racist motives when they are claimed. Unsupported or misrepresented claims of racism can stoke the embers of divisiveness that already smolder in many communities and fan them into flame. Baseless claims also serve to diminish the experiences of those who have endured hardship, pain, and even death at the hands of individuals and institutions whose avowed purpose is to defend and serve the community. It is as important to imagine and work toward social justice and to mitigate or eliminate racism and prejudice as it is irresponsible to improperly identify racism or prejudice without examining all of the available facts. Because accusations are leveled in a song or dramatized in a film, the artists enjoy a certain immunity from legal prosecution and an autonomy within the public domain where their artistry is particularly admired by millions of ardent fans who do not necessarily question the message, much less the messenger. But if artists do not choose to adhere to stricter ethical considerations, then what is left to ensure the consumer that a message "based upon a true story" reflects the veracity of the events that occurred?

The answer is that there are no such assurances: the burden of recognizing and subverting messages falls to the consumer of media (Khatchadourian, 1978) who simply must be more diligent in seeking for truth and more critical in their interactions with popular culture media. And they *must* care about such truths if they are to deserve to participate in a democracy since they are empowered to choose from among themselves who will lead them, and such choice should be informed by critical and thoughtful consideration. This diligent truth-seeking will not simply develop in consumers without instruction in CML skills, and the best place for that instruction to occur is in the school. This has significant implications for teachers since such instruction necessitates a shift in curricular focus and possibly in pedagogical approach (Hendrix-Soto, 2016; Robertson & Scheidler-Benns, 2016). The development of CML skills in school will help students navigate their daily lives where they are incessantly bombarded by media messages, which in turn helps them to become more informed consumers, not to mention arrive at a better understanding of the importance of their active and thoughtful participation in a democratic society.

CML IN THE CLASSROOM

Teens have been identified as being "more media savvy, knowledgeable, and immersed in media culture than their teachers" (Kellner & Share, 2007, p. 17), but they are no more likely to engage in critical analysis of media messages than adults and may even feel unable to engage critically with media, perhaps through lack of an understanding of CML or a perceived lack of agency. Or they may simply refuse to engage, as with teens who enjoy music but refuse to critique or even listen to song lyrics (Gainer, 2007). This could be viewed as a conscious refusal to engage with the lyrics, since a teen listener might not want "her music to be co-opted by didactic, adult-centered, finger-waving righteousness . . . [and instead] claim ignorance of the meaning and continue to enjoy her music thoroughly without allowing guilt to hamper the pleasure" (Gainer, 2007, p. 106), thus distancing herself from the social message of the media in order to free herself from ideology.

In any case, a refusal to engage critically with media may be seen as particularly troublesome and even irresponsible behavior for a citizen in a democratic society, especially in an age of multimedia bombardment where messages are unconsciously absorbed to construct consumers (Kellner & Share, 2007). Such a refusal suggests tacit approval of the message through a passive acceptance of the media: a lack of critical engagement with media suggests that CML should be introduced into the classroom early and often. It can be difficult to engage emotionally with media yet simultaneously distance one's self from it intellectually. Artistic and commercial constructs, especially media (Kellner & Share, 2005), are supposed to be compelling creations that move the consumer emotionally, though not "to a point at which media-delivered selective truths, or even lies, gain uncritical acceptance" (Marsh, 2006, p. 338).

The power to move an audience emotionally has been discussed above in both the Jewison (1999) film *The Hurricane* and Dylan's (1994) song "Hurricane," both of which elicit strong emotional reactions in the audience, and it is our emotional reaction which can mislead us unconsciously since we are moved to action through our emotions, bypassing reason and logic (Marsh, 2006). In other words, the audience may not recognize the message on a conscious level, or that intellectual recognition of a message may be overshadowed by an emotional reaction to it. From a CML perspective, the crucial elements include recognition of a message by the audience, a perceived agency to respond, and a deliberate, conscious choice over one's reaction to that message, and a breakdown in this chain of responses suggests a lack of true critical thought on the part of the audience and a commensurate need to emphasize these skills in the classroom in order to encourage critical thinking.

In *Democracy and Education*, Dewey (1916) argued the importance of education for a strong democratic society, observing that "a government resting upon popular suffrage cannot be successful unless those who elect and who obey their governors are educated" (p. 101), and literacy is a fundamental element in the education process. Although decoding, fluency, and comprehension form the basic building blocks of textual literacy which support our full participation in our culture and society (Kellner & Share, 2007), in our increasingly multimedia-driven society, media literacy must also compose a crucial element of our educational system (Baker-Bell, Stanbrough, & Everett, 2017; French & Campbell, 2019; Harshman, 2017, 2018), for it is through CML that consumers will be able to arm themselves against dubious information or one-sided arguments in the form of media messages and become activists themselves. According to Kellner and Share (2005), "Media literacy helps people to use media intelligently, to discriminate and evaluate media content, to critically dissect media forms, to investigate media effects and uses, and to construct alternative media" (p. 372), while "critical media literacy involves cultivating skills in analyzing media codes and conventions, abilities to criticize stereotypes, dominant values, and ideologies, and competencies to interpret the multiple meanings and messages generated by media texts" (p. 372) as well as ways to resist media manipulation. The increasing preponderance of media messages "in the home and community suggests that there is an urgent need to help students learn how to evaluate such messages for their social, political, economic, and aesthetic contents" (Alvermann, Moon, & Hagood, 1999, p. 4) so that students may consciously control their reaction to those media messages and thus resist being subconsciously manipulated through their passive acceptance of those media messages.

A consumer must first recognize the possibility of manipulation before being able to exercise the tools to undermine that manipulation and consequently assume agency over their construction as consumers (Cadiero-Kaplan, 2002; Lewison, Flint, Van Sluys, & Henkin, 2002). An understanding of CML can help "make us aware of how media construct meanings, influence and educate audiences, and impose their messages and values" (Kellner & Share, 2007, p. 4), as well as how the identities of consumers themselves, and especially children and young people, are constructed by media culture, a process which is "frequently invisible and unconscious" (Kellner & Share, 2005, p. 372). It is through individuals "who are media literate, critically savvy, and morally engaged" (Vande Berg et al., 2004, p. 226) that an informed citizenry in global society who recognize how media can mislead, construct, or position the consumer (Alvermann et al., 1999; Harshman, 2018; Kellner & Share, 2007) can compose the foundation of a literate electorate and thus strengthen our democracy.

THE SEDUCTIVE NATURE OF MEDIA

The compelling nature of song and film can be seen in terms of Plato's concept of the oral spell (Marsh, 2006) and McLuhan's (1964) notion of cool versus hot media. The oral spell suggests the enchanting and seductive nature of an orator's voice which transfixes the listener in an aural fascination, making the argument seems particularly appealing to the listener. This enthralling orality exists apart from the logical arguments of the speaker, even beyond the intrinsic ethos conveyed within an oral text, to impact the audience on a subconscious level, almost hypnotizing them. The more captivating the speaker, the more intently an audience participates in the message, and the more reason and critical thought *decrease*, unless one can interrupt the message in some way (Marsh, 2006). Plato's concept of the oral spell can explain how songs can seduce a listener, for the more compelling the song, the less able is the listener to disrupt the message. This theory also increases the culpability of Dylan, a brilliant singer-songwriter by any standards, in producing a biased and one-sided song that is catchy and acoustically appealing and thereby enhances the oral spell Dylan casts. Its persuasiveness is built upon the emotion it induces in the listener, rather than upon logical arguments it might present through the lyrics.

To the extent that the appeal of Dylan's song as an artistic production conflicts with an individual's disposition toward Carter's guilt, a cognitive dissonance (Festinger, 1957) is created within the listener. The resulting psychological discomfort may impel the listener to modify their beliefs or attitudes in some way by feeling persuaded by their enjoyment of the song and the arguments contained within it, by disliking the song that presents a view so wildly at variance with their own preconceptions (Elliott & Devine, 1994), or possibly by engaging in some kind of rationalization that could allow both conflicting ideas to exist simultaneously in their minds, embodying the Orwellian notion of "doublethink" (Orwell, 1949). Whether the listener would be swayed by the aesthetic enjoyment they experience from Dylan's (1994) song, not to mention their preconceptions of him as an artist, or by the extent of their knowledge of the facts of the crime, or even by their own innate idealistic or racist sentiments is determined by each individual. In any case, the question remains: Can a listener both enjoy Dylan's song *and* believe in Carter's guilt? The answer could be found in Gainer (2007) who relates the story of a teen who intentionally keeps herself aloof from overt political messages in her music in order to allow herself to enjoy the music "without allowing guilt to hamper her pleasure" (p. 106). If a listener could accomplish this task (i.e., enjoy Dylan's music while deliberately ignoring his message), then one could mitigate the effects of the cognitive dissonance.

More troubling even than the seductiveness of a song is that of a film, which is an example of McLuhan's (1964) concept of cool media. To McLuhan, hot media are highly focused, single-sensory products that afford less audience participation than cool media. Music is an example of a hot medium, since it involves only the auditory sense. Consider that one can engage other senses or perform other activities (e.g., multitasking) while listening to the radio: cooking, cleaning, driving, even reading a book are all eminently possible. A cool medium is one that involves multiple senses (McLuhan, 1964), making the performing of additional tasks much more difficult or even effectively impossible. Watching television or a film, for example, is much more immersive, being multisensory, than listening to a song, however compelling the music might be.

One cannot effectively watch a film and read a book or drive a car, for example. Cooking, cleaning, or eating might be possible, since they are primarily tactile in nature, while watching a film involves auditory and visual senses. (Possibly the ultimate in multisensory experiences—the epitome of cool media—might be virtual reality immersive gaming or multisensory cinema experiences, in which a person might experience visual, auditory, tactile, olfactory, and even gustatory stimuli.)

Film, applying McLuhan's (1964) concepts, is a cool medium and would by nature increase audience participation in the experience by involving multisensory stimulation (i.e., auditory and visual); hence, film and television, neither of which "foster dialogue with mass audiences" (Marsh, 2006, p. 343), reduce the possibility of an authentic interruption of the message and thereby increase their potential to seduce an audience. In this way, the power of the Jewison (1999) film to manipulate audiences even more than the Dylan (1994) song can be seen in its suppression of analytical thought through multisensory immersion, not to mention the fact that the film is many times longer than the song. This further emphasizes the need for some degree of self-regulation of the veracity of media messages among artists and the need to apply CML skills among consumers when interacting with media messages.

For example, Jewison's (1999) depiction of the Carter-Giardello fight involves visceral images of the boxing match, complete with loud, thudding blows and flying droplets of blood, sweat, and spit, followed by audience groans and expressions of disbelief and frustration as the bloody and beaten Giardello is announced the winner, despite Carter clearly dominating the match throughout the scene. An audience member, caught up in the violence of the match through its auditory and visual images, can easily be swayed into feeling the same frustration when witnessing such an obvious miscarriage of justice. Considering the real-life result of the match suggested that Giardello won the fight by all accounts, including Carter's own, Jewison has obviously eschewed any degree of self-regulation in order to maximize the effect of the medium.

ETHICAL IMPLICATIONS

In discussing ethical obligations in the production of media, Gibbons (2012) notes the importance of establishing "expectations for truth and/or authenticity in youth media productions," and if youth are expected to adhere to ethical standards of "truth and/or authenticity" (p. 256), then should not commercial artists such as singer-songwriters and filmmakers also adhere to the same or even more stringent standards since they are professionals? Perhaps they should be held to higher ethical standards, but this is not, and should not be, an artistic mandate: if we are to privilege artists as social and political critics, their art must not be regulated externally, even on ethical grounds, in order to allow them the freedom to address issues of social justice and equity without fear of official reprisal or legal limitation.

If artistic production should be unregulated by society, as Khatchadourian (1978) maintains, then it follows that only the artist may decide what message their art transmits and what elements it includes and excludes, and in the case of artists who choose to present historical events, whether and to what extent their art might fully realize the event and present multiple perspectives if not objectively, then at least accurately. From this perspective, artists have a responsibility to the consumer only insofar as they recognize that responsibility.

Consequently, it is then incumbent upon the consumer to discern the veracity of the message, rather than simply take the word of the artist, or risk being manipulated unwittingly. This discernment, as noted previously, is enhanced through the development of CML skills.

We may choose to enjoy a media message for its own sake, intentionally divorcing it from the *intent* of its message, but we must be cautious that we are not simultaneously relinquishing our democratic duty as citizens to remain as informed an electorate as we are able. By remaining ignorant, whether willfully or through a lack of critical competence, of messages conveyed through the media, we risk surrendering partial control over our intellectual lives, thereby giving up our decision-making capabilities and allowing ourselves to be swayed unconsciously. Actively questioning these messages by using CML skills can enable us to maintain control over our perceptions and develop informed conclusions. This is not to suggest that CML implies an automatic resistance to a media message; rather, an understanding of CML and an ability to apply those skills entails knowledge, agency, and empowerment.

REFERENCES

Alvermann, D. E., Moon, J. S., & Hagood, M. C. (1999). *Popular Culture in the Classroom: Teaching and Researching Critical Media Literacy*. New York, NY: Routledge.

Baker-Bell, A., Stanbrough, R. J., & Everett, S. (2017). The stories they tell: Mainstream media, pedagogies of healing, and critical media literacy. *English Education*, *49*(2), 130–151.

Booth, W. C. (1998). Why ethical criticism can never be simple. *Style*, *32*, 351–364.

BoxRec. (2009, March 15). The Ring magazine's annual ratings: 1964. *BoxRec*. Retrieved from https://boxrec.com/media/index.php/The_Ring_Magazine%27s_Annual_Ratings:_1964.

BoxRec. (2012, January 09). The Ring magazine's annual ratings: 1966. *BoxRec*. Retrieved from https://boxrec.com/media/index.php/The_Ring_Magazine%27s_Annual_Ratings:_1966.

Bradley, D. (2018). Artistic citizenship: Escaping the violence of the normative (?). *Action, Criticism, and Theory for Music Education*, *17*(2), 71–91.

Brown, P. (2001). The hurricane—Ode to a psychopath. *The Pat Brown Criminal Profiling Agency*. Retrieved from http://www.patbrownprofiling.com/article1.html.

Cadiero-Kaplan, K. (2002). Literacy ideologies: Critically engaging the language arts curriculum. *Language Arts, 79*(5), 372–381.

Campbell, M. S., & Martin, R. (Eds.) (2006). *Artistic Citizenship: A Public Voice for the Arts.* New York, NY: Routledge.

Carter, R. (1974). *The Sixteenth Round: From Number 1 Contender to Number 45472.* New York, NY: Lawrence Hill Books.

Carter v. Rafferty, 621 F. Supp. 533 (U.S. Dist. 1985). Retrieved from https://law.jus tia.com/cases/federal/district-courts/FSupp/621/533/1368171/.

Chaiton, S., & Swinton, T. (1991). *Lazarus and the Hurricane: The Freeing of Rubin "Hurricane" Carter.* New York, NY: St. Martin's Press.

Ciardi, M., Gray, G., & Johnson, M. (Producers), & Hancock, J. L. (Director). (2002). *The Rookie* [Film]. United States: 98 MPH Productions.

Cleveland, M. (1975). 'Hurricane' leads me to question Dylan's judgment. *The Herald-News.* Retrieved from http://www.graphicwitness.com/carter/cleveland .html.

David, M. (2016). The correspondence theory of truth. In E. N. Zalda (Ed.), *The Stanford Encyclopedia of Philosophy.* Retrieved from https://plato.stanford.edu/arc hives/fall2016/entries/truth-correespondence/.

De Haven, C., & Pizzo, A. (Producers), & Anspaugh, D. (Director). (1986). *Hoosiers* [Film]. United States: Cinema '84.

Deal, C. (n.d.). Hurricane Carter: The other side of the story. *Graphic Witness.* Retrieved from http://www.graphicwitness.com/carter/.

Dewey, J. (1916). *Democracy and Education.* New York, NY: The Macmillan Company.

Diverlus, R. (2016). Re/imagining artivism. In D. J. Elliott, M. Silverman & W. Bowman (Eds.), *Artistic Citizenship: A Public Voice for the Arts* (pp. 189–210). Oxford, UK: Oxford University Press.

Dyck, R. (2014). Youth education for social responsibility. *Systems Research and Behavioral Science, 32*(2), 168–174.

Dylan, B. (1994). Hurricane [Song]. On *Bob Dylan's greatest hits volume 3* [Album]. New York, NY: Legacy.

Elliott, A. J., & Devine, P. G. (1994). On the motivational nature of cognitive dissonance: Dissonance as psychological discomfort. *Journal of Personality and Social Psychology, 67*(3), 382–394.

Elliott, D., Silverman, M., & Bowman, W. D. (2016). *Artistic Citizenship: Artistry, Social Responsibility, and Ethical Praxis.* Oxford, UK: Oxford University Press.

Festinger, L. (1957). *A Theory of Cognitive Dissonance.* Redwood City, CA: Stanford University Press.

French, S. D., & Campbell, J. (2019). Media literacy and American education: An exploration with détournement. *Journal of Media Literacy Education, 11*(1), 75–96.

Fried, R.N., & Woods, C. (Producers), & Anspaugh, D. (Director). (1993). *Rudy* [Film]. Culver City, CA: TriStar Pictures.

Gainer, J. (2007). Social critique and pleasure: Critical media literacy with popular culture texts. *Language Arts, 85*(2), 106–114.

Gibbons, D. (2012). Developing an ethics of youth media production using media literacy, identity, and modality. *Journal of Media Literacy Education, 4*(3), 256–265.

Gibbons, T. (1979, October 31). "The Chief" a dedicated lawman. *The Herald-News.* Retrieved from https://alchetron.com/Vincent-DeSimone#vincent-desimone-2b0b 1820-7b32-4fd2-8efc-068f9fbcf29-resize-750.jpeg.

Goodpaster, M. (2019, February 9). How the movie *Eight Men Out* created a false narrative about Shoeless Joe Jackson. *The Grueling Truth.* Retrieved from https:// thegruelingtruth.com/baseball/eightmenoutfalsenarrativeshoeless-joe-jackson/.

Goodpaster, M. (2020, February 12). Why the movie *Hoosiers* was nowhere near as good as the true story of Milan 1954. *The Grueling Truth.* Retrieved from https:// thegruelingtruth.com/basketball/movie-hoosiers-nowhere-near-good-true-story-m ilan-1954/.

Gross, M. (1964, October 24). A match made in the jungle. *Saturday Evening Post, 237*(37), 76–78.

Harshman, J. (2017). Developing globally minded, critical media literacy skills. *Journal of Social Studies Education Research, 8*(1), 69–92.

Harshman, J. (2018). Developing global citizenship through critical media literacy in the social studies. *Journal of Social Studies Research, 42*(2), 107–117.

Hendrix-Soto, A. (2016). Moving English classrooms toward critical possibilities. *English Journal, 106*(2), 22–28.

Hirsch, J. S. (2000). *Hurricane: The Miraculous Journey of Rubin Carter.* Boston, MA: Houghton Mifflin.

History vs. Hollywood (n.d.). *The Blind Side (2009).* Retrieved from https://www.his toryvshollywood.com/reelfaces/blindside.php.

Humphreys, B. I. (1977). Correspondence. Retrieved from http://www.graphicwi tness.com/carter/humph1.html.

Jacobi, J. (2019, September 23). Things about the real Rudy that the "Rudy" movie purposely misrepresents. *Ranker.* https://www.ranker.com/list/sad-rudy-ruettiger -facts/jim-jacobi.

Jewison, N., Palmer, P., & Schwary, R.L. (Producers), & Jewison, N. (Director). (1984). *A Soldier's Story* [Film]. Los Angeles, CA: Columbia Pictures.

Jewison, N., Bernstein, A., & Ketcham, J. (Producers), & Jewison, N. (Director). (1999). *The Hurricane* [Film]. Universal City, CA: Universal Pictures.

Johnson, B., Kosove, A., & Netter, G. (Producers), & Hancock, J. L. (Director). (2009). *The Blind Side* [Film]. Los Angeles, CA: Alcon Entertainment.

Kellner, D., & Share, J. (2005). Toward critical media literacy: Core concepts, debates, organizations, and policy. *Discourse: Studies in the Cultural Politics of Education, 26*(3), 369–386.

Kellner, D., & Share, J. (2007). Critical media literacy, democracy, and the reconstruction of education. In D. Macedo & S. R. Steinberg (Eds.), *Media Literacy: A Reader* (pp. 3–23). New York, NY: Peter Lang Publishing.

Khatchadourian, H. (1978). Artistic freedom and social control. *The Journal of Aesthetic Education, 12*(1), 23–32.

Lewison, M., Flint, A. S., Van Sluys, K., & Henkin, R. (2002). Taking on critical literacy: The journey of newcomers and novices. *Language Arts, 79*(5), 382–392.

Marsh, C. (2006). Aristotelian ethos and the new orality: Implications for media literacy and media ethics. *Journal of Mass Media Ethics, 21*(4), 338–352. doi: 10.1207/s15327728jmme2104_8.

McLuhan, M. (1994). *Understanding Media: The Extensions of Man* (2nd ed.). Cambridge, MA: MIT Press.

Merron, J. (n.d.). 'The Rookie' in real life. *ESPN.* Retrieved from http://www.espn.com/page2/s/closer/020410.html.

Mirisch, W. (Producer), & Jewison, N. (Director). (1967). *In the Heat of the Night* [Film]. United States: The Mirisch Corporation.

Mulshine, P. (2000, February). A hurricane victim tells the story of being beaten by Carter. *Newark Star-Ledger.* Retrieved from http://www.graphicwitness.com/carter/character-mulshine.html#:~:text=A%20Hurricane%20victim%20tells%20the,of%20being%20beaten%20by%20Carter&text=The%20movie%20%22The%20Hurricane%22%20claims,story%20of%20a%20boxer's%20life.&text=Six%20weeks%20later%2C%20the%20tough,floor%20of%20his%20hotel%20room.

Neuenschwander, J. A. (2009). *A Guide to Oral History and the Law* (2nd ed.). Oxford, UK: Oxford University Press.

Orwell, G. (1949). *1984.* New York, NY: Signet Classics.

Phelan, M. (2019, November 18). What's fact and what's fiction in *Ford v. Ferrari. Slate.* Retrieved from https://slate.com/culture/2019/11/ford-v-ferrari-fact-vs-fiction-le-mans-ken-miles.html.

Phillips, T. (2000, February 23). Denzel Washington and Norman Jewison. *The Guardian.* Retrieved from https://www.theguardian.com/film/2000/feb/23/guardianinterviewsatbfisouthbank.

Pillsbury, S. (Producer), & Sayles, J. (Director). (1988). *Eight Men Out* [Film]. Los Angeles, CA: Orion Pictures.

Raab, S. (1999, December 28). Separating truth from fiction in *The Hurricane. NY Times.* Retrieved from https://archive.nytimes.com/www.nytimes.com/library/film/122899hurricane-film.html?scp=95&sq=exoneration%252520issues&st=Search.

Reply brief of Carter v. Rafferty, 621 F.Supp. 533 (U.S. Dist. 1985). Retrieved from http://www.graphicwitness.com/carter/sarokinresponse.html#point1.

Rhodin, P., & Murray, R. (1971, May 1). Student clashes flare at Easton High School. *The Morning Call, 5.* Retrieved from http://www.newspapers.com.

Robertson, L., & Scheidler-Benns, J. (2016). Critical media literacy as a transformative pedagogy. *Literacy Information and Computer Education Journal, 7*(1), 2247–2253.

Rumley, E. (2020, June 22). More than 200 march for peace, against racial injustice in Paterson. *Tap into Paterson.* Retrieved from https://www.tapinto.net/towns/paterson.

SBS (2000, March 15). Interview with Norman Jewison and Denzel Washington. *The Movie Show.* Retrieved from https://www.sbs.com.au/guide/video/11676739992/Interview-with-Norman-Jewison-and-Denzel-Washington.

Scott, A. (2020, March 2). 49 years after racial "riot" rocked Easton High School, lessons learned still reverberate today. *The Morning Call.* Retrieved from https://www.mcall.com.

Schofield, J. (2012). The archaeology of sport and pastimes. *World Archaeology,* *44*(2), 171–174.

Simon, A. (2012, November 15). Norman Jewison: In the eye of the storm [Reprint]. *Venice Magazine.* Retrieved from http://thehollywoodinterview.blogspot.com/200 8/03/norman-jewison-hollywood-interview.html.

Urban Cinefile. (n.d.). *Jewison, Norman: The Hurricane.* In the Heat of the Hurricane. Retrieved from http://www.urbancinefile.com.au/home/view.asp?a=3397 &s=Interviews.

Vande Berg, L. R., Wenner, L. A., & Gronbeck, B. E. (2004). Media literacy and television criticism: Enabling an informed and engaged citizenry. *American Behavioral Scientist, 48*(2), 219–228. doi: 10.1177/0002764204267266.

von Tunzelmann, A. (2014, April 24). The Hurricane: The facts of Rubin Carter's life story are beaten to a pulp. *The Guardian.* Retrieved from https://www.theguardian .com/film/2014/apr/24/the-hurricane-rubin-carter-denzel-washington.

Chapter 5

Telling the Story of Youth, Sports, and Disability in the Television Series, *Friday Night Lights*

Ewa McGrail, J. Patrick McGrail, and Alicja Rieger

Sports and involvement in sports are a significant part of life for many children and young adults in the general population in the United States (Physical Activity Council Report, 2019). Young people with disabilities are also keenly interested in sports, although this cohort participates somewhat less in sports or other extracurricular athletic activities, in comparison to their peers without disabilities (Lankhorst et al., 2015; U.S. Government Accountability Office, 2010).

Sports participation can affect athletic identity in young people with disabilities (Piatt et al., 2018). This is because sporting culture and sports communities exert a strong influence on society in general (Lee, Cornwell, & Babiak, 2012; Macri, 2012). Coaches, team players, and other staff members provide sport-playing youth with guidance, role models, and skills relevant not just to sports but also to life, especially with respect to their emotional, social, and physical well-being. Thus, taking on social roles such as *athlete*, *teammate*, or *friend* empowers youth with disabilities to advocate for themselves and others, especially in combating harmful beliefs and stereotyping practices within ableist culture and communities (Aytur et al., 2018; Groff & Kleiber, 2001; Hebblethwaite & Curly, 2015; Lundberg, Taniguchi, McCormick, & Tibbs, 2011).

In addition to the real-world influences that mitigate and alter the social development of young people of all abilities who play sports, televisual characterizations of disability, and disability-accessible sports and athletes with a disability also powerfully mediate, affect, and amplify perceptions of real-world individuals with disabilities by their peers and society at large (Carter & Williams, 2012; Purdue & Howe, 2013; Zhang & Haller, 2013). These characterizations also affect the self-perceptions of the individuals who consider themselves disabled (Brittain, 2004). While studies have examined media portrayals of elite disability athletics (e.g., Brooke, 2019; Rees, Robinson, & Shields, 2019; Kim, Lee, & Oh, 2017), few studies have investigated televisual portrayals of young, preadult athletes with a disability in a school setting and the role sports and sports involvement plays in their lives and in the lives of their peers.

This chapter explores the representation of youth with disabilities in the television program *Friday Night Lights* (*FNL*) (Berg, 2007), which was critically acclaimed for its naturalistic depiction of young sporting lives in the small, fictional Texas town called Dillon (Heffernan, 2006). In particular, the analysis focuses on the depictions of quad rugby and young athletes with disabilities and the sociocultural values that these televisual characterizations convey about youth, sports, and disability.

SPORTS AND YOUTH IDENTITY

Youth's involvement in sports contributes to their social identity development (i.e., a collective self) resulting in "improved peer relationships and friendships, school engagement" and personal growth in areas such as "self-control, effort, teamwork and social responsibility" (Anderson-Butcher, 2019, p. 185). "Within sport, athletes learn to cooperate with others, to compete, to deal with success and failure, to develop self-control, and to take risks "(Smith & Smoll, 2012, p. 6). Further, Smith and Smoll contend that "important attitudes are formed about achievement, authority, and persistence in the face of difficulty" (p. 6). A sense of worth and belonging are other positive outcomes of a sports team's influence on youth's social identity development (Bruner et al., 2017). In this chapter, the analysis is focused on wheelchair, or *quad* rugby players' social identity depiction in *FNL*, especially peer relationships within the quad rugby team and between those players and their peers without a disability.

Peer influence within youth team sports also affects an individual athlete's self-concept formation and behavior response toward teammates and peers. Limited research has shown "that sports participation is associated with specific psychosocial outcomes such as interpersonal relationships, self-esteem, and overall quality of life, particularly among adolescents" (Bedard, Hanna, & Cairney, 2020, p. 353). The ways in which sports teammates interact with their peers influence the individual youth athlete's social behavior. Specifically, teammate prosocial behaviors, that is, "acts that are intended to help or benefit others (e.g., encouragement)," and antisocial behaviors, that is, "acts that are harmful or put others at a disadvantage (e.g., verbal abuse)," tend to reinforce both prosocial and antisocial behaviors, respectively, among individual athletes (Benson & Bruner, 2018, p.120). Children and youth with disabilities also experience prosocial (e.g., inclusion, friendship) and antisocial behaviors (e.g., teasing) in interaction with peers in physical activity and sports settings (Martin, 2010).

Other motivational factors may regulate individual youth athletes' development of self and self-perception through participation in sports. For example, adolescents and young adults with physical disability who participate in sports report a positive physical self-concept, that is, how they see themselves in terms of "sport competence, physical condition, body attractiveness and physical strength" (Scarpa, 2011, p. 38). They also experience self-esteem and a sense of self-worth, which is one way they evaluate themselves (Scarpa, 2011). Similarly, adolescents with physical disabilities who conveyed "strong perceptions of overall self-concept, strength, endurance, and flexibility reported more favorable self-esteem compared with individuals expressing weaker self-perceptions in the four noted predictor variables" (Shapiro & Martin, 2010b, p. 304). Involvement in sports also enhances the "sense of self-concept, independence, ability and corresponding pride" in Paralympic athletes (Pack, Kelly, & Arvinen-Barrow, 2017, p. 2063).

Collectively, these studies suggest that playing sports can be a powerful force in identity development and an equally strong socializing environment for youth with and without disabilities (Shapiro & Martin, 2010a). This work explores both the aspects of athletes' identity that *FNL* depicts and the aspects it leaves out. In the area of social identity, it examines the representation of relationships, friendships, and teamwork within quad rugby and between players and peers without a disability and the extent to which prosocial or antisocial behaviors are on display.

SPORTS CULTURE AND DISABILITY
IN FICTIONAL TELEVISION

While young characters with disabilities occasionally appear in television dramas (e.g., *Breaking Bad* [Gilligan et al., 2008]; *Glee* [Brennan, Falchuk, & Murphy, 2009]; *Degrassi: The Next Generation* [Hood, Moore, & Schuyler, 2002]), portrayals of young *athlete* characters with a disability in television have been rarer (Woodburn & Kopić, 2016). When such stories appear, they tend to appear in documentaries (e.g., *Tin Soldiers* [Duffy & Sassano, 2020]; *Swim Team* [Stolman, 2016]; or *She's Got Grit* [Padwo-Audick & Downing, n.d.]).

This state of affairs reflects a more general trend in the media landscape that lionizes nonfictional sports by able-bodied persons, and gives short shrift to athletes with disabilities and sporting events such as the Paralympics, particularly when compared to the traditional Olympic Games (Rees, Robinson,

& Shields, 2019; Scharfenberg, 2018; Solves, Pappous, Rius, & Kohe, 2019). This shortage in coverage and disability representation signals a lack of voices and perspectives of this marginalized social group in television and popular culture (Ellis, 2016; Stewart & Spurgeon, 2019; Wagmeister, 2016). It mirrors some of the prejudices of ableist culture and communities with respect to disability and sports (Ellis & Goggin, 2015; Mallett, 2011).

In fictional entertainment, unlike in news production, writers and directors are freer to create character amalgams and worlds which, while they are like our own, may be purposefully constructed to comment on issues and struggles of the day. Creative producers can thus create programs and films that attempt to address the concerns of previously marginalized groups. One such program that enjoyed critical acclaim during its run is *FNL* (Berg, 2007). This program had comparatively many scenes throughout its first season that focused on quad rugby athletes even though the overall focus was about American high school football in a small town. In the first episode, during a Friday night game, Jason Street, the young quarterback, acquires a critical injury and loses the use of his legs. In the aftermath of the injury, Jason, desirous of continuing in his identity as an athlete, joins a quadriplegic rugby (*quad* rugby) team. Because of the program's comparatively unusual emphasis on quad rugby and young athletes with a disability, as well as its prominence and availability for analysis, it was chosen for intensive study.

Using media analysis techniques based on Berger's adaptations of coding, signs, and cinematography as a form of intertextuality (Berger, 2005), this qualitative analysis (Altheide & Schneider, 2013; Kohlbacher, 2006) examines the depiction of quad rugby, young athlete Jason Street's attraction to it, and his interaction with his newfound rugby teammates who have similar disabilities in *FNL*. It also explores the social and cultural goals for these representations through the following questions:

RQ1: Which aspects of sports activity and lifestyle appear in the portrayal of disability youth quad rugby in *FNL*?
RQ 2: Which personal attributes show in the portrayal of quad rugby youth athletes?
RQ 3: What sociocultural values do the portrayals of disability quad rugby and young athletes reveal?
RQ4: How do sports affect relationships and engagement among youth with and without disability?

Media Analysis and Meaning

Television entertainment, rather than being a structural free-for-all, adheres to time-honored storytelling techniques, no matter what the subject matter may be. As Potter (2019) writes, "The formulas are the guides; that is, they tell storytellers what elements are available to put into their stories and how those elements should be assembled" (p. 196). On the receiving end, "Because we as the audience also understand these formulas (albeit unconsciously and intuitively) we can easily follow the progression of the action" (Potter, 2019, p. 196). *FNL* is one such story, and as evident in the questions for this study, this work examines the elements the producers put together to tell the story about youth, sports, and disability in the show.

Every dramatic story features a protagonist that struggles against an obstacle or antagonist, who may or may not be a person. Sometimes that antagonist is an object, or an institution (Potter, 2019). In *FNL*, the protagonist is Jason, who struggles to regain his athletic identity in the aftermath of the disabling injury he acquires while playing football. In the scenes recounting his experiences after his injury, the ostensible antagonist is his physical disability—although it is less a battle against, and more a negotiation with, the new reality with which he must contend in his daily life and sports life activities. A much stronger opponent is the "invisible" enemy, namely, the sociocultural values and attitudes that a society associates with a disability. All of this is rendered for television on physical film in a remarkably realistic and naturalistic way (Heffernan, 2006). Pizer (1995) notes that these descriptive terms "bear social and moral valences that are frequently attributed to any work designated as realistic or naturalistic, whatever the specific character of the work. The real and the natural . . . suggest the genuine and actual shorn of pretension and subterfuge" (p. 3).

Therefore, the techniques of realism and naturalism by the visual storytellers attempt to bring the elements of a challenging disability and the interpersonal angst it causes in Jason Street's life closer to the viewer and to render it in a way that seems realistic and truthful. In recent years, realism has been employed with more frequency on television; it is a trope popular with critics such as Moore (2006) who wrote that *FNL* was "breathtaking in how it captures ordinary life set against extraordinary passions and world-class skills" (para. 5).

However, it is important to understand that realism, like romanticism or expressionism, is an aesthetic approach, and can be rendered via cinematic technique. The actual characters and situations may seem lifelike, but they are all merely choices that cinematographers, scenic designers, directors, and actors make (Wolfe, 1981). These artistic choices may be thought of as signs or codes that direct viewers to feel and see the world of the program in a certain way. The audience members may laugh when a joke is told by a TV character, but the humor engaged in by the character is not spontaneous; it was created by writers and brought to life by an actor. This quality of *seeming real* must be understood both as intentional and as a complex of semiotic codes.

According to Berger (2005), "Codes are highly complex patterns of associations that all members of a given society and culture learn" (p. 30). As such, "these codes, or 'secret structures' in people's minds, affect the ways that individuals interpret the signs and symbols they find in the media and the ways they live" (Berger, 2005, p. 30). In the context of this analysis, a sports activity such as quad rugby or football is an assemblage of codes as a collection of rules, behaviors, and norms that tell players what to do and what to value. The viewers or audience members have access to these *secret structures* and they use them to understand this sports activity, to evaluate player performance and to interpret the messages that this highly codified system carries. In like manner, codes apply to disability sports, athlete's lifestyle, and athletic identity, and they carry sociocultural values attached to them.

Jason's injury was caused by football, and the overall thrust of *FNL* is the explorations of a small town's identity being caught up in football and its joys and sorrows. Berger's (2012) theoretical orientation toward coding and signs, therefore, seemed particularly appropriate to this study, given also that he adds an entire chapter in the fourth edition of *Media Analysis* to the signs and codes of American football (Berger, 2012). He writes,

> Football is an interesting subject for the semiotician because the game is simultaneously full of signs and a signifier of some importance. . . . It is not unusual for 60,000 people or more to gather together for a game, and with television coverage sometimes millions of people watch a game, which means that the entire country "becomes" a football stadium. (Berger, 2012, p. 153)

While the *secret structures* or codes alluded to above are pervasive, this does not mean that they are always readily apparent. Members of mass media audiences would experience frequent cognitive dissonance (Festinger & Carlsmith, 1959) if television jolted them into complete awareness of attitudes and situations that had not been previously clear to them. Fictional televisual stories must seem naturally created and flow organically, in order to be accepted by the audience. Bal (2017) argues that in order for the narrative system of a work to seem realistic, the setting, camerawork, dialogue, and acting, or what is sometimes called the mise-en-scène (Monaco, 2009), must be made to seem "self-evident or necessary. This is so that the inflections of the presentation, the attributions of qualities and the ideological machinations remain invisible" to the viewer (p. 27). In other words, the persuasive elements of a film or television program only infrequently employ pure rhetoric; dialogue, setting, character relationships, and acting usually come together in a naturalistic way, which can conceal ideological meaning and sociocultural elements in the program.

This analysis concentrates on the setting, color, tone, acting, and dialogue in the television episode as the most powerful conveyances for the presentation of the ideologies inquired about in the research questions. Television dialogue, for example, consists of not only paragraphs of persuasive material but also a presumedly improvised give-and-take among and between multiple characters. The settings that a television episode employs, particularly when a show is on location, work together with dialogue and shot composition to render a world, a "cognized model" (Wolf, 1999, p. 19) seemingly fully inhabited by the characters, within which viewers find themselves. Therefore, the sociocultural meaning that the dialogue, setting, and mise-en-scène convey is best structurally analyzed at the scenic and then the episodic level, because characters interacting with one another through a script in a directed scene of color and spectacle create the total meaning of a scene. Scenes together create the meaning and narrative flow of the episode, which itself is a narrative element of the serial television program as a whole, which is in turn a complex of semiotic signifiers and codes that comments heavily on the social environment.

This analysis also draws heavily on the dialogue in the acting script to uncover "not only the manifest content of the material . . . but also so-called latent content" (Kohlbacher, 2006, Basic Ideas section, para. 1) in those scenes that portray quad rugby sports, quad athletes, and their abled and disabled peers in *FNL*. Manifestness and latency together form the ideological meaning and sociocultural elements that are conveyed to the viewers. While dialogue itself conveys manifest meaning, the context in which the words are said, which encompasses both the actor's choices and the director's scenography, is where the sometimes more important latent content may be found.

SCENE SELECTION

Although *FNL*, like most fictional television dramas, explores a variety of characters, themes, and issues over the course of its five-season run, this analysis concerns itself with how it treated the issue of the sudden onset of disability of one of its chief characters, a football athlete who then transitions to sports played exclusively by those with disabilities. It is therefore confined to the scenes featuring Jason Street, the young athlete who becomes permanently disabled due to a serious American football injury. Many of the studied scenes also include Herc, another character who had been an exceptional athlete prior to his disability. Herc is an experienced but flinty and outspoken quad rugby player with rough manners who simultaneously exasperates Jason and inspires him to accept his new status and to consider joining Herc's quad rugby team.

The bulk of the analysis is thus of the scenes featuring interactions between Jason Street and Herc, although related scenes in which other characters appear with Jason and have dialogic interaction with him have also been chosen. Thus, included are the characters of Jason's on-again, off-again girl-friend, Lyla Garrity, and his new significant other, Suzy Quinlan. A scene with Jason and Lyla's father, Buddy Garrity, and one with Jason and football coach Eric Taylor are also included, because the sociocultural content about disability were particularly evident in these scenes. The analysis is limited to the first season because of the need to analyze scenes in depth, and because the scenes establish for the rest of the program's seasons the characters' overall profiles.

There were a total of twenty-two episodes of *FNL* in Season One. In table 5.1, there is a complete list of the episodes from which analyzed scenes were taken, and the approximate timing information for those scenes within each episode. To choose relevant scenes from the twenty-two episodes in Season One, the scenes that were putatively about Jason, disability, and sports were determined by watching each episode and carefully determining the content of such scenes. Following this, it was determined that eleven of the twenty-two episodes (50 percent) featured significant material about Jason Street, his growing acceptance of his disability and his gradual adoption of quad rugby. From these eleven episodes, a total of twenty-eight scenes were analyzed. Studied scenes averaged just less than two minutes in length (117 seconds) and there were from one to five studied scenes in each episode. Every stud-ied scene features Jason Street, and twenty-four of the twenty-eight (85.7 percent) scenes feature the major speaking character named Herc. Several scenes also have other named and unnamed quad rugby teammates, such as Corey (who, like many in the supporting cast, has a disability in real life), as well as Jason's on-again, off-again girlfriend, Lyla Garrity, her father Buddy, Jason's football coach Eric Taylor, and Jason's new girlfriend, Suzy Quinlan.

Scene Analysis

In this qualitative analysis, the sociocultural elements for which evidence was sought are the sociocultural attitudes alluded to in the RQs: (1) *sports activ-ity and sports lifestyle*, (2) *personal attributes of the (dis)abled athletes*, (3) *social structures and stereotypes* (of disability), and (4) *the impact of quad rugby on peer relationships and engagement*.

In the first part of our analysis, the scenes were analyzed separately for two properties—the *presence* of the above attitudinal themes and the *valence* of those themes. After analysis of each studied scene, these themes were assigned numbers that represented a most-least metric with respect to the strength or presence of these different sociocultural elements. Afterward, the overall

Table 5.1   FNL Episodes Analyzed by authors McGrail, McGrail, and Rieger, 2020.

Season/Episode#/Name	Air Date	Number of Analyzed Scenes	Timing of Scenes (Based on DVDs)
Season 1, Episode 4 "Who's Your Daddy"	October 24, 2006	4	5:11–5:52, 7:43–9:25, 22:23–24:28, 31:52–33:43
Season 1, Episode 5 "Git'er Done"	October 30, 2006	2	12:18–13:38, 18:43–19:55
Season 1, Episode 7 "Homecoming"	November 14, 2006	1	17:05–18:40
Season 1, Episode 8 "Crossing the Line"	November 28, 2006	5	12:20–13:44, 17:56–20:32, 25:43–28:03 33:33–36:22, 38:56–40:30
Season 1, Episode 11 "Nevermind"	January 3, 2007	1	10:48–12:42
Season 1, Episode 13 "Little Girl I Wanna Marry You"	January 24, 2007	3	17:38–18:24, 21:58–24:01, 30:26–32:16
Season 1, Episode 15 "Blinders"	February 7, 2007	2	21:12–22:58 31:11–32:20
Season 1, Episode 16 "Black Eyes and Broken Hearts"	February 14, 2007	1	22:42–23:41
Season 1, Episode 17 "I Think We Should Have Sex"	February 21, 2007	3	04:46–6:11, 15:35–18:07, 22:12–24:53
Season 1, Episode 18 "Extended Families"	February 28, 2007	4	02:50–04:02, 11:12–12:39, 19:26–20:03, 21:23–22:56
Season 1, Episode 19 "Ch-ch-ch-ch-Changes"	March 21, 2007	2	1:49–3:00, 3:44–6:21

episodic mean of the numbers was derived from the scenic numbers, in order to indicate the average presence of that element in the episode in which the scene appeared. In the second step, a number corresponding to the perceived valence, or positivity/negativity, was similarly applied to each sociocultural value found in the studied scenes, around a central point of neutrality in order to indicate the overall positivity or negativity of characterization in the episodes.

Specifically, in step one, the strength, or presence, of the sociocultural values with Jason, Herc, and others was coded by the first two authors as to whether these were *predominant* (Rating 5), *very noticeable* (Rating 4), *somewhat noticeable* (Rating 3), *barely present* (Rating 2), or *not apparent or not applicable* (Rating 1). It was not assumed that these structures would be available in every studied scene; if a sociocultural value was not in evidence, it was given a rating of "1."

Then in step two, the valence, or positivity or negativity, of these values in each studied scene was also coded, using the scale *5 = very positive, 4 = positive, 3 = neutral, 2 = negative, 1 = very negative*. Positivity and negativity were adduced by the authors as to how they felt that the studied scene valued or provided positive or negative coverage to the given sociocultural value.

It is important to note that these analytic numbers are qualitative descriptive data, however, and they should not be misinterpreted as quantitative data. The data were analyzed inductively to identify emerging patterns in youth athlete disability representations in the scenes selected for study. They represent the impressions of these values by the authors. In a macro view, they may be thought of as an aid in assessing how "fair" the program is to the activities portrayed in it, particularly quad rugby and the young men with disabilities who play it.

The research questions were used as broad areas for investigation and to group identified patterns into the themes presented in this work. As previously indicated, the analysis focused on the ways in which the manifest and latent content (Kohlbacher, 2006) together formed the ideological meaning and sociocultural elements that the *FNL* series conveyed to the viewers.

THE GRITTY WORLD OF QUAD RUGBY AND JASON'S SEARCH FOR A NEW IDENTITY

The findings are organized around the research questions. The overall strength (presence) and valence (levels of positivity and negativity) of research questions are explained in an overview and they are also displayed in figures 5.1 and 5.2. This is followed by a discussion of the themes within each research question.

Overall Strength (Presence) and Levels of Positivity

Figures 5.1 and 5.2 display evidence for the perceived existence of each of the four sociocultural values inquired into in RQs 1 through 4: (1) *sports activity and sports lifestyle*, (2) *personal attributes of the (dis)abled athletes*, (3) *social structures and stereotypes* (of disability), and (4) *the impact of quad rugby on peer relationships and engagement*.

As we can see in figure 5.1, the issue of sports lifestyle (RQ1) was not perceived as present in every scene to a degree which would permit its analysis. It was absent in Episode 4, "Who's Your Daddy" (aired 11/02/06), and

COMPARATIVE STRENGTH OF THE FOUR RESEARCH QUESTION VALUES

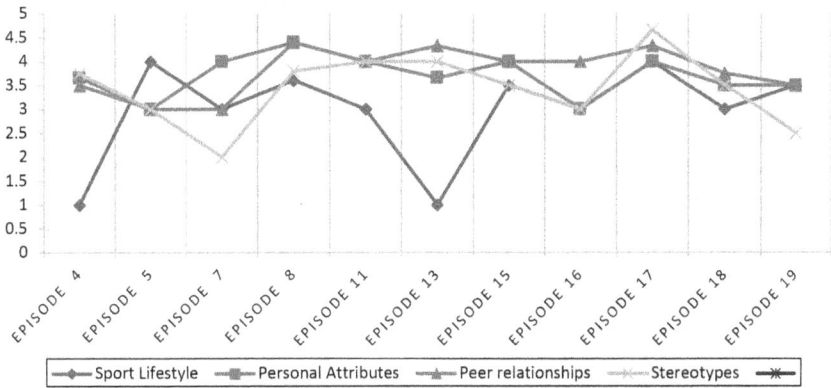

Figure 5.1 Comparative Strength of the Four Research Question Values. Note: 5 = Predominant, 4 = very noticeable, 3 = somewhat noticeable, 2 = barely present, 1 = not noticeable or not applicable. *Source*: Graph created by authors.

COMPARATIVE VALENCE OF THE FOUR RESEARCH QUESTION VALUES

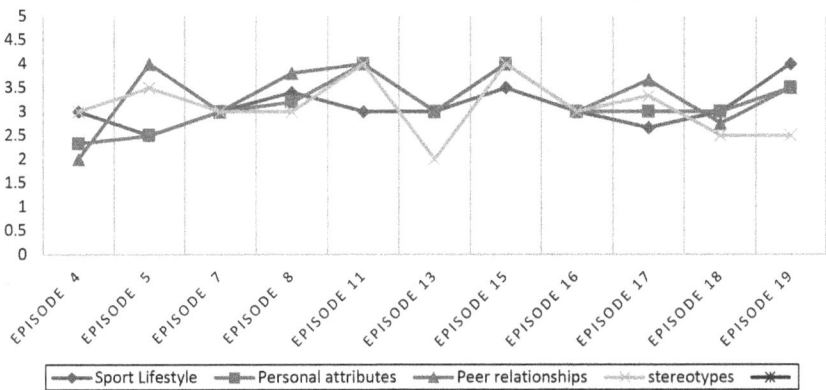

Figure 5.2 Comparative Valence of the Four Research Question Values. Note: 5 = very positive, 4 = positive, 3 = neutral, 2 = negative, 1 = very negative. *Source*: Graph created by authors.

Episode 13, "Little Girl I Wanna Marry You" (aired 01/24/07). The issue of sports lifestyle was discussed most prominently in Episode 5, "Git 'er Done" (aired 11/8/06).

The two most prominent sociocultural values that were identified in the studied scenes were personal attributes (RQ2) and peer relationships (RQ4).

The mentions, suggestions, and presentation of these two values lay above the average point of 3 on our scale. Moreover, unlike as with sports lifestyle, these values appeared in every studied scene. The issue of stereotypes (RQ3) was perceived as present in most studied episodes, with the exception of Episode 7, "Homecoming" (aired 11/14/06), and Episode 19, "Ch-ch-ch-ch-Changes" (aired 03/21/07), where it was barely noticeable.

In terms of valence (positivity and negativity), figure 5.2 shows that sports lifestyle (RQ1) was the most consistently portrayed in terms of positivity. Although not appearing in every scene or episode, when it was shown, it averaged a valence of approximately "3." Peer relationships (RQ4) enjoyed the greatest positivity in the scenes studied, with a majority of scenes at 3.5 or above. Stereotypic portrayals, which are inquired into with RQ3, also sometimes averaged a 4 in terms of positivity. It is possible for a stereotypical portrayal to be deemed "positive" even if it veers from realism and conformance with the lived experience of the group it describes. Examples of this exist particularly in Episode 11, "Nevermind" (aired 01/12/07), and Episode 13, "Little Girl I Wanna Marry You" (aired 01/24/07).

The discussion of the discovered themes for each question follows. It includes the notes on the cinematic techniques that have been rendered to portray the representations of disability that these themes convey.

RQ1: Which aspects of sports activity and lifestyle appear in the portrayal of disability youth quad rugby in *FNL*?

Overall, in comparison with the enthusing crowds and colorful pageantry of the Friday night football games in which Jason Street was previously involved, the world of quad rugby is depicted televisually as a gritty, gray world of metallic appurtenances that exist only to physically support the players with a disability. The wheelchairs have been customized by hand and are not designed to be attractive modes of transportation; they are designed to take a beating and to be instruments of offense to other players. The players' characters are not explored to the same degree as those from Jason's former football team; however, the sardonic Herc is presented in a three-dimensional way. Overall, the quad rugby players are portrayed as older, wiser, and more world-weary than the young, idealistic high schoolers from whose company Jason has emerged.

Jason's newfound acquaintance Herc is openly dismissive of Jason's initial "medical" wheelchair but he ignites Jason's competitive gaming sense. Gradually, he leads Jason into the world of competitive wheelchair *quad* rugby. Jason's natural athleticism soon provides him with an advantage, and he proves his merit as a wheelchair rugby player. He is crushed, however, when he is not chosen to go to Beijing for an important Paralympic tryout.

The themes of *Being Good at It* and *the Specter of Injury* that are discussed next reveal the tensions between athletic aspirations and the reality of injury that Jason and his teammates have to negotiate as part of their new athlete lifestyles.

Being Good at It

The desire to be good and successful at a sport marks the lifestyle of a committed athlete. These aspirations are most directly referenced in Episode 5, Scene 2, in the following exchange between Herc and Jason:

Herc: "Hey. I hurt ya?"
Jason: "Sorry. (looking at a picture of Herc as abled athlete) When was that?"
Herc: "That was a while back. (Chuckles) Oh, you're getting good at that [i.e., rugby]. Look at you. Very nice. (Groans)"
Jason: "Herc . . . What's your injury?"
Herc: "Same as you. C7-T1. Got our fingers. We're the lucky ones around here."
Jason: "Oh, yeah. Real lucky. (snickers)"
Herc: "It's all relative, QB."
Jason: "How . . . How long before you started playing quad rugby?"
Herc: "About a year. Of course, I wasted a good six months drowning in a sea of self-pity." (*FNL*, "Git 'er Done" aired 11/8/06)

In the above scene, it is evident that Herc, like Jason, had been a successful athlete before his injury. Although it is never directly stated in the program which sports Herc had formerly played, the fleeting glimpse of the picture shows someone who appears to be in track garb, so perhaps Herc was a track star. It is clear in this scene that Jason and Herc are still emotionally healing from their respective unsettling separations from the sports at which they had been previously successful, and which had formed their identities. Their previous sports lifestyles had been initially punctured with helplessness and self-pity following serious injuries, as have real-life athletes in previous research (Timler, McIntyre, Rose, & Hands, 2019). Nevertheless, Jason and Herc also hold athletic competence and accomplishments in obvious high esteem as they both desire to excel at a new sport, which is for them quad rugby.

As such, the *FNL* series gives these young athletes credit for their talent and skill, suggesting to the viewers that disability does not define them but rather refines their athletic identity. This positions them as athletes first who secondly happen to have a disability (Pack et al., 2017). This is an attempt by Berg and the other *FNL* showrunners to create a piece in opposition to the perception of athletes with disability by the public who do not view them "'as real' athletes'" even though they "strongly perceived themselves as athletes" (Martin, 2010, p. 52)

Scenically, there is a grayness and sense of claustrophobia to this and many of the scenes that feature Herc and Jason. This might symbolize that the journeys back into success that Herc and Jason have undertaken require a great deal of grit and persistence in their sports practice and in terms of their states of mind in order for them to be high achievers again. Borrowing from the psychology of color (Kaya & Epps, 2004), the gray color in these scenes might also represent the losses, fears, and depression that they need to overcome in their journeys, with not particularly picturesque trajectories ahead of them.

The Specter of Injury

Quad rugby is a full-contact sport. According to the International Wheelchair Rugby Federation (n.d.), "Contact between wheelchairs is not only permitted, but is in fact an integral part of the sport as players use their chairs to block and hold opponents" (Wheelchair Rugby Federation, n.d., para. 1). *FNL* has several scenes of quad rugby in which the jarring, full-contact nature of the sport is dutifully explored. The specter of injury due to the sport is also mentioned; at one point, when Jason expresses an avid desire to join Herc's quad rugby team in the Paralympic tryouts, he is cautioned (fruitlessly) by his physical therapist in Episode 8, "Crossing the Line":

Jason: "You tell the boys here that I'm gonna come scrimmage on Thursday? I'm ready. I told you I'm ready."
Phil: "Jason, you're not ready."
Jason: "Phil, come on. Every day it's about how great my progress has been, how unusual I am. What's the worst that could happen? I fall out of my chair, break my neck? Oh, wait, that already happened, didn't it?" (*FNL*, "Crossing the Line" aired 12/07/06)

Phil then proceeds to enumerate various injuries that might happen to Jason if he pushes too hard, but Jason does not seem to care or comprehend fully the potential risks involved and Phil is forced to make it even more clear to him:

Phil: "You don't seem to know what that means, so let me spell it out for you. Those little bits of bone are all that's protecting your spinal cord at your injury site. Know how you can use your hands? You screw up your fusion, no more grip. Then what? I want you to think long and hard about this before you do it." (*FNL*, "Crossing the Line" aired 12/07/06)

As evident in the exchange between Phil and Jason, this full-contact sport carries certain risks. Nevertheless, for those who are already disabled and are playing it, it is a visible badge of self-esteem and perceived mastery within disability athletics. These values shape their self-concept (Scarpa, 2011) and contribute to self-worth perceptions which these characters use to evaluate themselves and their athleticism (Shapiro & Martin, 2010b). The portrayal of quad rugby as a sport that is as rough and uncompromising as ordinary American football positions these athletes as capable of competitive sports, which is normally considered not possible for people with disabilities (Hardin & Hardin, 2004). It also gives this Paralympic team sport and these athletes a strong footing, at least in the fictional sports world of *FNL*. The representation here is again unlike that in the real world, where this sport is less known and given less visibility in media in comparison to the coverage of team sports played by able-bodied persons, especially during the traditional Olympic Games (Rees et al., 2019; Scharfenberg, 2018; Solves et al., 2019).

Scenographically, the scene is shot in a relaxed social setting with Jason, Herc, and the other quad players, and not as an exchange exclusively between Jason and his trainer Phil. After Phil's cautionary words about further injury for Jason, the others dismissively hoot and call Phil "Captain Bringdown." The group power of the quad players within this scene is representative of prosocial team behavior (Benson & Bruner, 2018) that reinforces Jason's determination to continue to play quad rugby.

Playing the sport of quad rugby has yet another function in *FNL*. It defeats the stereotypical and ableist perceptions of disability athletes as being "weak, passive, or frail" (Lindemann & Cherney, 2008, p. 108) and of what they can or cannot do as a result of physical impairment. In a sense, in his exchange with Phil, Jason challenges the medical assessment of his physical (dis)ability and of the society's expectations of disability athletes (Lindemann, 2008).

RQ2: Which personal attributes show in the portrayal of quad rugby youth athletes?

The theme that emerged most strongly in response to this question is that of struggle as associated with transitioning from one identity to another. The many facets of this struggle are presented next.

Identity Struggles

In all of the scenes in Season One of *FNL* that depict quad rugby players, the character of Herc is most prominent. A few other players are featured and have a few lines, such as Corey and some other unnamed characters, but

Herc acts as the voice of the group. Herc is a loud, intelligent, unrepressed, unapologetic, crude, and sometimes sexist raconteur who befriends Jason even as his jibes and hyper-personal comments and questions visibly irritate him. Herc may be said to be comfortable in the new skin of an athlete with a disability. Jason, on the other hand, struggles with this identity. The following scene from Episode 8, "Crossing the Line" (aired 12/07/06), is a classic example:

Herc: "Come on! You ain't got nothing on me, baby! Come on, boy! Come on! Let's go."
Jason: "Ain't you got some medals or something, huh? Attaboy. (Laughs) Don't feel bad. I was All-Conference last year."
Herc: "Yeah, that don't mean you're ready to get on the court yet. I'm telling you, Phil's telling you, your doctor is telling you. Even your cute little cheater's telling you."

In response, Jason defends his girlfriend. Herc comes back with the following accusation:

Herc: "You think as long as you hold on to that girlfriend, the girlfriend you had when you could walk, you can avoid the reality of being one of us." (*FNL*, "Crossing the Line" aired 12/07/06)

In this scene, Herc is challenging Jason to accept and affirm his new identity, by "claiming disability" with pride and by "identifying oneself as disabled" (Haslett, Choi, & Smith, 2020; Lindemann & Cherney, 2008, p. 108). Herc's role in this process is that of a fellow athlete more advanced than Jason in the process of being transformed into a new self, whose role is to "welcome him to the club and to instruct him in how to manage himself physically and psychically" (Goffman, 1963, p. 36). Clearly Herc's encouragement and guidance serve as teammate prosocial behaviors, that is, they are "acts that are intended to help or benefit" Jason (Benson & Bruner, 2018, p.120). Jason is, however, not ready yet for the transition into a new community fully as he is trying to hold onto his girlfriend who is the remnant of his successful pre-disability athletic identity as a quarterback on a football team:

Jason: "Dammit, Herc! Argh! She's all I got, man." (*FNL*, "Crossing the Line" aired 12/07/06)

As such, his fight to keep Lyla Garrity in his life is an attempt to keep connected to the earlier identity of a successful able-bodied athlete. It may also serve as Jason's attempt to validate his self-image among the new rugby peer players as someone who has an able-bodied girlfriend as an "asset," something most of his peers with a disability do not have.

The scene is shot in a narrow hallway in which there is little room to maneuver. The scene visually suggests stricture and confinement. This may be so that the theme of conflict and struggle are made more manifest.

Later, in another scene, Jason admits this struggle to his former coach Eric Taylor when he discusses his doubts on his fitness for quad rugby, as the two move around in quad wheelchairs:

Jason: "Try it again. Everyone says I'm not ready for this game. Everyone says I shouldn't be at the scrimmage tonight. Doctors, parents. Yeah? Lyla."
Taylor: "What do you say?"
Jason: "I say I am ready. I don't know, it's just my whole life I've been thinking about football, you know? Football, football, football. That's all. Nothing else. I think about what it used to feel like. Able to compete. To be able to be a part of something, you know? And I feel like. . . . Like that whole part of me is just empty now. It's just gone. Maybe they're right. Maybe it's too soon." (*FNL*, Episode 8, "Crossing the Line" aired 12/07/06)

What is striking about this scene is how it is shot. As Jason and Coach Taylor move slowly about an empty basketball court in wheelchairs, the long shot reveals a setting sun in the window in the corner, and the scene is bathed in a dying light. Metaphorically, Jason is portrayed as raging "against the dying of the light" (Thomas, 1952, Stanza 1) associated with his former identity of football athlete. At the same time, he is attracted to quad rugby because it permits him to be part of something he had in football.

Jason's uncertainty and ambivalence are understandable, and as Goffman (1963) notes, it is even expected from the individuals transitioning from a life without disability into a life with disability and dealing with the stigma attached to it. Goffman explains,

> As already suggested, when the individual first learns who it is that he must now accept as his own, he is likely, at the very least, to feel some ambivalence; for these others will not only be patently stigmatized, and thus not like the normal person he knows himself to be, but may also have other attributes with which he finds difficult to associate himself. (p. 37)

Despite this ambivalence, Jason is ready to undertake the journey to "re-inscribe" his disability (Lindemann, 2008, p. 113) and his identity as a wheelchair rugby player into something he had had as an able-bodied athlete when he played football. Quad rugby, as displayed in *FNL*, permits the character of Jason Street to grow into a man, a proud man with a disability, as well as a proud athlete with a disability, overcoming what he had lost in one sport and working to become yet again a great athlete, this time in another sport.

The other quad athletes are portrayed as a merry, reckless group, who enjoy hijinks and practical jokes. In one scene, the character Corey, a small man who is an amputee, hides under the sink and surprises a woman seeking cleaning products (Episode 17, "I Think We Should Have Sex" aired 02/21/07). The daredevil and macho manners of the athletes portrayed in *FNL* that they exhibit during the game function as "communicative performances of (dis)ability" (Lindemann, 2008, p. 98), where "athletes' physical displays of aggression and hard hits on the court" (Lindemann & Cherney, 2008, p. 110) symbolize agency on the part of players with disabilities. In *FNL*, the characters carry such performances over into the social settings as well, as evident in Episode 17.

Also, Herc's use of crude language and descriptions of the difficult aspects of life with a disability might be perceived as a form of agency. This is because he has not succumbed to self-pity, wallowing, and helplessness but rather has faced his tough reality head on, with resourcefulness, a goal-driven agenda and determination to become yet again a successful athlete.

RQ3. What sociocultural values do the portrayals of disability quad rugby and young athletes reveal?

The stereotypes that were evident and reinforced in the portrayal of young athletes with a disability in *FNL* stemmed from limited societal understanding of life with a disability and sexuality. They are captured under the themes of *Not Being Able to See Beyond the Status Quo* and *Not Gonna Happen*, respectively.

Not Being Able to See beyond the Status Quo

In Episode 13, "Little Girl I Wanna Marry You," Jason's confrontation with Lyla's father, Buddy, in a harsh "cards on the table" scene, reveals both forms of stereotype:

Jason: "Why'd you set Lyla up on a date with Ty Johnston?"
Buddy: "Why?"
Jason: "Yeah. Why? What, you need me to answer it for you? Because if I was still the quarterback and wasn't the town cripple, you wouldn't be setting your daughter up on dates with college boys." (*FNL*, "Little Girl I Wanna Marry You" aired 1/24/07)

Initially, Buddy does not take the bait and he explains that Lyla met with Ty Johnston to help him with a term paper. Jason presses on:

Jason: "You don't want your little girl to end up with me, so you're just trying to show her that there are other choices out there. Bigger fish in the sea, huh?" (*FNL*, "Little Girl I Wanna Marry You" aired 1/24/07)

To appease Jason and dodge his question, Buddy insists that he and his family have always supported him. Jason, however, demands the truth and Buddy gives it to him:

Buddy: "You want me to be honest with you, son? Do you?"
Jason: "Please."
Buddy: "I love that little girl in there. That's my daughter. And I want her to have a great life. And I'm real uncertain about the future here. I mean, how's she gonna get money? How are you gonna get money? You gonna go to college? Is she gonna go to college? Are you gonna have babies? Can you have babies? Can you? Can you have children, Jason?"
Jason: "We haven't quite answered that yet." (*FNL*, "Little Girl I Wanna Marry You" aired 1/24/07)

At this time, Buddy takes the opportunity to spell out his concerns:

Buddy: "Well, what if you can't? And what if you can, Jason? When that little baby's crying upstairs in the night, who's gonna go up and take care of him? I don't want Lyla to be a caregiver her whole life, son. I know that's a bitter pill to swallow and I'm sorry I have to say it to you. And Lyla Garrity, she loves you. She'd follow you into hell. Are you sure you wanna lead her there?" (*FNL*, "Little Girl I Wanna Marry You" aired 1/24/07)

In this scene, the Buddy Garrity character is pushed by Jason past the niceties to reveal his true thoughts. He speaks as a stereotypical "normal" abled father might, who is frightened of his daughter's reduced prospects at marrying a person with a disability. However, the scene clearly presents a biased view when it suggests that his daughter Lyla might never have a full life if she should marry Jason, a person with a disability.

The scene is shot, as many are, with Jason and his friends post-disability, at night. The two men are outside, in the driveway, and are completely alone. The sole sources of light are the artificial lights from the street and garage, and they bathe the characters in an eerie glow. The loneliness in the scene symbolizes the society's tendency to isolate and separate Jason-like individuals with a disability from the rest of the community. The artificial lighting combined with an eerie glow suggests the feelings of fear, discomfort, and guilt within the society around the individuals with a disability (Ellis, 2019).

Buddy Garrity's fears are therefore the result and reflection of the social stigma that is typically attributed to individuals with disabilities who are perceived as "notnormals" (Goffman, 1963, p. 5) and who are thus seen as incapable of having a normal life and performing everyday life activities, which in this case, involves taking care of a life partner or having a family. As per the individual model of disability (Ellis, 2019, p. 24), Buddy Garrity places the disability problem on Jason rather than locating it within the community that he represents. In particular, he is unable to deal with it and find ways to support Lyla, his daughter, and Jason having a life together, going to college, and reinventing their life as a couple with Jason as an individual with a disability. In other words, the problem is not Jason and Jason-like individuals but rather, the Buddy Garritys within the ableist world who fail to see beyond the status quo and who operate within the traditional frames of reference in regards to what is possible for couples with a partner with a disability.

In another scene in an earlier episode, "Who's Your Daddy" (Episode 4), Herc is trying to bring to Jason's attention other stereotypical reactions from the able-bodied friends, peers, family, and community members around him with which he will have to learn to deal: an *invisible* enemy. This is in response to Jason accusing him of not knowing "anything about my life":

Herc: "Actually, I know everything about your life. Let me write down the next two years for you. You see, you're still in the golden 'everyone rallies around you' phase. Yeah, they'll start to get bored with that in about six weeks and then all the letters and cards and visits and prayers will die down dramatically."
Jason: "All right, just shut up."
Herc: "In another three months after that, the girlfriend is going to tell you all about how you're different people now and how you need to find out who you are apart. That'll be the end of her ass." (*FNL*, "Who's Your Daddy" aired 11/02/06)

He then tells him how he is going to lose more people because of the lawsuit to secure funds for his medical care and how his parents will get a divorce because of too much stress.

Just after Jason makes good on his promise to do something to Herc if he does not stop talking, he flings a cup of water at Herc. It is obvious that beyond the extreme impoliteness, Herc is actually trying to let Jason know that his life is about to profoundly change, as his able-bodied friends discover that his injury is permanent and that Jason will need to live his life in a way that is very different from theirs, reinforcing the Us versus Them stereotype (Ellis, 2019).

Not Gonna Happen

Stereotypic portrayals in *FNL* also concerned sex and sexuality. A good example is the following exchange when Jason inquires with Herc if he will be able to have sex again, in Episode 11 ("Nevermind" aired 01/12/07):

Herc: "Yeah. Not gonna happen. At least not for a while anyway." (People talking; Herc burps)
Jason: "Why not?"
Herc: "Dude, you're like a newborn baby. You don't know how to do anything. Look, man, whatever worked for you before may not work now. You know? You gotta figure out what turns you on, you know?" (*FNL*, "Nevermind" aired 01/12/07)

Jason queries further:

Jason: "Will I ever be able to . . ."
Herc: "What? Shoot fireworks?"
Jason: "Yeah."
Herc: "Have super-happy fun time?"
Jason: "Yeah."
Herc: "Yes. Probably. Just maybe not every time. Look, nothing's like it was, you know? But don't look so glum, man. There's more to life than hit-it-and-quit-it, QB. Trust me." (*FNL*, "Nevermind" aired 01/12/07)

The scene is shot in a casual eatery, with Jason and Herc, who appear comfortable with speaking freely. It is nighttime. As we can see from the dialogue, there is a mixture of good advice and the typical *machismo* of normative masculinity (Lindemann & Cherney, 2008) on display in this scene. The issues of sex, sexuality, and disability are highly individual and unique to each person with or without a disability, and they are shaped by many factors, including self-esteem, self-concept, and psychological well-being (Brodwin & Frederick, 2010). Therefore, while the scene is portrayed with a certain naturalism, especially as it is acted, it may represent stereotypes of how sex and disability are actually lived in the real world.

Jason, who is influenced by the stereotypic gender expectations of masculinity that prevail within the society and within his community, is not sure if he can successfully perform sexual activities anymore (Brodwin & Frederick, 2010). In other words, in the show, Jason is shown struggling with how to envision his sexuality and sexual expression in his relationship with Lyla in the aftermath of his injury. His struggle may, therefore, reflect real-world able-bodied individuals who "make stereotypically incorrect assumptions about the sexualities of people with disabilities and their abilities to exercise agency in negotiating love and relationships" (Chappell, 2014, p. 1159).

At the same time *FNL* seeks to show its audience that a young man with a disability does not have to yield up all of the trappings of youthful masculinity; as Herc advises Jason, he is merely "like a newborn baby," who has to learn how to sexually function as a man all over again.

> RQ 4: How do sports affect relationships and engagement among youth with and without disability?

In *FNL*, high school American football serves as a salve for, and an escape from, a life that may otherwise be hard for the carefully portrayed working-class people of the fictional town of Dillon, Texas. Specifically, the boys and young men who play high school football are given special privileges, including "Rally Girls" who wait on them hand and foot, complete homework assignments for them, and even apparently provide sexual favors (although this horrifies football Coach Taylor's wife, Tami, the guidance counselor for the school). Disability changes everything. As a result, Jason's relationships with peers with and without a disability suffer. The theme of *Friendships Going Awry* reflects some of these relational changes and challenges.

Friendships Going Awry

Unsurprisingly, Jason Street's best friend is Tim Riggins, the fullback/running back of the Dillon Panthers, and his former teammate on this local high school football team. Riggins cannot bring himself to visit the "fallen" Jason in the hospital. Following his debilitating injury, Jason is laid up, and doubt about his full recovery begins to creep into the mind of his girlfriend Lyla. She is unfaithful to Jason on several occasions with Riggins. Jason begins to suspect that something may be going on and sees an intimate hug between them from the vantage point of a high window. After inviting Tim to a quad rugby match, Jason confronts him in a powerful scene:

Tim: (claps) "That is the Six I know. Man, I tell you, those hits. . . . I gotta take some notes. Great game, man. Tell you what, man . . ."

Jason: (punches Tim in the face) "Get up, Riggins. Get up and fight me, huh? Come on, coward. Come on, hit me! No. Steal my girl and you're not ready to fight me, huh?"

Lyla: "Jason!"

Jason: "Don't you dare, Lyla. Don't you dare. (to Tim) Come on. Look me in the face. I want you to. (Tim slinks away) Come back here. Come back here!"

Lyla: "Jason!"

Jason: (to Tim) "You gonna steal a cripple's girl but you won't fight a cripple, huh? You coward! You're a coward, Riggins! Always will be!" (*FNL*, Episode 8, "Crossing the Line" aired12/07/06)

Prior to Jason's confrontation, Tim and Lyla, reasonably certain that Jason is in the dark about their affair, cheer Jason and his teammates on at the quad rugby match. However, we see foreshadowing of the confrontation to come with Jason's snarling looks at Tim, while Tim seems unaware of the problem. The scrimmage match is shot expertly, with many cross shots and closeups that are blended together to create an exciting recreation of a quad rugby game. The obvious enjoyment and satisfaction of the players serves to buoy the sparse audience, which appears to be at least somewhat enthusiastic about the match. Against this backdrop of victory, Jason lashes out in rage and disappointment at Tim, and at the betrayal of his trust.

It has been argued that the highest passions occur with the deepest of friendships (e.g., Bagwell & Coie, 2004), and it is obvious that the friendship between these two young men forged in high school football is responsible for their extreme behavior. Jason is experiencing conflicting emotions. On the one hand, he is trying to show his able-bodied friend that he can fight and scrap with the best of them still. At the same time, his use of the term "cripple," which is an offensive term to persons in the disability community (Sylva & Howe, 2012), shows that he is not entirely comfortable with his new status and new athlete identity, although he begins to embrace disability as part of his developing identity.

This is an example of how the onset of disability in one who was previously uninjured can produce irrational fears, both in those acquiring the disability and in the able-bodied people around them as well. Those with the disability become "the other." As Jason Harris of the Burton Blatt Institute at Syracuse University points out, "Living in communities has made us look to things that bind us to be part of a group but also can lead to the 'outsider effect' where anyone who is not in the group is a threat" (Harris, 2016, para. 7). The idea here, reinforced also to some degree in the above scene with Buddy Garrity, is that disability produces the unreasonable fear that the newly disabled person is somehow "cursed" and meaningful life is over for that person (Ellis, 2019), instead of that new life requiring rehabilitation, the relearning of skills, and the seeking of new opportunities for identity development.

Tim Riggins eventually comes around to support Jason in developing his new identity and their friendship is revived. Lyla, his girlfriend, on the other hand, is unable to embrace Jason's new sports identity and to foresee their future as a couple and a future family. Like her father, Buddy Garrity, she is unable to envision a life together with an individual with a disability. This portrayal in *FNL* suggests that maintaining a romantic relationship with an individual with a disability is unlikely to succeed because of the belief that it will not work, a belief that has been observed in previous representations of disability on the big screen (Adams, 2015).

CONCLUSION

In the portrayal of sports and a sports lifestyle, quad rugby is presented as a full-contact sport that is an excellent identifier of self-esteem and perceived mastery within disability athletics even though it carries certain risks. The athletes who play it are shown to be strong, talented, and skilled individuals who aspire to be great athletes and who work hard to accomplish these goals. Their aspirations, talents, determination, and practice, rather than their disability, define their identity, lifestyles, and sports activity. As such, being involved in this sport is characterized as enhancing these characters' "sense of self-concept, independence, ability and corresponding pride," values also found in Paralympic athletes (Pack et al., 2017, p. 2063). At the same time, the show reveals the harsh reality of injury and the challenges young athletes face as they strive to gain athletic competence and navigate the challenges a disability has brought to their sports activity.

Collectively, however, the images of others' response to Jason's disability in *FNL* reinforce the stereotypical social views of disability as loss and a burden (Ellis, 2019), and ultimately as an experience too overwhelming for able-bodied peers, family, and community members. The losses as portrayed in the series include romantic relationships, friendships, families, along with social status, utility, and the attractiveness of disabled people to peers, friends, and members in the community (Watermeyer, 2014). Such cultural representations fail to consider the "real losses," which in fact are society's tendency to exclude, isolate, and depreciate people with disabilities (Watermeyer, 2014) as well as its failure to address such discrimination, to provide supportive environments, and most of all, to facilitate change in societal stereotypical attitudes and prejudice toward individuals with disability (Ellis). The picture of the community's response that Herc painted for Jason projects and makes available such a failure for the viewers' uptake. His cynical predictions are borne out in large measure, though not without growth and Jason's growing acceptance of his disability.

Cinematically, the show was shot on film with many closeups and extreme closeups, so that the characters' emotions are usually clearly visible. The show alternates a viewpoint where Jason's disability is viewed as the most vexing of tragedies, but also compassionately reveals that many young men who play quad rugby are reasonably well adjusted to their limitations.

There are issues that disability advocates have voiced, however. Both Scott Porter, who played Jason, and Kevin Rankin, who played Herc, are able-bodied actors. Disability advocates have noted that there are many talented actors with disabilities who could have played these, among many other roles (Harnett, 2000). Also, the viewer cannot help but notice the dark colors and lack of daylight and attractive backgrounds with which the scenes featuring Jason and the quad rugby players are shot. These visual elements form a subtext to the scenes that sometimes undermines Herc's gritty optimism and open-mindedness.

Nevertheless, *FNL* manages, within the strictures of broadcast television, to adroitly and convincingly portray the huge life change that befalls a promising young athlete following a disabling injury. It is clear that the television makers, especially Peter Berg, researched sports, disability, and quad rugby. However, they still approached it from the perspective of able-bodied television makers, as the two principal characters in our analysis were portrayed by abled actors. Being observant of this fact and of the gritty contours ascribed to the world in which Jason and the quad rugby players reside involves the viewer emerging from immersion in the narrative and viewing this well-liked television program critically. Critical media analysis techniques can help viewers see beneath the cinematography and actors' dialogue to the "secret structures" (Berger, 2005, p. 30) or codes that the visual artists transmit in their portrayal of youth disability on the ubiquitous small screen of television.

REFERENCES

Adams, R. (2015). Privacy, dependency, discegenation: Toward a sexual culture for people with intellectual disabilities. *Disability Studies Quarterly, 35*(1). Retrieved from https://dsq-sds.org/article/view/4185/3825

Altheide, D. L., & Schneider, C. J. (2013). *Qualitative Media Analysis* (2nd ed.). Thousand Oaks, CA: Sage.

Anderson-Butcher, D. (2019). Youth sport as a vehicle for social development. *Kinesiology Review, 8*(3), 180–187.

Aytur, S., Craig, P. J., Frye, M., Bonica, M., Rainer, S., Hapke, L., & McGilvray, M. (2018). Through the lens of a camera: Exploring the meaning of competitive sport participation among youth athletes with disabilities. *Therapeutic Recreation Journal, 52*(2), 95–125. doi: 10.18666/TRJ-2018-V52-I2-8774.

Bagwell, C. L., & Coie, J. D. (2004). The best friendships of aggressive boys: Relationship quality, conflict management, and rule-breaking behavior. *Journal of Experimental Child Psychology, 88*(1), 5–24.

Bal, M. (2017). *Narratology: Introduction to the Theory of Narrative* (4th ed.). Toronto, Canada: University of Toronto Press.

Bedard, C., Hanna, S., & Cairney, J. (2020). A longitudinal study of sport participation and perceived social competence in youth. *Journal of Adolescent Health,
66*(3), 352–359. doi: 10.1016/j.jadohealth.2019.09.017.
Benson, A. J., & Bruner, M. W. (2018). How teammate behaviors relate to athlete
affect, cognition, and behaviors: A daily diary approach within youth sport. *Psy-
chology of Sport & Exercise, 34*, 119–127. doi: 10.1016/j.psychsport.2017.10.008.
Berg, P. (2007). [Director]. *Friday Night Lights* [Television series]. Universal City,
CA: Universal.
Berger, A. A. (2005). *Media Analysis Techniques*. Thousand Oaks, CA: Sage.
Berger, A. A. (2012). *Media Analysis Techniques* (4th ed). Thousand Oaks, CA:
Sage.
Brennan, I., Falchuk, B., & Murphy, R. (Creators). (2009). *Glee* [Television series].
Los Angeles, CA: Fox.
Brittain, I. (2004). Perceptions of disability and their impact upon involvement in
sport for people with disabilities at all levels. *Journal of Sport and Social Issues,
28*(4), 429–452. doi: 10.1177/0193723504268729.
Brodwin, M. G., & Frederick, P. C. (2010). Sexuality and societal beliefs regarding
persons living with disabilities. *Journal of Rehabilitation, 76*(4), 37–41.
Brooke, M. (2019). The Singaporean Paralympics and its media portrayal: Real sport?
Men-Only? *Communication & Sport, 7*(4), 446–465.
Bruner, M. W., Balish, S. M., Forrest, C., Brown, S., Webber, K., Gray, E., . . .
Shields, C. A. (2017). Ties that bond: Youth sport as a vehicle for social identity
and positive youth development. *Research Quarterly for Exercise & Sport, 88*(2),
209–214.
Carter, N., & Williams, J. (2012). "A genuinely emotional week": Learning disability,
sport and television—Notes on the Special Olympics GB National Summer Games
2009. *Media, Culture & Society, 34*(2), 211–227. doi: 10.1177/0163443711430759.
Chappell, P. (2014). How Zulu-speaking youth with physical and visual disabilities
understand love and relationships in constructing their sexual identities. *Culture,
Health & Sexuality, 16*(9), 1156–1168. doi: 10.1080/13691058.2014.933878.
Duffy, B., & Sassano, M. J. (2020). *Tin Soldiers* [Documentary]. New York: Ben
Duffy & Michael J. Sassano Productions.
Ellis. K. (2016). *Disability Media Work: Opportunities and Obstacles*. New York,
NY: Palgrave Macmillan.
Ellis, K. (2019). *Disability and Digital Television Cultures: Representation, Access,
and Reception*. New York, NY: Routledge.
Ellis, K., & Goggin, G. (2015). Disability media participation: Opportunities, obsta-
cles and politics. *Media International Australia, 154*, 78–88.
Festinger, L., & Carlsmith, J. M. (1959). Cognitive consequences of forced compli-
ance. *Journal of Abnormal and Social Psychology, 58*, 203–210.
Gilligan, V., Moore, K., Porter, D., Cranston, B., Gunn, A., Mitte, R. J., Paul, A. . . .
(Producers). (2008). *Breaking Bad: The Complete First Season*. Culver City, CA:
Sony Pictures Home Entertainment.
Goffman, E. (1963). *Stigma: Notes on the Management of Spoiled Identity*. New
York, NY: Simon & Schuster.

Groff, D., & Kleiber, D. (2001). Exploring the identity formation of youth involved in an adapted sports program. *Therapeutic Recreation Journal, 35*(4), 318–332.

Hardin, M., & Hardin, B. (2004). The "supercrip" in sport media: Wheelchair athletes discuss hegemony's disabled hero. *Sociology of Sport Online, 7*(1). Retrieved from http://physed.otago.ac.nz/sosol/v7i1/v7i1_1.html.

Harnett, A. (2000). Escaping the evil avenger and the supercrip: Images of disability in popular television. *Irish Communication Review, 8*(1). Retrieved from http://arrow.dit.ie/icr/vol8/iss1/3.

Harris, J. (2016, October 4). The elephant in the room: The fear of disability [Blog post]. Retrieved from https://www.jasonsconnection.org/blog/the-elephant-in-the-room-the-fear-of-disability/.

Haslett, D., Choi, I., & Smith, B. (2020). Para athlete activism: A qualitative examination of disability activism through Paralympic sport in Ireland. *Psychology of Sport & Exercise, 47,* 1–9.

Hebblethwaite, S., & Curley, L. (2015). Exploring the role of community recreation in stroke recovery using participatory action research and photovoice. *Therapeutic Recreation Journal, 49*(1), 1–17. Retrieved from https://js.sagamorepub.com/trj/article/view/5433/4909.

Heffernan, V. (2006, October 3). *Friday Night Lights*: On the field and off, losing isn't an option [Review]. *The New York Times.* Retrieved from http://www.nytimes.com/2006/10/03/arts/television/03heff.html?_r=0.

Hood, K., Moore, Y., & Schuyler, L. (Creators). (2002). *Degrassi: The Next Generation* [Television series]. Toronto, Canada: Epitome Pictures and Bell Media.

Kim, K. T., Lee, S., & Oh, E-S. (2017). Athletes with disabilities in the Paralympic Games: A framing analysis of television news. *Managing Sport and Leisure, 22*(4), 255–275.

Kaya, N., & Epps, H. H. (2004). Relationship between color and emotion: A study of college students. *College Student Journal, 38*(3), 396–405.

Kohlbacher, F. (2006). The use of qualitative content analysis in case study research. *Forum Qualitative Sozialforschung / Forum: Qualitative Social Research, 7*(1). Retrieved from http://www.qualitative-research.net/index.php/fqs/article/view/75/154).

Lankhorst, K., van der Ende-Kastelijn, K., de Groot, J., Zwinkels, M., Verschuren, O., Backx, F., [HAYS study group]. (2015). Health in adapted youth sports study (HAYS): Health effects of sports participation in children and adolescents with a chronic disease or physical disability. *Springer Plus, 4,* 796. doi:10.1186/s40064-015-1589-z.

Lee, S. P., Cornwell, T. B., & Babiak, K. (2012). Developing an instrument to measure the social impact of sport: Social capital, collective identities, health literacy, well-being and human capital. *Journal of Sport Management, 27,* 24–42.

Lindemann, K. (2008). "I can't be standing up out there": Communicative performances of (dis)ability in wheelchair rugby. *Text and Performance Quarterly, 28*(1/2), 98–115.

Lindemann, K., & Cherney, J. (2008). Communicating in and through "murderball": Masculinity and disability in wheelchair rugby. *Western Journal of Communication, 72*(2), 107–125.

Lundberg, N., Taniguchi, S., McCormick, B., & Tibbs, C. (2011). Identity negotiating: Redefining stigmatized identities through adaptive sports and recreation participation among individuals with a disability. *Journal of Leisure Research, 43*(2), 205–225. doi: 10.1080/00222216.2011.11950233.

Macri, K. J. (2012). Not just a game: Sport and society in the United States. *Inquiries Journal, 4*(8). Retrieved from http://www.inquiriesjournal.com/articles/1664/not-just-a-game-sport-and-society-in-the-united-states.

Mallett, R. (2011). Representing disability in an ableist world: Essays on mass media. *Disability & Society, 26*(7), 891–893.

Martin, J. J. (2010). The psychosocial dynamics of youth disability sport. *Sport Science Review, 29*(5–6), 49–69. doi: 10.2478/v10237-011-0032-9.

Monaco, J. (2009). *How to Read a Film, Movies, Media and Beyond*. New York, NY: Oxford.

Moore, F. (2006, October 1). Much-honored "Eyes on the Prize" documentary returns to television. Retrieved from https://www.ocala.com/news/20061001/much-honored-eyes-on-the-prize-documentary-returns-to-television

Pack, S., Kelly, S., & Arvinen-Barrow, M. (2017). "I think I became a swimmer rather than just someone with a disability swimming up and down:" Paralympic athletes' perceptions of self and identity development. *Disability & Rehabilitation, 39*(21), 2063.

Padwo-Audick, D., & Downing, T. (n.d.). *She's Got Grit* [Video web film series]. Washington, DC: Creative Strategies Media and Spark Media.

Physical Activity Council's (PAC) Report on Participation. (2019). The physical activity council's annual study tracking sports, fitness, and recreation participation in the U.S. Jupiter, FL: Sports Marketing Surveys USA.

Piatt, J., Kang, S., Wells, M. S., Nagata, S., Hoffman, J., & Taylor, J. (2018). Changing identity through sport: The Paralympic sport club experience among adolescents with mobility impairments. *Disability and Health Journal, 11*(2), 262–266. doi: 10.1016/j.dhjo.2017.10.007.

Pizer, D. (1995). Introduction: The problem of definition. In D. Pizer (Ed.), *The Cambridge Companion to American Realism and Naturalism: Howells to London* (pp. 1–19). Cambridge, UK: Cambridge University Press. doi: 10.1017/CCOL0521433002.

Potter, W. J. (2019). *Media Literacy* (9th ed.). Thousand Oaks, CA: Sage.

Purdue, D., & Howe, P. (2013). Who's in and who is out? Legitimate bodies within the Paralympic Games. *Sociology of Sport Journal, 30*(1), 24–40.

Rees, L., Robinson, P., & Shields, N. (2019). Media portrayal of elite athletes with a disability – A systematic review. *Disability and Rehabilitation, 41*(4), 374–381.

Scarpa, S. (2011). Physical self-concept and self-esteem in adolescents and young adults with and without physical disability: The role of sports participation. *European Journal of Adapted Physical Activity, 4*(1), 38–53.

Scharfenberg, D. (2018). Why do Americans ignore the Paralympics? *Palaestra, 32*(2), 15–17.

Shapiro, D. R., & Martin, J. J. (2010a). Athletic identity, affect and peer relations in youth athletes with physical disabilities. *Disability and Health Journal, 3*(2), 79–85.

Shapiro, D. R., & Martin, J. J. (2010b). Multidimensional physical self-concept of athletes with physical disabilities. *Adapted Physical Activity Quarterly, 27,* 294–307.

Smith, R. E., & Smoll, F. L. (2012). *Sport Psychology for Youth Coaches: Developing Champions in Sports and Life.* Lanham, MD: Rowman & Littlefield.

Solves, J., Pappous, A., Rius, I., & Kohe, G. Z. (2019). Framing the Paralympic Games: A mixed-methods analysis of Spanish media coverage of the Beijing 2008 and London 2012 Paralympic Games. *Communication & Sport, 7*(6), 729–751.

Stewart, K., & Spurgeon, C. (2019). Researching media participation by listening to people with disability. *Media, Culture & Society,* 1–18. doi: 10.1177/0163443719890536.

Stolman, L. (Director). (2016). *Swim Team* [Documentary]. Short Hills, NJ, United States: Woodland Park Productions.

Sylva, C., & Howe, P. D. (2012). The (in)validity of superscript representation of Paralympian athletes. *Journal of Sport and Social Issues, 36*(2), 74–194. doi: 10.1177/0193723511433865.

The International Wheelchair Rugby Federation. (n.d.). *Introduction to Wheelchair Rugby.* Retrieved from https://www.iwrf.com/resources/iwrf_docs/Introduction-to -Wheelchair-Rugby-2012.pdf.

Thomas, D. M. (1952). *The Poems of Dylan Thomas.* New York, NY: New Directions Publishing. Retrieved from https://poets.org/poem/do-not-go-gentle-good-night.

Timler, A., McIntyre, F., Rose, E., & Hands, B. (2019). Exploring the influence of self-perceptions on the relationship between motor competence and identity in adolescents. *PLoS One, 14*(11), 1–15. doi: 10.1371/journal.pone.0224653.

U.S. Government Accountability Office. (2010). *Students With Disabilities: More Information and Guidance Could Improve Opportunities in Physical Education and Athletics.* (Report No. GAO-10-519). Retrieved from https://www.gao.gov/ assets/310/305770.pdf.

Wagmeister, E. (2016, July 13). Able-bodied actors play 95% of disabled characters in top 10 TV shows, says new study. *Variety.* Retrieved from http://variety.com/2 016/tv/news/disabled-actors-television-study-1201813686/.

Watermeyer, B. (2014). Disability and loss: The psychological commodification of identity. *Psychology Journal, 11*(2), 99–107.

Wolf, E. (1999). Cognizing cognized models. *American Anthropologist, 101* (1), 19–22.

Wolfe, C. (1981). Fictional realism: Watt and Bazin on the pleasures of novels and films. *Literature Film Quarterly, 9*(1), 40–51. Retrieved from https://www.jstor .org/stable/43796161.

Woodburn, D., & Kopić, K. (2016). The Ruderman white paper on employment of actors with disabilities in television. Retrieved from https://www.rudermanfound ation.org/wp-content/uploads/2016/07/TV-White-Paper_final.final_.pdf.

Zhang, L., & Haller, B. (2013). Consuming image: How mass media impact the identity of people with disabilities. *Communication Quarterly, 61*(3), 319–334. doi: 10.1080/01463373.2013.776988.

Chapter 6

Transforming Diabetes Stigma

The Role of Counternarrative in Sports Media

Cynthia Martin

My son was diagnosed with type 1 diabetes (T1D) during the summer before entering the third grade. The story of his diagnosis is unremarkable when compared to thousands of other children and young adults who are diagnosed each year. He was drinking and urinating a lot, but we attributed it to being on a summer swim team for the first time. Yes. My husband and I assumed he was swallowing a lot of pool water as he learned to swim butterfly. But when we went on vacation in early July, I knew something was wrong. My active, beach-loving son was taking naps and waking in the middle of the night to drink gallons of water. Upon our return home, we took him to the doctor, who immediately sent us to the ER at a children's hospital an hour away. My son's blood glucose (BG) was almost 1000 mg/dL. To put that in perspective, a person who does not live with diabetes has a BG of 70–80 when fasting and 120–130 immediately after eating. My son's BG was so high, he had also developed diabetic ketoacidosis, which occurs when excess glucose in the blood cannot be flushed by the kidneys, making one's blood acidic. He was a sick boy.

While my son received insulin via a drip for three days in the pediatric intensive care unit, my husband and I took a crash course to learn how to care for him. We suddenly found ourselves thrust into the roles of nurse, doctor, endocrinologist, nutritionist, mathematician, phlebotomist, and more. It was overwhelming. We wondered if our son would ever be able to sleep over at a friend's house again or attend summer camps, get back into the pool to swim on a team or to play any sport for that matter. Filled with overwhelming anxiety and fear about the new life with diabetes our son was to lead, we did what every other parent new to diabetes did—we turned to the internet.

What we found was not reassuring. Most media representations focused on the poor lifestyle choices often associated with type 2 diabetes (T2D) and on the devastating complications caused by poor disease management. Where were the portrayals of kids and adults managing diabetes and living their best lives filled with family, sports, and travel? We wanted models, and there were very few to be found.

Like most disabilities, diabetes is both misrepresented and underrepresented in the media, which often confuse and conflate different types of the disease.[1] At the same time, there aren't many affirming examples of characters with diabetes in popular media. A character with diabetes is often either used to teach a valuable lesson about lifestyle or a part of some tragic storyline. For example, in the movie *Memento* (Todd, Todd, & Nolan, 2000), a woman living with T1D administers multiple insulin shots to commit suicide. In *Steel Magnolias* (Stark, Stone, White, & Ross, 1989), the main character lives with T1D but has negative complications such as repeated seizures. Many such negative portrayals of the disease show it as problematic, even fatal.

Characters who live a healthy, positive life with diabetes, type 1 or type 2, are largely absent from the screen. They are also absent from sports media or are featured primarily when there is controversy. Gary Hall, Jr., a ten-time Olympic medalist diagnosed with T1D in 1999, was lauded for his victories in the pool, but when he declared during a 2008 press conference that U.S. swimming suffered from a doping problem, he became the target of the media (and athletes) across the globe (Vinton, 2008). The press accused him of being soured because he didn't qualify for the Olympic team. Worse, they distorted diabetes and presented it as something that gave him an advantage in the pool. *The Daily News* ran a headline that read "Diabetic Olympian Gary Hall blasts dopers, while life depends on insulin," likening insulin therapy to performance enhancing drugs and suggesting Hall was somehow hypocritical to suggest swimmers were illegally using steroids (Vinton, 2008). The media treated Hall just as it treats many people who live with diabetes—as deviant. Vinton's (2008) article, which appeared in *Daily News*, presented Hall's insulin use as a choice instead of as the lifesaving necessity it was. The article ignored Hall's accomplishments and success in the pool, choosing instead to focus on his insulin use and the fact that he didn't qualify for the U.S. Olympic swim team at the age of thirty-four.

The media plays an important role in creating a social identity for, and in influencing people's views of, individuals who live with diabetes (Da Silva & Toledo, 2019; Lins, Melo, Alves, & Silva, 2019). For this reason, positive representation of individuals who live with diabetes is crucial. Working in critical media literacy (CML) studies in education, scholars call for transgressive narratives that resist dominant portrayals of disability (Broderick et al.,

2010). Drawing on critical race theory and gender studies, they explain how counternarratives (also called counterstories) tell the story of experience that is often marginalized by dominant discourse. Milner and Howard (2013) argue that such narratives "represent non-mainstream stories which represent other truths, and other experiences that directly refute hegemony" (p. 542). Solórzano and Yosso (2001) suggest the use of counternarratives to reframe and rewrite "deficit" stories. Counternarratives of diabetes and disabilities, more generally, in sports are needed to counter the often-inaccurate representations of the disease in the media. Such portrayals could also potentially empower children, teens, even adults, who live with diabetes and who may feel isolated because of their disease.

This chapter provides a brief overview of diabetes and examines sources of misunderstanding and stigma that surround the disease. It then explores narratives of diabetes in general media and sports media, calling attention to the often-inaccurate and stigmatizing portrayals of the disease. It then looks to the potential of counternarrative in transforming the discourse that surrounds diabetes by offering more accurate depictions of athletes who live with diabetes. Ultimately, this chapter not only calls for more positive media coverage of athletes who live with diabetes but also issues an invitation to scholars to fill the gap in research regarding representation of athletes with diabetes.

WHAT IS DIABETES? REALITY AND STIGMA

One of the greatest challenges faced during post-diagnosis is the fairly commonplace misunderstandings of diabetes, especially type 1. Well-meaning friends and family encourage diets or carb-cutting entirely. They may assure parents that diabetic youth will outgrow the disease, which is untrue. A common misconception is that behaviors can preclude type 1 from progressing to type 2 through lifestyle changes.[2] In general, people are very much aware of T2D, but have very little understanding of type 1.

Types of Diabetes

Diabetes mellitus is a name given to a group of metabolic disorders that result in hyperglycemia or higher-than-average levels of glucose in the blood (Sladek, 2018).[3] While diabetes is often portrayed as a singular disease in the media, several forms or types exist. T1D, once known as juvenile diabetes and the type of diabetes my son lives with, strikes most often—though not always—during childhood, adolescence, or early adulthood. It is caused by an autoimmune disorder in which white blood cells attack the pancreas and kill insulin-producing beta cells. In a matter of weeks, the autoimmune attack kills the pancreas, which stops producing insulin entirely. Without insulin, the body's cells cannot convert glucose to energy, making glucose levels in the blood excessively high. Excessive levels of BG for an extended period of time can lead to kidney failure, blindness, neuropathy, and eventual death. For these reasons, those who live with T1D must inject or pump insulin for the rest of their lives to survive. The cause of type 1 is unknown, but it is believed that a virus triggers the autoimmune response that leads the white blood cells to attack one's pancreas. There is no cure and it cannot be reversed (Juvenile Diabetes Research Foundation, 2020).

T2D, also known as insulin-resistance, occurs when the pancreas produces insulin as it should, but the body's cells become resistant to it so that the body requires more and more insulin to support the conversion of glucose to energy. Whereas T1D occurs over a relatively brief period of time—usually a few weeks—T2D generally occurs over a period of years as cells become more and more resistant to insulin. Type 2 is most often, though not always, associated with diets high in carbohydrates and with sedentary lifestyles. It can often be controlled by diet and exercise but may require oral medication or insulin to control ("Diabetes," 2019). Like type 1, type 2 has a genetic component and runs in families. As such, individuals who are a healthy weight can develop T2D, which is then often referred to as "lean diabetes" (Wiginton, 2019). See table 6.1 for a comparison of types 1 and 2 diabetes.

Other types of diabetes occur less frequently. Gestational diabetes (GD) occurs during pregnancy and resolves itself after delivery though women who develop GD are at greater risk for developing T2D later in life. Latent autoimmune diabetes in adults (LADA) occurs as a slow progressing form of T1D after the age of thirty. It is often diagnosed as T2D at first but will eventually require insulin injections. Those diagnosed with LADA test positive for the antibodies that indicate an autoimmune disorder ("What is LADA?," n.d.). Monogenic forms of the disease involve the mutation of a single gene that leads to diabetes-like symptoms but do not present exactly as type 1 or type 2. Maturity onset of diabetes in the young (MODY) is the most common form of monogenic diabetes ("What is Monogenic Diabetes?," n.d.). In addition, there are other forms of diabetes related to other diseases.

Diabetes and Stigma

Arguably, diabetes is one of the most misunderstood and most vilified diseases today. Few other diseases are associated as much with shame and blame as diabetes (Furuta, 2020). Diabetes stigma refers to perceptions of exclusion, blame, or judgment because one has diabetes (Major & O'Brien, 2005). An overwhelming body of research supports findings that people with diabetes often feel stigmatized for having the disease (Liu et al., 2017). Those who

Table 6.1   A Comparison of Type 1 and Type 2 Diabetes

	Type 1 Diabetes	Type 2 Diabetes
Definition	An autoimmune disorder in which white blood cells attack insulin-producing pancreas beta cells, destroying the pancreas's ability to make insulin	Cells become resistant to insulin and become unable to use insulin to convert glucose to energy
Causes	Linked to genetics, can be spontaneous	Linked to genetics, obesity, lifestyle
Occurrence	Most often strikes in childhood	Most develops in mid-to-late adulthood
Progression	Develops over a short period of time (weeks)	Develops over years beginning with insulin resistance toward insulin dependency
Symptoms	Symptoms include excessive thirst, increased urination, headaches, fatigue	Most often symptomless until complications arise
Cure	Does not have a cure	Does not have a cure, but may be temporarily reversed or halted with lifestyle changes
Treatment	Requires insulin daily to manage disease	Can be managed with lifestyle changes and oral medication
Incidence	Accounts for 5% of diabetes	Accounts for 90-95% of diabetes

Source: Adapted from Diabetes: The differences between types 1 and 2 (2019). *Medical News Today*. Retrieved from https://www.medicalnewstoday.com/articles/7504#treatment.

live with type 1, especially children and adolescents, perceive this stigma to an even greater extent. A study (Liu et al., 2017) conducted in association with the diaTribe Foundation and dQ&A revealed 52 percent of people with T2D and 76 percent with T1D who were surveyed perceived stigma, with the highest rates being reported by parents of children who live with type 1. In another study, 93 percent of people with diabetes (types 1 and 2) who were surveyed believed T1D was stigmatized with 52 percent reported experiencing negative stereotyping, discrimination, and rejection associated with their disease (Browne, Ventura, Mosely, & Speight, 2014, 2016). This stigma is often internalized and can result in adverse effects such as poor disease management, depression, and anger. Liu et al. also reported feelings of stigma affected disease management and prevented those who live with the disease from disclosing the disease to friends, family, and health-care professionals. Gredig and Bartelsen-Raemy (2017) found people with diabetes not only reported experiencing stigma but nearly all participants (over 3,300) also reported being discriminated against in the workplace, school, and social activities because of their condition. Analysis of data further suggests that perceived stigma correlates with low self-esteem, psychological distress, and depressive symptoms (Gredig & Bartelsen-Raemy, 2017).

These findings are even more pronounced in youth with diabetes, who report feeling ashamed and angry about their disease and who express a desire to feel "normal" (Jeong, Quinn, Kim, & Martyn-Nemeth, 2018). Adolescents and young adults in the study reported behaving in ways that can have deleterious effects on their health and management of their disease, including not checking their BGs and not dosing insulin so as not to draw attention of others. Diabetes is often deemed to be an invisible disease, but for a newly diagnosed child or teen, management of the disease can seem very visible and very alienating (Schatz, 2016).

Absence and Stigma: The Public Narrative of Diabetes

Diabetes, and notably T1D, is largely seen as an invisible disease because those who live with it do not necessarily bare physical markers of the disease (Schatz, 2016). Unfortunately, diabetes is also often "invisible" or absent in sports media, especially sports media for children. A review of *Sports Illustrated Kids* print edition over the thirteen-year period between 2006 and 2019 yielded three articles written about an athlete who lives with diabetes. "Drive to Overcome" is an article about IndyCar driver, Charlie Kimball (Martin, 2013). "Throwback" is an article about Adam Morrison who played for the Charlotte Bobcats basketball team (Gramling, 2006–2007). "Super Sam" is an article about NBL player, Sam Fuld (Gagne, 2011). In addition, the SIKids .com website, which supports the print journal, featured four other articles on athletes who live with diabetes (Canning, 2014; Ciampaglia, 2013; Neubauer, 2015; Tapper, 2012).

Research on representation of children with diabetes is likewise limited. Published studies focusing on representation of disability in sports media for children have focused largely on disabilities that can be seen. A study examining representation of young athletes who live with disability in *Sports Illustrated Kids* found that of 7,092 photos that appeared in the journal from July 1996 to June 1999, only 24 featured children with disabilities (Hardin, Hardin, Lynn, & Walsdor, 2001). None of the twenty-four photos appeared in advertisements or on covers of the magazine. As the authors note, the numbers are "embarrassing and illustrate the exclusion of persons with disability in sports media" (Hardin et al., 2001). So, too, is the limited representation of diabetes in sports media for kids.

News coverage of diabetes, on the other hand, has been plentiful, but that coverage fails to differentiate between types 1 and 2. Using the generic term "diabetes," the media unfortunately tends to portray the disease as a costly burden on hospitals, insurance companies, and the general public. Rock (2005) examined four major North American newspapers, *Toronto Star, The Globe and Mail, Newsweek,* and *Time* during the period of 1988–2001 for articles about diabetes. Several of the articles presented diabetes as an "insidious problem" (p. 1836). *Newsweek* went further, framing diabetes in one of its two articles as "sinister." Other language that appeared in headlines of the articles include "villain" in reference to obesity and "couch potatoes" referring to people who live with diabetes (p. 1836). While Rock attempted to isolate articles about type 2 from type 1, she noted the challenge of doing so. An initial literature review of media covering the release of the Centers for Disease Control and Prevention (CDC) "National Diabetes Statistics Report" in 2014 found headlines were plagued with terms such as *alarming* (Paddock, 2014), *suffer* (Goldberg, 2014), *burden* (American Diabetes Association, 2014), and *costs* (Papenfuss, 2014; Shute, 2014). Such headlines create a narrative of diabetes and those who live with diabetes as burdensome.

In other instances, the media associate shame and blame with the disease. Advice columnists, in particular, waged a battle against those living with diabetes throughout the 1990s and early 2000s. Ann Landers (1997) suggested in a response to a letter about a drunk driver who happened to live with diabetes that those living with diabetes should not be permitted to drive. All but ignoring the fact that the driver was intoxicated, Landers instead directed her attention on diabetes, making it seem like someone who lives with the disease is somehow deficient and unable to be trusted to engage in the daily activity of adult living. A year later, she continued her assault, writing, "A person who would inject himself or herself at the dinner table in the presence of others exhibits gross insensitivity and very poor manners" (Landers, 1998). Again, her advice suggested a lack of empathy while relegating those who live with the disease to the margins of society as undesirables.

A decade later, Ms. Manners (2014) advised a reader with diabetes that instead of checking his BG in his seat on the airplane, he should be doing so in the cramped restroom of the plane: "Absent an emergency, medical applications (like bodily functions and grooming) are properly done out of sight meaning in private or in a restroom" (Miss Manners, 2014). The association of lifesaving management of a disease to bodily excretion demonstrates a lack of understanding and compassion. In addition, these examples from Landers and Miss Manners suggest diabetes is a disease that should remain hidden and invisible and that those who live with diabetes should feel shame.

Other instances of misunderstanding and misrepresentation of diabetes are rooted in gross generalizations about personal behavior and responsibility. Sports media mogul and CEO of CrossFit, Greg Glassman, invoked the ire of the diabetes community in 2015 when the company's Twitter account tweeted an image of a Coca-Cola bottle with the slogan "open diabetes," headlined with a quotation from Glassman: "Make sure you pour some out for your dead homies—Greg Glassman" (CrossFit, 2015). The T1D community was incensed by this tweet because it failed to distinguish type 2 from type 1, and because the tweet suggested people who live with diabetes are to blame for having a disease. Discussing the incident, Huffington Post commentator and T1D advocate, Riva Greenberg (2015), observed, "Once again, [t]ype 1s have been scooped up in the shame-mongering diabetes net" (para. 2). Greenberg's criticism alludes to the fact that not only does Glassman's tweet reflect a lack of understanding of diabetes but it suggests Glassman is, above all else, a "story-seller" which Share, Mamikonyan, and Lopez (2019) describe as agents of the media or corporations who are "more interested in peddling ideas and products than informing, enlightening, inspiring, or challenging" (p. 2). The irony here is not lost. As a leader in the fitness industry, Crossfit should serve the very population Glassman is so determined to demonize with his "open diabetes" tweet.

SPORTS MEDIA, REPRESENTATION, AND THE SUPERCRIP STEREOTYPE

As the examples above suggest, criticism of the media for its stigmatizing representation of people living with diabetes, and chronic disease and disability, more generally, is warranted. Sports media, on the other hand, has been criticized for its lack of representation and for sensationalizing disability when featuring stories about athletes (Howe, 2008; Silvia & Howe, 2012). Lins et al. (2019) argue these stories are often aligned with commercial interests in that the soul intent is to draw viewers and readers. Beacom, French, and Kendall (2016) note that stories about athletes who live with disease or disability almost always focus on the personal "tragedy" of the athlete, commodifying the disability as emotional appeal to create a sympathetic story (p. 57). As such, these stories aren't about athletic accomplishment so much as they are about disability. The narratives aren't about athletic triumph, but more about triumph over disease, what Silva and Howe (2012) term the "achievement syndrome" (p. 174). Lins et al. (2019) and Marques, Gutierrez, Almeida, Nunomura, and Menezes (2014) further argue the discourse surrounding athletes with disability commodifies the disability of the athlete as a kind of emotional appeal; the athletes' abilities and talent are secondary to the stories of the disabilities. Even in coverage of the Paralympic Games, it was found that athlete biographies focused more on the disability and rarely showed video footage of athletes engaged in their sport (Lins et al., 2019).

Further, such stories often defer to stereotypes and perpetuate "supercrip" narratives, which Schalk (2016) explains has its origins in late nineteenth-century freak shows and disability photography, but more contemporarily suggests a narrative based on a stereotype of people who overcome their disabilities and are seen as inspirations simply for engaging in the mundane activities of everyday life or who are portrayed as superhuman for doing so (Schalk, 2016; Silva & Howe, 2012). These stories almost always focus on perceived "lack" stemming from disability and the overcoming of said "lack" (Schalk, 2016, p. 74). As such, these narratives underemphasize experiences that depict stress, depression, and other negative influences and overemphasize personal traits such as willpower and determination. The message thus conveyed is that with hard work and effort, any disability can be overcome (Scott, 2006). Such stereotypes are often presented in order to appeal to emotions and sell a feel-good story (Silva & Howe, 2012). Others criticize supercrip stories because they believe it sets the bar too high for all people with disabilities (Leavitt, 2013). Scholars such as Lins et al. (2019), Howe (2008), and Marques et al. (2014) suggest these *success-despite-disability* stories undermine the potential empowerment associated with sports participation by presenting unrealistic or hyperbolic portrayals of athletes.

Yet more recently, scholars have questioned the blanket dismissal of supercrip narratives. Schalk (2016) argues for a more critical assessment of the many ways *supercrip* is articulated in both narratives and scholarship about the narratives. Others have suggested such narratives may have positive associations for some who live with disability. Kama (2004) and Linton (2006) acknowledge these narratives can have a positive influence in the lives of people with disabilities, especially as inspiration for others to pursue sports and activity. Berger (2009) also points to these narratives as important sources of role models for younger athletes.

As these scholars acknowledge, portrayals of athletes with disabilities play an important role in the empowerment and agency of young people who live with disability and chronic disease. Their stories can serve important roles in not only motivating athletic participation but also challenging stigma associated with disability and disease, especially diabetes. In addition, a reevaluation of supercrip narratives can provide a gateway for more accurate portrayals of those who live with disability. Such counternarratives can challenge inaccurate and harmful representations in the media while also effecting transformative change in that they provide a means for those who live with disability or chronic disease to resist dominant discourses and to challenge hegemonic power relations that relegate them to the margins (Broderick et al., 2012, p. 828). In so doing, such counternarratives present the potential to transform the way the public perceives disability and disease and the way those who live with disability perceive themselves.

COUNTERNARRATIVES AND SPORTS MEDIA: SPORTS PARTICIPATION AND ATHLETES WITH DIABETES

Research suggests people with diabetes, and any disability more generally, have more to gain from sports participation because doing so increases strength and overall health, improves self-esteem by countering stigma, and increases self-confidence (In the Spotlight, n.d.). Participation can also decrease anxiety and depression, which is especially important given that people with disabilities experience mental health issues at a rate greater than the general population (In the Spotlight, n.d.). As Tozer, an endurance athlete and cofounder of the Diabetes Sports Project, explains in an interview with Kasper of the Bravest podcast,

> What sports and athletics . . . teach people, especially kids, is phenomenal— things like teamwork and commitment and how to win, how to lose with dignity and class. . . . I attribute a lot of my success on and off the field [even] in the workplace to my sporting career. (Kasper, 2016)

Indeed, the benefits of being active are well known but for those who live with chronic disease or disability, activity and especially sports can seem like an unattainable goal when faced with portrayals of athletes based on the "supercrip" stereotype.

Diament (2014) and J. Martin (2013) affirm the need for greater representation of athletes with disabilities, noting that one in two people with disabilities do not get enough exercise. The Juvenile Diabetes Research Foundation (2013) reports similar statistics for people with T1D. For those living with type 1, exercise can present an obstacle to good glucose control because activity, especially aerobic activity, makes the body metabolize insulin faster, increasing the risk of hypoglycemia (low BG) (Briscoe, Tate, & Davis, 2007). Finding that magical balance between consuming carbohydrates, dosing insulin so the body can convert those carbs to energy, and engaging in aerobic activity takes time and patience. For these reasons, many people who live with diabetes may be hesitant to engage in sports (Juvenile Diabetes Research Foundation, 2013) or may simply give up trying to find that perfect formula of carbs and insulin to sustain energy without experiencing adverse symptoms of low BG.

For athletes who are diagnosed or disabled mid-career, counternarratives can mean the difference between continuing with one's passion and sport and giving up on life. Gary Hall Jr., an Olympic swimmer who was diagnosed in 1999 while training for the Sydney Olympics, revealed how his diagnosis almost scared him away from exercising and continuing with swimming: "Being told I would never swim competitively again did not motivate me at all. I was suicidal. When I first started back, it was with a reckless determination that I would live my life as I had [before diagnosis]" (Staff, 2019, You were told section, para. 1). However, the challenges of managing his BG especially during the 2000 Sydney Olympic games led to dangerously high and dangerously low BGs that affected Hall's performance and endangered his life. He said, "My blood sugar levels were dangerously high for the 4 x 1000 freestyles relay . . . we lost the race and I'm pretty sure I had ketoacidosis. . . . A team manager found me barely conscious. My blood sugar was 28" (Staff, 2019, How did you handle section, para. 1). Instead of giving up, however, Hall realized he had an opportunity to make a terrifying diagnosis a little "less scary for some kid and their family" (Staff, 2019, Were there any unexpected section, para. 2). He has since retired from competitive swimming and spends his time lobbying Congress, running camps for young people with T1D, and speaking about the disease to raise awareness. He understands well the importance of serving as a role model for youth who are newly diagnosed because he, himself, didn't have one (Stein, 2020).

In addition, counternarratives that depict athletes with diabetes or chronic disease can educate the public and correct misconceptions about disease and disability. Jessica Cripps (2018), a contributor to *Insulin Nation*, notes media stories involving diabetes too often:

> Feed the ignorant public view that there is just one generic type of diabetes that can be caused due to a one-off event (eating too much sugar). . . . I rarely see an accurate representation of what I know my condition to be. . . . Educating the public is important, but representation for those living with the condition is even more crucial. A child dreams of becoming an athlete because they see an athlete succeeding on television. (para. 7)

Counternarratives that accurately represent diabetes, especially T1D, not only have the potential to educate the public about the disease but can potentially challenge the stigma associated with the disease by depicting people with diabetes as athletes, two identities that current discourse posits as contradictory and mutually exclusive of one another. Such confrontation of current thinking is the real benefit of counternarratives, which Harter et al. (2007) suggests offer real possibilities for change. Yet these counternarratives are few and far between.

Getting it Right: Telling the Story of the Athlete with Diabetes

More than anyone, children facing a diagnosis of diabetes or any chronic disease or disability need models to motivate and show them their diagnosis should not deter them. Who is better to realize this than athletes who live with T1D and who have lived through diagnosis, themselves? Understanding the importance of role models and, importantly, their stories, Tozer explains,

> People used to think five to ten years ago, maybe you shouldn't play sports, maybe you shouldn't go do this because of your diabetes [but] role models out there are giving that hope and helping shift the mindset of what type 1 is all about. (in Kasper, 2016)

He explains that not everyone is going to have a warrior-like mentality that enables them to forge new ground when it comes to achieving in the face of diabetes. He stated, "Those are the people that really need athletes to be there as role models. . . . People are starting to have a more positive outlook on it [diabetes] because there are role models out there achieving these incredible feats" (Tozer in Kasper, 2016). Tozer also explains how beneficial and important it is for those living with diabetes or any chronic disease to find their way to health, and he understands that getting stories out there is the first step. "If we can share our stories and our accomplishments, especially with [t]ype 1, whether it can be in the type 1 community or outside of it, [we can] change people's lives and . . . inspire and educat[e]" (in Kasper, 2016). Importantly, Tozer calls for athletes to tell their stories, which is not only a source of empowerment for other athletes, but for the storytellers, themselves. Mora (2014) notes that when counternarratives "come from the margins," they do more than relay a story; they empower and give agency to those individuals and communities: "By choosing their own words and telling their own stories, members of marginalized communities provide alternative points of view, helping to create complex narratives truly presenting their realities" (Mora, 2014, What is it?, para. 1).

Sports media also plays an important role in portraying counternarratives. For example, an article by Weiner (2015) offers brief biographies of professional athletes who live or lived with diabetes, including baseball hall of famer, Ron Santo, hockey hall of famer, Bobby Clarke NHL player, Max Domi, and National Football League players, Jay Cutler and Patrick Peterson. Weiner points out how these players served as role models or inspirations for other athletes with diabetes, noting that Santo served as a mentor for the much younger Sam Fuld, a former Major League Baseball outfielder, who also lives with diabetes. Weiner also notes Clarke's success as a hockey player was inspiration for Max Domi (Weiner, 2015). Bar Down, the website of Canada's TSN sports network, also featured a story about Max Domi's admiration for his role model, Bobby Clarke. The article describes Domi's utter disappointment when he was diagnosed with T1D at the age of twelve because he had always dreamed of playing professional hockey. His discovery soon after diagnosis that Bobby Clarke shared his disease inspired him to keep playing (Marin, 2019). Again, stories that convey accurate portrayals of diabetes and that feature athletes who live with the disease engaging in their sport have the potential to inspire and motivate young athletes who may be facing uncertainty when they are diagnosed.

Sports media stories such as the above suggest media portrayals of counternarratives are increasing. In their examination of media representation of para-athletes at the 2014 Glasgow Commonwealth Games, McPherson, O'Donnell, McGillivray, and Misener (2016) found that the tone of the coverage almost unequivocally was positive and encouraging while avoiding the condescending "aww factor" (Ellis, 2009). Lins et al. (2019) argue that media has the means and reach to challenge current models that present disability as a condition to be cured or overcome, and instead offer a space where the community of people with disabilities can find acceptance. Counternarratives that tell stories of athletes who live with disability and chronic disease are integral to this transformation.

Gold Fever, the Gold Standard of Representation

Perhaps the most evident example of successful counternarrative is the three-part BBC Sports documentary *Gold Fever* (Mirzoeff & Davidson, 2000), which offers an excellent model for addressing chronic disease or disability in sports stories. *Gold Fever* follows the four members of the British coxless four Olympic crew over a three-year period leading up to the 2000 summer games in Sydney. The team members were each given a camera and asked to keep a video diary of their lives while training. Fewer than three months into training, team member and four-time Olympic Gold medalist Steve Redgrave was diagnosed with diabetes and required to inject insulin to live. Instead of commodifying the diagnosis or turning it into a spectacle, the documentary balances the diagnosis with not only the grueling training regimen Redgrave and his team members followed but also other big events in Redgrave's life and in the lives of the other crew members. In a blog post on *RowingRelated*, Tufnell (2018), editor of *Row360* magazine, notes, "The series, comprising mainly intimate video diaries recorded by the four athletes, shows everything from Redgrave's diabetes diagnosis to the birth of his daughter between training camps, erg testing, and tough selection decisions." The producers do an excellent job of ensuring Redgrave's diagnosis doesn't dominate the narrative, while simultaneously eschewing the conventions of the *supercrip* narrative by humanizing the disease and showing the raw emotion Redgrave feels after he is diagnosed and while he is training. In two different segments, Redgrave confesses the diagnosis has him feeling down and depressed, a very real consequence of living with a chronic disease. Redgrave also acknowledges his discomfort of managing his disease in front of the camera: "This is the worse time to do it [inject insulin] because you are right in front of everybody where they can all see you." And yet, after this confession in his video diary, Redgrave administers an insulin shot in his abdomen in full, close-up view of the camera.

At a time when Ann Landers and Miss Manners advised readers to hide their disease and conduct the business of disease management out of the public eye, Redgrave injects insulin on camera because that insulin injection is a fact of his daily life. His acceptance of the disease and his determination to continue to train communicates to people with diabetes everywhere that one doesn't have to put life or one's goals on pause because of diabetes. In doing so, he becomes a role model not only for the millions of people world-wide who live with diabetes but also for those who are fortunate enough not to. Tufnell (2018) explains just how much the documentary, and Redgrave, impacted his life:

> In August 2000, I was 11 years old and just about to start at an English boarding school, which happened to have a rowing team. It was my mother who spotted the show in the TV listings and suggested I watch it one evening; having never yet rowed, I was instantly hooked.

> I remember waiting impatiently for each new episode to air for those three weeks at the end of those summer holidays; I was utterly inspired. I went straight to sign up for the rowing team as soon as the new school term started and never once looked back.

Beyond serving as a role model, Redgrave's story serves another important purpose. Though it is not revealed explicitly, Redgrave explains in the documentary that he dealt with diabetes eight years earlier but had been able to control it through diet and exercise. In interviews after the Olympics took place, Redgrave admitted he lives with T2D and that it ran in his family ("Sir Steve Redgrave's," 2019). Seeing a fit and successful gold medal-winning Olympian doesn't exactly fit the dominant narrative that type 2 is the result of laziness. Redgrave's story provides a powerful counternarrative to the stigmatizing hegemonic perception that T2D is solely a disease of lifestyle and that the only people who get diabetes are overweight, inactive couch potatoes. On the contrary, as Redgrave repeats in interviews on his nutrition and lifestyle website and in the documentary, even the most fit lifestyles cannot stand up to genetics (Mirzoeff, 2000; "Sir Steve Redgrave's," 2019).

THE IMPORTANCE OF "GETTING IT RIGHT"

In his address at the 2016 ADA conference, Desmond Schatz noted diabetes is invisible to everyone except those who live with the disease. He noted that

20–30 percent of children present with diabetic ketoacidosis at diagnosis, and that some of those children will die because of it. He calls for the diabetes community to pressure governments and the media worldwide to pay attention. Schatz (2016) says, "We have to turn diabetes from a highly invisible disease to a very powerful and highly visible disease."

Though *Gold Fever* accurately represents an individual with diabetes, the documentary seems to be the exception, rather the rule. There are plenty of athletes, both professional and collegiate, who live with T1D and whose stories could offer much to the public conversation about diabetes. Because diabetes is seen as an invisible disease, accurate representation is crucial, especially as such representations influence perceptions of the disease and support for funding research (Schatz, 2016). The Juvenile Diabetes Cure Alliance (2019) reported that NIH-funded type 1 research was cut in half between 2016 and 2018, from \$320 million to \$168 million, following a trend in the decrease for general diabetes research (from \$322 million to \$200 million) (Juvenile Diabetes Cure Alliance, 2019, Key Highlights, para. 3). The lack of funding moves us back decades in the search for a cure. The media has the eyes and ears of America. Privileging stories of athletes who live with diabetes could move the conversation forward again by raising awareness of the disease and by ensuring children and adults, alike, who live with diabetes have positive portrayals and role models to look up to.

In addition, there is limited research on sources of diabetes stigma and on media representation of athletes who live with diabetes. Just as counternarratives that portray athletes living active, healthy lives with diabetes are so crucially necessary to redirect public perceptions of the disease, so, too, is scholarship that examines sources of diabetes stigma and how individuals who live with diabetes are portrayed in the media. Scholars working in CML studies, disability studies, health communications, and medical rhetoric have an important role to play in countering hegemonic discourse that portrays diabetes as deficit and individuals who live with diabetes as society's undesirables.

NOTES

1. In this chapter, I rely on Silva and Howe's (2012) definition of disability as "a comprehensive term that includes the social, cultural, and individual factors that have an impact on the experiences of people with impairment" which "restricts individual abilities compared to the mainstream population." As a chronic disease, diabetes falls under and is specifically mentioned in Section 504 of the Rehabilitation Act, which governs access to public services by those who live with disability. The nonmedical scholarship on diabetes, which still today is quite limited, primarily falls under disability studies and the emerging discipline of medical rhetoric. I draw on both fields

of scholarship in this chapter, but I rely most heavily on the former. Because of the limited amount of research on the representation of people with diabetes, I also rely heavily on and apply research on disability.

2. Even though T1D and T2D are different diseases with different causes, the nomenclature erroneously suggests a progression of disease from type 1 to type 2. Those who are uninformed about the different types of the disease may conflate or confuse type 1 with prediabetes, a condition of progressing insulin resistance that precedes the development of type 2. As I explain in this chapter, the stigma associated with type 2, with its common roots in obesity and sedentary lifestyle, transfers to T1D—an autoimmune disorder—because of this lack of understanding and clarity of nomenclature.

3. The categorization I use in this chapter to describe the different types of diabetes has been commonly used for the last twenty years. Current research published by Emma Ahlquist et al (2018), however, argues for a more robust system of five clusters that acknowledge the high heterogeneity of the disease. The proposed classification system focuses clusters around patient characteristics and risk of complications, devoting a cluster to severe autoimmune diabetes (type 1) and breaking down type 2 into four clusters along a continuum of severity, ranging from severe insulin deficient diabetes (cluster 4) to mild age-related diabetes (cluster 1).

REFERENCES

Adichie, C. (2008). The Dangers of a Single Story. *TEDGlobal2009* [TedTalk]. Retrieved from https://www.ted.com/talks/chimamanda_ngozi_adichie_the_dange r_of_a_single_story?language=en#t-1065184.

Ahlquist, E., Storm, P., Käräjämäki, A., Martinell, M., Dorkhan, M., Carlsson, A., . . . Wessman, Y. (2018). Novel subgroups of adult-onset diabetes and their association with outcomes: A data-driven cluster analysis of six variables. *The Lancet: Diabetes and Endocrinology, 6*(5), 361–368.

American Diabetes Association. (2014). Economic burden of prediabetes up 74 percent over five years. *Cision PR Newswire.* Retrieved from http://prnewswire.com/ news-releases/economic-burden-of-prediabetes-up-74-percent-over-five-years-283 384841.html.

Beacom, A., French, L., & Kendall, S. (2016). Reframing impairment? Continuity and change in media representations of disability through the games. *International Journal of Sport Communication, 9*, 42–62.

Berger, R. (2009). *Hoop Dreams on Wheels.* New York, NY: Routledge.

Briscoe, V., Tate, D., & Davis, S. (2007). Type 1 diabetes: Exercise and hypoglycemia. *Applied Physiology, Nutrition and Metabolism, 32*, 576–582.

Broderick, A. A., Hawkins, G., Henze, S., Mirasol-Spath, C., Pollack-Berkovits, R., Clune, H. P., . . . Steel, C. (2012). Teacher counternarratives: Transgressing and "restorying" disability in education. *International Journal of Inclusive Education, 16*(8), 825–842.

Browne, J., Ventura, A., Mosely, K., & Speight, J. (2014). "I'm not a druggie, I'm just a diabetic": A qualitative study of stigma from the perspective of adults with type 1 diabetes." *BMJ Open, 4*(7).

Browne, J., Ventura, A., Mosely, K., & Speight, J. (2016). Measuring the stigma surrounding type 2 diabetes: Development and validation of the type 2 diabetes stigma assessment scale (DSAS-2). *Diabetes Care,* 1–8.

Ciampaglia, D. (2013). Two-time NBA champ Ray Allen's next opponent: Diabetes. *Sports Illustrated Kids.* Retrieved from https://www.sikids.com/hoop-head/ray-allens-next-opponent-diabetes.

Canning, B. (2014). Ryan Reed's race against diabetes. *Sports Illustrated Kids.* Retrieved from https://www.sikids.com/kid-reporter/ryan-reeds-race-against-diabetes.

Cripps, J. (2018). How diabetes is both invisible and sensational. *Insulin Nation.* Retrieved from https://insulinnation.com/living/how-diabetes-is-both-invisible-and-sensational/#:~:text=In%20this%20respect%2C%20diabetes%20is,in%20fact%2C%20isn't.

CrossFit. (2015, June 29). Open diabetes [Twitter moment]. Retrieved from https://twitter.com/crossfit/status/615539464232902656/.

Da Silva, E., & Toledo, M. (2019). The misuse of social media and the propagation of incorrect information about diabetes. *Journal of Diabetes Research Therapy, 5*(1), 1.

Diabetes: The differences between types 1 and 2 (2019). *Medical News Today.* Retrieved from https://www.medicalnewstoday.com/articles/7504#treatment.

Diament, M. (2014). CDC: 1 in 2 with disabilities physically inactive. *Disability Scoop.* Retrieved from https://www.disabilityscoop.com/2014/05/07/cdc-physically-inactive/19343/.

Ellis, K. (2009). Beyond the aww factor: Human interest profiles of paralympians and the media navigation of physical difference and social stigma. *Asia Pacific Media Educator, 19*, 23–35.

Furuta, R. (2020, February 4). Living "with" diabetes, but "for" something else. *Patients Rising.* Retrieved from https://patientsrising.org/diabetic-stigma/?gclid=CjwKCAjwxLH3BRApEiwAqX9arSJwPQGCCwDcpssEajI7k-d7QVTi5Eh735v9Z-LX32Qxd6nxgPhqtRoC2psQAvD_BwE.

Gagne, M. (2011). Super Sam. *Sports Illustrated Kids, 23*(5), 22.

Goldberg, H. (2014). 29.1 Million Americans now suffer from diabetes. *Time.* Retrieved from https://time.com/2853077/americans-diabetes/.

Gramling, G. (2006–2007). Throwback. *Sports Illustrated Kids, 18*(12), 44–45.

Gredig, D., & Bartelsen-Raemy, A. (2017). Diabetes-related stigma affects the quality of life of people living with diabetes mellitus in Switzerland: Implications for healthcare providers. *Health and Social Care in the Community, 25*(5), 1620–1633.

Greenberg, R. (2015, June 29). People disgusted by CrossFit's 'Open Diabetes' Coke tweet. *Huffington Post.* Retrieved from https://www.huffpost.com/entry/people-disgusted-by-cross_b_7721848.

Hardin, B., Hardin, M., Lynn, S., & Walsdor, K. (2001). Missing in action? Images of disability in Sports Illustrated for Kids. *Disability Studies Quarterly, 21*(2). Retrieved from https://dsq-sds.org/article/view/277/303.

Harter, L., Scott, J., Novak, D., Leeman, M., & Morris, J. (2007). Freedom through flight: Performing a counternarrative of disability. *Journal of Applied Communication Research, 34*(1), 3–29.

Howe, P. (2008). From inside the newsroom: Paralympic media and the production of elite disability. *International Review for the Sociology of Sport, 43*(2), 135–150.

In the spotlight: Sports and type 1 diabetes. (n.d.). *T1 Everyday Magic.* Retrieved from https://www.t1everydaymagic.com/in-the-spotlight-sports-and-type-1-dia betes/.

Juvenile Diabetes Cure Alliance. (2019, July 15). NIH T1D funding cut in half. Retrieved from http://thejdca.org/nih-funding-cut-in-half#:~:text=Type%201% 20focused%20research%20was,%24322m%20to%20%24200m.

Juvenile Diabetes Research Foundation. (2013, February 13). Don't sweat it! Exercise and type 1 diabetes. Retrieved from https://www.jdrf.org/blog/2013/02/21/don t-sweat-it-exercise-and-type-1-diabetes/.

Juvenile Diabetes Research Foundation. (2020). Diabetes basics. Retrieved from https ://www.jdrf.org/t1d-resources/about/.

Jeong, Y., Quinn, L., Kim, N., Martyn-Nemeth, P. (2018). Health-related stigma in young adults with type 1 diabetes mellitus. *Journal of Psychosocial Nursing Health, 56*(10), 44–51.

Kama, A. (2004). Supercrips versus the pitiful handicapped: Reception of disabling images by disabled audience members. *Communications, 29*(4), 447–466.

Kasper, C. (Host) (2016). Building strength through little victories and supporting the next generation of type 1 athletes with Eric Tozer. *The Bravest Podcast* [Audio Podcast]. Retrieved from https://www.thebravestlife.com/002.

Landers, A. (1997, September 10). Diabetics not dangerous. *Sun Sentinel.* Retrieved from https://www.sun-sentinel.com/news/fl-xpm-1997-09-10-9709090182-story .html.

Landers, A. (1998, November 22). Ferret lover wants wildlife laws changed. *News & Record.* Retrieved from https://www.greensboro.com/ferret-lover-wants-wildlife-laws-changed/article_3a138395-6108-5d02-a9fa-1f7ba1c70736.html.

Leavitt, S. (2013). *Disability, identity and media: Paralympians in advertising.* [Unpublished master's thesis]. University of Lethbridge, Lethbridge, Calgary. Retrieved from https://opus.uleth.ca/bitstream/handle/10133/3294/LEAVITT_ST ACEY_MA_2012.pdf?sequence=3&isAllowed=y.

Lins, S., Melo, C., Alves, S., & Silva, R. (2019). "Our voices, our meaning": The social representations of sports for Brazilian athletes with disabilities. *Adapted Physical Activity Quarterly, 36*, 42–60.

Liu, N., Brown, A., Folias, A., Younge, M., Guzman, S., Close, K., & Wood, R. (2017). Stigma in people with type 1 or type 2 diabetes. *Clinical Diabetes, 35*(1), 27–34.

Linton, Simi. (2006). *My Body Politic: A Memoir.* Ann Arbor, MI: University of Michigan Press.

Major, B., & O'Brien, L. (2005). The social psychology of stigma. *Annual Review of Psychology, 56*, 393–421.

Marin, C. (2019). Max Domi and Bobby Clarke shared an awesome moment before Thursday's Game. *BarDown*. Retrieved from https://www.bardown.com/max -domi-and-bobby-clarke-shared-an-awesome-moment-before-thursday-s-game-1. 1394414.

Martin, J. (2013). Benefits and barriers to physical activity for individuals with disabilities: a social-relational model of disability perspective. *Disability and Rehabilitation, 35*(24), 2030–2037.

Martin, P. (2013). Drive to overcome. *Sports Illustrated Kids, 25*(6), 38.

Marques, R., Gutierrez, G., Almeida, M., Nunomura, M., & Menezes, R. (2014). Media approach to paralympic sports: Brazilian athletes' standpoint. *Movimento, 20*(3), 989–1012.

McPherson, G., O'Donnell, H., McGillivray, D., & Misener, L. (2016). Elite athletes or superstars? Media Representation of para-athletes at the Glasgow 2014 Commonwealth Games. *Disability and Society, 31*(5), 659–675.

Milner IV, H. R., & Howard, T. C. (2013). Counter-narrative as method: Race, policy and research for teacher education. *Race Ethnicity and Education, 16*(4), 536–561.

Mirzoeff, E. (Producer) & Davidson, S. (Director). (2000). *Gold Fever* [Documentary]. London, UK: British Broadcasting Corporation.

Miss Manners. (2014, February 18). Miss Manners: Future grandchild is worth chilly reception at shower. *The Washington Post*. Retrieved from https://www.washingt onpost.com/lifestyle/style/miss-manners-future-grandchild-is-worth-chilly-recept ion-at-shower/2014/02/04/470657d0-8a98-11e3-833c-3398f9e5267_story.html.

Mora, R. (2014). Counternarrative. *Key concepts in intercultural dialogue, 36*. Retrieved from https://centerforinterculturaldialogue.files.wordpress.com/2014/10 /key-concept-counter-narrative.pdf.

Neubauer, R. (2015). Young athlete doesn't let diabetes stop her from playing football. *Sports Illustrated Kids*. Retrieved from https://www.sikids.com/kid-reporter/ diabetes-cant-stop-kelliann-keogh.

Paddock, C. (2014). Diabetes rise in the US is "alarming," say CDC. *Medical News Today*. Retrieved from https://www.medicalnewstoday.com/articles/278140.

Papenfuss, M. (2014, November 19). Obesity costs world $2 trillion a year. *UPI Top News*. Retrieved from Newspaper Source Plus. Retrieved from https://www.upi .com/Top_News/World-News/2014/11/19/Obesity-costs-world-2-trillion-a-year/1 351416449186/.

Rock, M. (2005). Diabetes portrayals in North American print media: A Qualitative and Quantitative Analysis. *America Journal of Public Health, 95*(10), 1832–1838.

Schalk, S. (2016). Reevaluating the supercrip. *Journal of Literary & Cultural Disability Studies, 10*(1), 71–86.

Schatz, D. (2016). Diabetes: Confronting the "invisible" disease. *Medscape*. Retrieved from https://www.medscape.com/viewarticle/864806#:~:text=Diabetes %20is%20invisible%20to%20everyone,children%20dying%20of%20diabetic %20ketoacidosis".

Scott, C. (2006). Time out of joint: The narcotic effect of prolepsis in Christopher Reeve's *Still Me. Biography: An Interdisciplinary Quarterly, 29*(2), 307–328.

Share, J., Mamikonyan, T., & Lopez, E. (2019). Critical media literacy in teacher education, theory, and practice. *Oxford research encyclopedia of education*. Retrieved from https://oxfordre.com/education/view/10.1093/acrefore/9780190264093.001.0001/acrefore-9780190264093-e-1404.

Shute, N. (2014). What diabetes costs you, even if you don't have the disease. *NPR*. Retrieved from https://www.npr.org/sections/health-shots/2014/11/20/365279289/what-diabetes-costs-you-even-if-you-dont-have-the-disease.

Silva, C. & Howe, P. (2012). The (in)validity of supercrip representation of paralympian athletes. *Journal of Sport and Social Issues, 36*(2), 174–194.

Sir Steve Redgrave's winning ways with type 2 diabetes. (2019). *Health Awareness*. Retrieved from https://www.healthawareness.co.uk/diabetes/sir-steve-redgraves-winning-ways-with-type-2-diabetes/.

Sladek, R. (2018). The many faces of diabetes: Addressing heterogeneity of a complex disease. *The Lancet: Diabetes and Endocrinology, 6*(5), 348–349.

Solórzano, D., & Yosso, T. J. (2001). From racial stereotyping and deficit discourse toward a critical race theory in teacher education. *Multicultural Education, 9*(1), 2.

Staff. (2019). Olympic swimmer Gary Hall Jr. talks competing as a diabetic. *Future of Personal Health*. Retrieved from https://www.futureofpersonalhealth.com/diabetes/olympic-swimmer-gary-hall-jr-talks-competing-as-a-diabetic/.

Stark, R., Stone, A. & White, V. (Producers), & Ross, H. (Director). (1989). *Steel Magnolias* [Motion picture]. Culver City, United States: Rastar.

Stein, A. (2020). Interview with Olympian Gary Hall. *HealthDay*. Retrieved from https://consumer.healthday.com/encyclopedia/diabetes-13/misc-diabetes-news-181/interview-with-olympian-gary-hall-644303.html.

Tapper, C. (2012). 10 questions with . . . Carlos Boozer. *Sports Illustrated Kids*. Retrieved from https://www.sikids.com/10-questions/10-questions-20.

Todd, S., & Todd, J. (Producers), & Nolan, C. (Director). (2000). *Memento* [Motion picture]. Santa Monica, CA: Summit.

Tufnell, B. (2018). Featured video: Row360 editor Benedict Tufnell's favorite, 'Gold Fever'. *Rowing Related*. Retrieved from https://www.rowingrelated.com/2018/03/featured-video-row360-editor-benedict-tufnell-rowing-video.html.

Vinton, N. (2008). Diabetic Olympian Gary Hall blasts dopers, while life depends on insulin. *Daily News*. Retrieved from https://www.nydailynews.com/sports/more-sports/diabetic-olympian-gary-hall-blasts-dopers-life-depends-insulin-article-1.349585.

Weiner, A. (2015). 5 notable athletes who overcame diabetes. *Sportscasting*. Retrieved from https://www.sportscasting.com/5-notable-athletes-who-overcame-diabetes/.

What is LADA? (n.d.), *Beyond Type One*. Retrieved from https://beyondtype1.org/what-is-lada-diabetes/.

What is monogenic diabetes? (n.d.), *Beyond Type One*. Retrieved from https://beyondtype1.org/what-is-monogenic-diabetes/.

Wiginton, K. (2019). Can you get diabetes if you are thin? *WebMD*. Retrieved from https://www.webmd.com/diabetes/features/do-thin-people-get-diabetes#:~:text=You%20don't%20have%20to,It's%20called%20lean%20diabetes.

Chapter 7

Languaging Actions in Sports Media and Students' Writing about Sports

Richard Beach and Limarys Caraballo

By refusing to "stick to sports," like their critics demanded, athletes weren't posing for attention, or showing disrespect for their country and their flag. Instead, they were tapping into the widespread frustration with racial inequality that's on vivid display, through social unrest in cities across the country—and the world. (Gregory, 2020, np)

Recent headlines in the national and international media demonstrate that many athletes are unwilling to remain "neutral" on controversial topics. Nonetheless, popular athletes like Colin Kaepernick have recently reframed that discourse: according to a *Time Magazine* article, "by refusing to 'stick to sports,' like their critics demanded, athletes weren't posing for attention, or showing disrespect' for their country and their flag. Instead, they were tapping into the widespread frustration with racial inequality that's on vivid display, through social unrest in cities across the country—and the world" (Gregory, 2020, np). Initially, the National Football League (NFL) distanced itself from Kaepernick, but as the national racial justice movement gained increasing public support, "the league now says it encourages players to express themselves—and its new commitment to social-justice causes will be hard to miss" (Beaton, 2020, np).

Adopting a critical media perspective involves analyzing how media sports reporters and commentators employ play-by-play descriptions of games and matches to build and promote relations with audiences as a commercial, merchandising venture to maintain those audiences. This use of language involves the "mediatization" (Birkner & Nolleke, 2016, p. 368) of sports, as shaped by commercial/corporate discourses for framing a sports team as a corporate brand designed to appeal to media audiences. Analyzing promotional use of language involves perceiving language as action or *languaging* for enacting relations with media audiences (Beach & Bloome, 2019; Beach & Beauchemin, 2019; Linell, 2009).

This chapter provides an analysis of reporters' and commentators', as well as professional sports players' use of languaging that serve team owners' corporate/commercial interests. This use of languaging helps to promote teams as a brand, to maintain high ratings by readers or viewers, and to provide a reflection of the "mediatization" of language (Birkner & Nolleke, 2016) based on commercial/corporate discourses.

We also provide examples of twelfth-grade adolescents' languaging as portrayed in their writing about their involvement in sports. These students were part of a research study conducted in 2017 with twelfth-grade students enrolled in an English class in an upper-Midwest high school (Beach & Aukerman, 2019; Beach & Beauchemin, 2019) (all students included in this chapter are identified by pseudonyms). As part of that study, students wrote reports that described their participation in different social contexts, including sports. They also responded to their teacher's prompts to write reflections on their narratives and "mini-ethnography" writing.

In writing about their engagement in sports, these adolescents adopted different purposes related to enacting their roles and relations as members of sports teams by portraying their own unique experiences for enacting identities and intimate relationships through sports participation.

We contrast these two uses of languaging by comparing sports commentary/ reporting in a commercial media world versus students' portrayal of participation in sports to define the limitations of media representations of professional athletes in the media world. These commercial media representations of sports often preclude professional athletes' unique, human qualities given the need to highlight and promote the team itself as a brand. In contrast, students were more likely to portray their unique, human qualities in their writing.

Teachers could then draw on these students' experiences in sports to have them critique how the languaging in commercial media commentary and reporting precludes players' unique, human experiences with sports. They can also have students examine how this commercialization thwarts players' efforts to use their public platforms to effect change. Exposing the "mediatization" (Birkner & Nolleke, 2016, p. 368) of professional athletes can thus disrupt the mainstream narrative of sports as "neutral", deepen students' critical literacies, and support more humanizing and justice-oriented identities among all who engage in sports.

LANGUAGING ACTIONS IN SPORTS
COMMENTARY AND REPORTING

Sports commentary and reporting involve using language as actions or languaging for enacting relations with others (Beach & Bloome, 2019; Beach

& Beauchemin, 2019; Linell, 2009). In using language as actions, "the meaning of language is created through co-action; words come to mean whatever is congenial to those who are in relationship" (Gergen, 2011, p. 188). Rather than focusing solely on what people are *saying*, a languaging perspective focuses on what people are *doing* in using language as actions to enact relations with others. From a languaging perspective, "language, action, and perception are seen as inseparable" (Jensen, 2014, p. 73). Commentators/reporters use languaging actions to create and maintain loyal fans who identify with the commentator's or player's descriptions of a game or match.

A primary focus of languaging theory is how language serves a "medium-as-doingness" for defining the "in-between" meaning of interactions to enact relations (Bertau, 2014, p. 528). Analyzing how languaging serves to enact these relations with audiences involves focusing not only on the speaker/writer or their audiences as autonomous entities but also on the nature of the "in-between" meanings constituting their relationships. In social interactions, two people may sense how their utterances are serving to *open up* versus *close down* their connection (Jensen, 2014). "Language mediates the living individuals to each other, and by doing this it offers forms to the relation, forming its specific dynamics, enabling and constraining specific space-times as the between of the subjects" (Bertau, 2014, pp. 527–528). For example, after a soccer match, a player may share specific descriptions of her moves associated with scoring a winning goal with her media audience enacting in-between, intersubjective meanings of being *close to* or *tied-in* with her fanbase.

In her theory of reader-response, Rosenblatt (1939/1996) locates these "in-between" meanings in the transaction *between* the reader and text. Similarly, Bakhtin (1993) describes how people use languaging actions to enact positive relations with others. When a teacher quotes a student's insightful comment to a class, the teacher is using languaging to create a positive relationship with that student.

Bakhtin (1993) also describes the use of language for "double-voicing" certain underlying discourses as belief systems constituting "in-between" meanings in a social or cultural world (Gee, 2014). Within the social world of professional sports such as the NFL, reporters or commentators are continuing "double-voicing" a discourse of high-stakes, competition between teams related to the belief that every game "counts" in terms of teams making or not making playoffs. If a game no longer "counts" for making playoffs, then attendance and viewership may decline. This "double-voicing" of language fosters and maintains fan viewership related to promoting high viewer ratings that help to please advertisers within the large commercialization of sports.

In responding to this languaging in sports coverage, readers or viewers create "in-between" meanings (Bertau, 2014) in their transactions with reporters or commentators. For example, they describe being *engaged by* or *caught up* in a reporter's description of a team winning a championship game. These "in-between" meanings reside not solely in the reporter/commentator or their audience, but rather in the transaction between the two. When a commentator characterizes a game as having a "thrilling ending," the meaning of those words depends on their audiences' shared "in-between" meanings based on their perceptions of the game as having a "thrilling ending" within the context of a sports world.

Languaging as Embodied Actions and Emotions

The fact that these in-between meanings involve being close to, tied-in, engaged by, or caught up through reporters'/commentators' or players' languaging consists of the use of embodied actions and emotions for enacting relations with their audiences (Jensen, 2014; Linell, 2009; Madsen, Karrebaek, & Moller, 2016). These embodied actions and emotions function as the "glue" or "grease" shaping "in-between" meanings in interactions based on their embodied actions and emotions unfolding in an interaction (Jensen, 2014, p. 9). For example, they describe how a "thrilling ending" evokes certain emotions.

Whereas all players enact embodied actions and emotions as "linguistic bodies" (Di Paolo, Cuffari, & Jaegher, 2018) for interacting with other team members (Gordon, 2003; Kyselo, 2014), media representations of sports do not typically capture the more intimate relations embedded within these languaging actions. Media representations are more likely to frame languaging actions through neutral narratives of a game or match. For example, a commentator may note how a soccer player yells "pass" to another player in a game or how a quarterback changes a play when he perceives certain defenses. That involves the use of "team cognition" for engaging in collaborative, shared interactions (Eccles, 2010; Santos, Duarte, Davids, & Teoldo, 2018). In contrast, in their written narratives about playing sports as part of a research study (Beach & Bloome, 2019; Beach & Beauchemin, 2019), student-athletes portrayed their languaging actions associated with more specific details about their embodied actions and emotions associated with their participation in games or matches.

This focus on languaging actions related to the portrayal of sports suggests the need to examine how sports commentators/reporters, as well players involved in media representations of professional sports, employ languaging based on their commercial agendas (e.g., Beach & Beauchemin, 2019; https://tinyurl.com/y89o3668).

Commercial Agendas Shaping Languaging Actions in Media Sports Broadcasts

Media broadcasts/reporting frame professional sports events based on commercial/corporate agendas associated with achieving high viewer ratings based on attracting and maintaining large audiences. These high ratings are essential for acquiring payments for advertisements to include in broadcasts (Birkner & Nolleke, 2016; Fuller, 2006; Musto, Cooky, & Messner, 2017). In the case of newspaper reports of sports events, sportswriters appeal to readers to maintain their newspapers' readership and subscriptions.

The success of professional sports teams also stems from how they achieve positive media coverage to enhance their fan base given that media coverage/ commentary does influence positive perceptions of a team (Birkner & Nolleke, 2016; Gunther & Storey, 2003). Most of a team's revenue derives from contracts with media outlets; for example, in 2019, only one-fourth of the Minnesota Twins baseball team's revenue came from gate receipts (Schafer, 2020).

This synergy between professional sports teams and media outlets leads to the need for the media to maintain their audience fan base. This synergy then leads team owners, coaches, and players to use the media to project a positive media image for teams to maintain their fan base both in terms of ticket sales and viewership. When Roger Goodell and other NFL executives tried to pressure team owners to sign Colin Kaepernick, team owners rejected doing so because they were concerned about their "image" with their fan base:

> For many owners, it always came back to the same thing. Signing Kaepernick, they thought, was bad for business. An executive from one team that considered signing Kaepernick told me the team projected losing 20% of their season ticket holders if they did. (Lockhart, 2020, np)

In June 2020, amid the protests about the murder of George Floyd, NFL commissioner Roger Goodell went beyond blaming the owners to state in a video,

> We, the NFL, condemn racism and the systematic oppression of Black people. We, the NFL, admit we were wrong for not listening to NFL players earlier and encourage all to speak out and peacefully protest. We, the NFL, believe Black Lives Matter. . . . I personally protest with you. . . . Without Black players, there would be no National Football League. (Montgomery, 2020, np)

In the examples that follow, the analysis shows how commentary/reporting about commercial sports reflects commercial/corporate discourses shaping media representations of professional sports. This analysis suggests the need to engage students in critical media literacy (CML) analysis of how these discourses shape and limit sports commentary/reporting. We build on examples of students' writing about their participation in sports as the basis for engaging them in critical analysis of commercial/corporate commentary/reporting to further develop their CML.

Using Languaging to Dramatize Games/ Matches or Players' Actions

To engage their audiences, sports reporters and commentators use languaging as actions to dramatize the significance of a particular game/match or player's actions and skills in ways as a means of promoting the team's media image (Meân & Halone, 2010). They often dramatize the "eventness" (Bakhtin, 1984) related to the significance of a game or match based on descriptions of the unexpected nature of a team's success to please television and radio network owners (Schwartz & Vogan, 2017).

In her *San Francisco Chronicle* newspaper report before the 2020 Super Bowl between the San Francisco 49ers and the Kansas City Chiefs, Ann Killion (2020b) dramatizes the game around the unexpected novelty of the 49ers being in the Super Bowl:

> New faces. New ideas. Maybe a new era? The 49ers are back in the ultimate game for the seventh time, but only the first time in seven years. Theirs is a team of youth and energy. Of crazy good chemistry and a certain degree of innocence. After a 4-12 season a year ago, this team could never have predicted that it would be trying to win the 49ers' sixth Lombardi Trophy on February 2. The 49ers are the best story of the year, thanks to their stunning turnaround and overwhelming defense. (p. B4)

Sports commentators or reporters also employ celebratory languaging about a player or team to foster positive relationships with players and coaches. Players and coaches then provide them with needed perceptions and quotes. For example, individual players serve as "heroes" who, in turn, then serve as spokespersons for a team or product (Drucker, 2008). As Rosen (2019) notes:

> The league is as much a televisual enterprise as an athletic one. For decades, it has reshaped the game and its rules to create the most exciting and cinematic show: kinetic live-action drama, a pageant of speed and violence and guts and glory, captured from every imaginable angle by a dozen or more cameras, including those that whiz above the gridiron on zip lines and others mounted at ground level inside end-zone pylons. The spectacle is overlaid with displays of patriotism and jingoism, games that begin with the unfurling of giant American flags and flyovers by military jets. The result is an aesthetic achievement and

a political one—corporate propaganda at its most bombastic and seductive. (p. 15)

In sharing narratives about events in a game or match, commenters and reporters employ languaging actions to dramatize the "eventness" (Bakhtin, 1984) of these events as deviations from the norms or discourses of a premium on winning or losing a game or match. In his report on the 49er coach, Kyle Shanahan, Matt Kawahara (2020) includes Shanahan describing his experience as an offensive coordinator for the Atlanta Falcons playing against the New England Patriots in the 2017 Super Bowl in which New England scored 25 unanswered points the final quarter to win 34-28:

> "But the whole narrative of 'If I just would've ran it, we would've won'—I know that wasn't the case. I know what went into that game and all the stuff that happened." Shanahan said the play he "regretted the most" came on 2nd-and-11 late in the fourth quarter. With the Falcons up 28-20 and on the Patriots' 23-yard line, Shanahan called for a pass that backfired when Ryan was sacked for a 12-yard loss. A holding penalty on the next play pushed the Falcons out of field-goal range, forcing a punt that led to the Patriots driving for the game-tying touchdown. "The last time down there, on (second down), I called a run and got a 2-yard loss and a holding call that put us out of field-goal range," Shanahan said. This time I went the opposite, tried to get the play to Julio (Jones), they played a different coverage. Didn't get the call I wanted, so I didn't like the call. I was hoping we could just get rid of it, but they had a pretty good rush. "But, yeah, I wish I didn't call that play on 2nd-and-11 that led to that sack." (p. B1)

The "eventness" of this narrative account revolves around the fact that the Falcons, who had a large lead in the game in the third quarter, might have won the Super Bowl were it not for this one problematic play call, an example of the use of languaging actions that engage readers.

Consistent with CML instruction, students could study celebratory, hyperbolic languaging related to the promotion of their own local professional sports team(s) related to the need to enhance a team's fan base. They could note how commentators or reporters may employ hyperbolic languaging to describe a team's success. They could also analyze television broadcasts involving cinematic, visual display as spectacle associated with promoting a team's image (Rosen, 2019).

Languaging Audience Relations through Color Commentary

Commentators and reporters also use languaging to dramatize their play-by-play descriptions through color commentary. This commentary includes the use of emotionally loaded words or visual metaphors for languaging about players' emotions or embodied actions to engage their fans or readers (Caballero, 2012).

This color commentary reflects cultural models (Lakoff & Johnson, 2011) or discourses (Caballero, 2012) consistent with corporate and commercial agendas (Lee, Williams, & Pedersen, 2016). Analysis of a Wimbledon 2008 final match between Roger Federer and Raphael Nadal identified metaphors associated with particular cultural models or discourses. For example, commentators portray tennis as "a struggle for dominance; players are rulers; and tournaments/titles are kingdoms" (Caballero, 2012, p. 709), as evident in this commentary:

> Federer, who had not dropped a set before the final, had to fight back from two sets down and saved three match points . . . Federer handed Nadal a third set point. This time Nadal found the first serve [. . .] to collect the opening set. . . . After chucking away a 3-0 lead in the second set, it looked as though [Federer] did not even want to be on Centre Court. (Caballero, 2012, p. 710)

Commentators depict this struggle for dominance through the use of metaphors of violence or motions as in

> the Spaniard ripped a forehand down the line, crunched an overhead and eventually held to 4-4. Nadal held two break points at 5-5, but Federer gunned an ace and a heavy forehand. Then at 7-7, Nadal swam straight through the Swiss tide and turned it. (Caballero, 2012, p. 719)

Metaphors of players as rulers within the context of tennis tournaments as kingdoms were evident in "Nadal usurps King Federer on the lawn" or "The reign falls at Wimbledon. Rafael Nadal, the prince, had become king" (Caballero, 2012, p. 719).

This use of metaphors as color commentary also reflects commercial and corporate cultural models. In her coverage of the 2020 NFL playoff game between the San Francisco 49ers and the Green Bay Packers for the *San Francisco Chronicle*, Ann Killion (2020a) describes the appeal of the San Francisco 49ers team to local fans. She uses languaging to define the relationship between the team and their fans through the use of financial and business metaphors. She entitles her article with the language that the team "gives fans something to *invest in*" and that "these 49ers are not a *hard sell*" (p. C4, emphasis added).

Students could analyze this use of languaging in sports commentary or reports in terms of use of words and metaphors such as "invest in" and "hard sell" reflecting business and corporate discourses. They may also investigate how their local professional sports teams' earnings depend heavily on television contracts, which in turn, depend on advertisers' willingness to equate portrayals of their products with a team's corporate image.

Use of Stereotypes in Media Coverage

Color commentary may also include languaging based on stereotypes related to race, class, gender, and nationality. For example, stereotypical descriptions of female athletes as uninspired relative to male athletes are used (Musto et al., 2017; Rada & Wulfemeyer, 2005; Smith, Myrick, & Gantz, 2019). Commentators rely on these stereotypes that serve to "systematize and simplify commentators' work. They act as a linguistic shorthand that guides how sports commentators read images and translate them into something meaningful for their national audiences" (Desmarais & Bruce, 2010, p. 342).

For example, in broadcasting international games and matches, commentators may use stereotypes associated with cultures of particular countries represented by teams from those countries in ways that conform to fans' stereotypes about those countries (Desmarais & Bruce, 2010). Even though this languaging of relations with audiences applies to both amateur and professional sports, it reinforces rather than challenges audiences' stereotypes or expectations about all teams, even when events during a game/match contradict those stereotypes.

Analysis of uses of stereotypes on televised broadcasts of national college games during the 2016 season identified instances of employing racial stereotypes (Merullo et al., 2019). Analysis of 1,455 broadcasts of NFL and NCAA football games found that commentators were more likely to refer to White players based on descriptors related to personality and intelligence while referring to non-White players more by their physical athleticism (Merullo et al., 2019). In one study, a commentator described a White quarterback's play: "'That shows you his football intelligence; [he's] not trying to force the play,' while the same commentator described the play of a Black defensive back as 'What's special about him? His size, length, and long arms'" (Schultz, Sheffer, & Towery, 2018, p. 32).

Analysis of commentators' broadcasts in the 2009 Softball College World Series described female softball players using words such as "kids," "girls," or "young ladies" in addition to focusing on their appearance in ways that stereotypes female athletes through infantilized languaging (McCallister & Mahone, 2012). Commentators also highlighted female players' emotions. For example, it is said that she "'needs to be a little bit more in control of not just her emotions but her pitches,' or 'She's usually her best when she's about 65, 66 miles per hour, so she might have some emotions play into this a little bit'" (p. 90).

Media commentary about female coaches also reflects sexist biases. Sexist perceptions of female basketball coaches influence actual games in which male referees treat female coaches differently than male coaches, and how referees also engage in subtle forms of sexual harassment with younger female coaches (Paulsen, 2020). This gender stereotype was evident in commentary about the University of Oklahoma basketball team who played the University of Connecticut team for the 2002 NCAA championship. The female coach of the Oklahoma team, Sherri Coale, was described as having obtained her job primarily because of the efforts of the male coach of the Connecticut team. The male coach was "portrayed as the 'master,' while Coale was relegated to a 'cheerleading' role" (Hallmark, 2006, p. 165).

In contrast to these sexist and racist portrayals, an article about gay, female San Francisco 49ers' assistant coach, Katie Sowers, as the first female coach participating in the 2020 Super Bowl, focused on her abilities as a coach (Killion, 2020c). The article quotes the 49ers coach, Kyle Shanahan, who states that "It's good she gets the attention to encourage other people" (B4). Sowers noted the value of such attention, stating, "In order to dream about something, you have to see it. . . . You have to know it exists. . . . You have to see the opportunity" (p. B4).

Given the use of sexist and racial stereotypes in commentary and reporting of both amateur and professional sports, students could identify instances of these stereotypes in media coverage and their own lives related to the effects of such languaging on players and their sense of agency as players. For example, students could examine how racist stereotypes highlight Black players' physical traits or sexist stereotypes may limit female athletes' self-confidence in their athletic ability.

Construction of Players' "Media Identities" through Languaging

Commercial media broadcasts also construct players' identities based on particular commercial and corporate agendas or discourses constituting the "mediatization" of sports associated with attracting viewer audiences to create fan loyalty to a team as itself a brand (Birkner & Nolleke, 2016). Commentators frequently interview professional athletes about their perceptions of their own or their team's performance. In these interviews, players employ languaging to highlight their team as a brand instead of focusing on their individuals identities (Birkner & Nolleke, 2016).

Players are therefore enacting "media identities" as a "public version of self that presents them positively to their audience and maintains their relationships with other members of their team," consistent with the commercial and corporate agendas shaping sports broadcasting (File, 2015, p. 442). An analysis of language employed in 160 televised post-match interviews with rugby and soccer team players from Europe and Oceania found that players

consistently shifted the focus of their perceptions away from praising themselves for their performance to focus on their team's overall performance
(File, 2015). In interviews with players on the international rugby team, players noted that their team identity is part of their job. One player noted that his
"biggest goal there was to not act like a sore loser . . . behind closed doors, it
was a bit different" (p. 456).

Analysis of players' interviews also found that players assumed that they
should not voice negative comments about their team, given the need to
promote the team itself versus voicing critical perspectives as a reflection of
their own identities (File, 2015). Players positioned themselves as accepting
the results of a game or match and referees' decision. "Players often indicated
a desire to actively avoid making positive remarks about their performance
and index a team-oriented self," given their concern with how any critiques
or negative comments could lead to issues with their relationships with other
players (File, 2015, p. 442). One player noted that in an interview, he tried
"not to get carried away . . . if you get carried away, you just get shot down"
(File, 2015, p. 8). When players do become emotionally "carried away,"
those interview events then become the subject of further media coverage
about themselves as opposed to their team.

In her articles about the San Francisco 49er's team for the *San Francisco
Chronicle*, Ann Killion (2020a) included interviews with players who praise
the team's "likability. This team, at least up to this point (and one always
has to be cautious about such generalizations), appears to be made up of
good guys who play hard and who like each other an awful lot" (p. C4). In a
follow-up story after the 49ers defeated the Green Bay Packers, Killion cited
an interview with the 49er quarterback, Jimmy Garoppolo, who would not
elaborate on his eight passes during the game. She writes: "He doesn't care.
He's going to the Super Bowl surrounded by teammates who also aren't worried about their own statistics but only the game's outcome" (Killion, 2020b,
C4).

Students could study instances of how local commenters' and reporters'
use of interview questions designed to shift the focus from having players
describe specific aspects of their personal lives to a focus on players' emphasis on identifying as "team players." This shift could include instances in
which star players typically praise contributions by *other* players rather than
describe *their* unique contributions.

Players' Languaging "Media Identities" through "Self-Branding"

Another aspect of professional sports players' "media identities" involves
how players engage in "self-branding" through advertising endorsements

of products. Audiences then equate specific associations with these players' identities with the meaning of products, such as when Roger Federer endorses products that equate an upper-middle-class set of associations related to a tennis star with a product.

Players also note how they can earn more money through endorsements than as players (Birkner & Nolleke, 2016). Analysis of autobiographies written by fourteen German and English soccer players included their descriptions of how media coverage of their performances shaped their athletic careers, including instances of losses in their income and status (Birkner & Nolleke, 2016).

Players also described how they perceived themselves as defined through and by the media. In his autobiography, and Frank Lampard (2006) writes, "'Even now, if I finish a game feeling that I haven't been as involved as I should, I will watch the TV highlights and read the reports to analyze my performance'" (p. 241) (Birkner & Nolleke, 2016, p. 375). The use of social media commentary during a game or match also frames the meaning of players' actions. For example, San Francisco 49er's running back, Dominque Mostert's record-breaking performance during the 2020 playoff game against the Green Bay Packers resulted in extensive media coverage of, and texting about, his performance (Branch, 2020), coverage defining his identity through social media languaging.

As noted earlier, Colin Kaepernick resisted adopting a "media identity" consistent with a professional football's commercial and corporate discourse. After his 2016 refusal to stand during the Star-Spangled Banner to protest racial injustice, followed by other players engaging in similar protests, owners of NFL teams refused to sign him despite his record with the 49ers as an outstanding quarterback. This exclusion led to his allegations of collusion by the NFL to punish him for his actions, resulting in the NFL negotiating an undisclosed financial agreement with him in February 2019, while also implying some admission of collusion (Kennedy, 2019). Enacting this agreement reflects how the NFL was willing to engage in languaging to attempt to keep Kaepernick from engaging in further protests, and how legal actions privileged the NFL over an individual player based on the need to present a positive media image for the NFL.

Then, in December 2019, in a further attempt to present a positive media image, the NFL planned to stage a media event at the Atlanta Falcons training facilities designed to portray Kaepernick demonstrating his skills to team scouts. According to Rosen (2019), the NFL requested that he sign a liability waiver discrediting any negative media perceptions of the NFL's collusion against him. The NFL had also planned to use an NFL camera crew to record the event so that they could edit the video to present their biased version of the event. Kaepernick refused to sign the waiver, moved the event to a local high school, and employed his videographers to create his online video. The video ends with his statement, "'Stop running from the truth. Stop running from the people. We'll let you know if we hear from them. Ball's in their court'" (p. 15). Through this statement, Kaepernick was using languaging to assert his version of the truth regarding the NFL's attempt to frame this media event according to their agendas. What began as an individual act of protest by Kaepernick and other players became a standoff between players and the corporate entities that attempt to frame their actions to maintain their positive media image.

In contrast to how languaging of commercial and corporate media serves to position their identities and relations with their team, players turn to alternative, noncommercial media through the use of online and social media sites. For example, *The Players' Tribune* (2014) site, founded by former New York Yankee baseball star, Derek Jeter, is designed and operated by players. Players share their writing about personal experiences with fans as a "space for athletes to self-brand without the interference of voices that might muddy the positive images they seek to build, promote, and exploit" (Schwartz & Vogan, 2017, p. 50).

Jeter and other players wanted to create a space that challenged media portrayals of their identities as idealized heroes with the context of promoting their teams' branding agendas through sharing their own personal, everyday lives. For example, Blake Griffin, a leading player on the Los Angeles Clippers, wrote a post about former Clippers owner Donald Sterling, who was banned by the NBA for his racist remarks. Griffin described Sterling's remarks as consistent with what he knew about Sterling's racism and why the team continued to play even when fans wanted the team to boycott further games. These personal insights are often not expressed in commercial media sports broadcasts (Schwartz & Vogan, 2017).

Students could analyze how the media positions players on their local teams as "media identities" based on compliance with the team's commercial branding. They could contrast how the media positions these players with examples of players critiquing their team's branding on sites such as *The Players' Tribune* (2014). They could also analyze advertisements in which players endorse certain products based on connections between a players' "media identity" image and the type or nature of the product. For example, Nike uses star NBA players to endorse their shoes to match the product with the media image of those players.

In their critical media analyses, students could examine the use of languaging actions to frame professional sports teams based on a discourse of commercial and corporate agendas for branding of teams and players to achieve positive fan/viewer responses and ratings.

STUDENTS' WRITING ABOUT
SPORTS PARTICIPATION

In contrast to this media framing of languaging through "mediatization" of sports (Birkner & Nolleke, 2016), analyses of adolescents' writing about their participation in sports represent a different use of languaging. Through their writing, adolescents portray their identities and relations with others through complex interactions within their teams and with competitors. Adolescents' involvement in sports itself contributes to learning to engage in languaging with others (Lamb, 2014; McLaren & Spink, 2018). In one study, students who played sports acquired increased communication practices compared with students who did not play sports (Ozturk, Ozbey, & Camlieyer, 2015). Furthermore, adolescents who assume the roles of team captains or mentors acquire the use of languaging for providing instruction or support for players. For example, student-athletes model how to share specific descriptors for planning individual plays for their peers (Naula-Rodríguez, 2018).

Students' Portrayals of Emotions, Embodied
Actions, and Racialized Encounters

Studies of adolescents writing about sports indicate that they focus on their perceptions, emotions, and relations with other players and family members involved in playing sports (Kent, 2014; Lamb, 2014; Parsons; 2014). Adolescents are also using languaging to portray their embodied actions and emotions associated with participation in games or matches (Lucas & Fleming, 2012). They employ languaging to engage in supportive peer interactions and assume leadership roles that enhance their self-confidence, interpersonal skills, and goal orientation (Cosh & Tully, 2014; Holt, Tink, Mandigo, & Fox, 2008).

Adolescents' participation in Midwest soccer clubs resulted in gains in their confidence and goal orientation, mainly through interactions with age groups different from their age groups (Hwang, Machida, & Choi, 2017). Youth soccer players noted how their interactions with other team members built cohesive relations (McLaren & Spink, 2018). Also, in the examples discussed below from Beach's research (Beach & Aukerman, 2019; Beach & Beauchemin, 2019), students portrayed their perceptions and emotions from the embodied actions of a well-coordinated dance team to the racial trauma experienced by Black athletes in a predominantly White sports team.

Students in Beach's research noted the practical importance of nonverbal communication with other players. One student, Jeff (2017), posited that "the research states that around 80% of communication is nonverbal, and for the varsity tennis players, that figure is around 100%. When greeting each other, no words are ever emitted from our mouths." Another student, Martha, described the use of languaging for identifying specific embodied actions in the context of her dance team: "We dance in such close proximity and go through so much together, we might as well be a hive mind" (Beach & Aukerman, 2019, p. 63). This languaging includes a specific vocabulary for efficiently explaining dance moves: "If our coach told us to do a six a la seconds into a triple coupé, we need to know what that means in order to execute it" (p. 63–64).

Students also described how their emotions as languaging actions conveyed the effects of racial trauma and shaped their responses to racial trauma in participating in games or matches. In writing a narrative about her experience in a basketball game against a rival school, Michelle (2017), who identifies as Black, describes one of her opponents tripping her. She complained to the referee, who then called a technical foul on her rather than on the other student. From her experience as a Black athlete, Michelle believes the referee's call was racially motivated:

I was now fuming with anger because not only did she get away with this, but I was now letting my team down. As I walked over to the bench, I had mumbled or so I thought it was a mumble, that the ref was stupid and it was because I was black. The whistle was blown and he slammed his hands into a "T" like form, indicating that I had gotten a technical foul. To make matters worse, I kicked my chair over and refused to sit down where my coach was trying to talk to me.

When she returns to the game, Michelle attempts a layup against the same opponent: "I decided to just take it into the paint myself and try to make something happen. I drive, digging my shoulder into the defender and going up for the layup. She falls, and a whistle is blown." Michelle then called for a charge, which she challenges, resulting in her receiving a technical foul and her being ejected from the game.

Michelle reflects on her emotions about her opponent, based on a "feeling of hate, disgust, and I just wanted to see her lose. I think the feelings were vice versa, she did not like me, and we both made it very clear that we did not like each other. I am certain of these emotions."

In her written reflection about her narrative, she describes the languaging she portrays in her writing. She notes that "the language I used was aggressive to show the feeling of hate and dislike toward the other person. I learned that feelings are temporary, so don't make permanent decisions that could affect me in the long run" (np). Michelle's languaging of this intense emotional response includes a passing reference to being mistreated "because I was Black." Yet, most of her narrative focuses on her intense response to the interpretation that they "did not like each other."

Michelle portrays her emotions based on an ethical, "I-thou" (Buber, 2000) concerns regarding power relations with others. Michelle recognizes how her anger over what she perceived to be unfair fouls against her shaped her perceptions of her opponent and the referee's perceptions of her as a Black player. However, she does not discuss the connection between her perception of this incident as racialized and her strong feelings of mutual "dislike." Arguably, the predominant public discourse of sports as transcending race and class may explain the minimization of racial microaggressions in sports participation. This discourse limits athletes' ability to perceive these issues and address their impact (Lee, Bernstein, Etzel, Gearity, & Kuklick, 2018).

In another example, an athlete describes an overtly racialized incident in which his coach intervened. Mitchell (2017), who identified as Black, describes playing in a hockey game where an opponent called him the N-word:

We take the faceoff, and the game begins. Both of us are being physical, skating fast, and are getting great shots towards the goalies. Suddenly, I hear someone call me the n-word. It was my first-time hearing somebody refer to me as the n-word. I did not know how to react. At first, I thought I misheard a player and kept going on with the game. But as time went on, I heard it more often. I was too scared to tell my coaches or my teammates because I thought that they would not care. I finally had the confidence to tell my coach and teammates the situation that had occurred. Surprisingly, my coach stopped the game and had a word with the other team's coach and teammates that had called me the n-word. Additionally, all of my teammates surrounded supporting me, knowing that this was a severe state of mind for me. Witnessing this, showed me that having people by your side making things so much easier.

Unlike Michelle, whose languaging of embodied emotions suggests she is bearing the brunt of this racial incident internally and individually, Mitchell's experience of an overt racial slur draws on languaging to describe feeling "too scared to tell my coaches or my teammates" because he thought "they would not care." In his "severe state of mind," Mitchell realized that confirming his team's indifference would be even more traumatic, but he finally garnered the confidence to speak up. Mitchell's courage to discuss this racialized experience led to a resolution that strengthened the team's morale, and most importantly, affirmed and supported Mitchell in negotiating this traumatic incident.

Teachers can use these adolescents' descriptions of embodied actions and emotions constituting their *own* unique experiences to disrupt the neutral and colorblind dominant discourse of mainstream sports (Lee et al., 2018). Students could then contrast their descriptions, emphasizing their own unique identities with how reporters and commentators, as well as how their actions and emotions contribute to the overall team's success. They may also contrast their critical portrayals of how race, class, or gender impacts their participation in sports in contrast to the degree to which sports coverage adopts a similar critical perspective.

Use of Self-Talk Constituting Relations

Languaging also includes self-talk or inner speech that consists of a range of voices echoing different discourses or perspectives (Bakhtin, 1984). People assume these different voices as self-talk in an inner dialogue as they expect or engage in interactions with others. For example, they might rehearse what they might say in a class discussion, job interview, or meeting with a doctor (Grossen & Orvig, 2011).

In sports events, players use self-talk for thinking about their use of specific strategies or practices during a game or match, thinking that reflects their own unique languaging of embodied actions and emotions associated with their identity as a player. Commentary and reporting often marginalize players' self-talk, given their focus on external physical versus mental actions.

A meta-analysis of nonprofessional athletes' use of self-talk found that they benefit from self-talk for engaging specific, novel tasks of focusing attention, building self-confidence, and controlling emotional reactions (Hatzigeorgiadis, Zourbanos, Galanis, & Theodorakis, 2011). Student-athletes use self-talk for motivating themselves using words such as "psyching up (e.g., 'let's go'), maximizing effort (e.g., 'give it all'), building confidence (e.g., 'I can do it'), and creating positive moods (e.g., 'I feel good')" (p. 349). For example, a first-time female marathon runner, Laura, employed self-talk through an inner dialogue between the competing voices of "Body" versus "Brain" about becoming overheated:

Body: "I hurt. You kill me. Please stop."
Brain: "Get off it. Only two more hours of it. Get used to it." (Tovares, 2010, p. 268)

In another example, Terri, running in a 35-mile ultra-runner event, adopts two different inner voices in her self-talk. The one voice associated with being self-critical of her pace is "The Pisser," who negatively pressures her while running: "You pathetic whimp [*sic*], you SHOULD be running stronger, get it together" (Tovares, 2010, p. 270). The counterpart to this voice, the inner voice that she names "The Rock," focuses on maintaining her pace: "Stay steady, this pace was your plan today, just get through the miles and you'll be fine" (Tovares, 2010, p. 270).

Adolescents in Beach's study also portrayed how their "self-talk" (Grossen & Orvig, 2011) shaped their performance (Hatzigeorgiadis et al., 2011). For example, they deride their play only to have other players or family members provide more positive perceptions of their play. In playing in the 2017 USTA Team Tennis National Championships in Orlando, Florida, Jeff (2017) lost his first match, leading to his self-talk critique:

> Wow, I sarcastically said to myself as I angrily packed my racquets into my bag. You are such a FAILURE. You had such a good first half of the match, but because you suck at tennis, you can't execute the win!

After receiving positive comments from peers and his father, he then played a second match in which he won the first set, but then lost the second set. This loss led to a tiebreaker in which each player kept winning. This led to his thought that

> "the bad luck demon arrived at my court, and I driveled my match point away, and it was tied up again. Oh no. There it goes. Gone. I pushed away all thoughts and distractions"

> He noted how . . . what reverberated through my mind was my dad and his wisdom. It changed me. When you are emotional is when you are not at your most rational, but I felt as if I was seeing the match more clearly than ever.

Jeff describes how his self-talk as languaging served to both demoralize him in his play as a "failure." At the same time, receiving support from his peers and father bolsters his self-confidence. These disclosures of self-talk, particularly self-deprecating self-talk, is rarely shared in media coverage of professional players descriptions of their participation in games or matches.

Tanya (2017) describes how she employs self-talk for supporting herself during track meets by "saying to yourself, 'I'm worth more than I have now. I'm faster than that stopwatch is showing'" (np). She describes her participation on her team through how "we laughed, cried, and prayed together. More importantly, We supported each other. Out there, on the track, we weren't just runners. We were more than a team; we were family."

Teachers could have students compare their portrayals of self-talk in their writing with the degree to which sports coverage provides access to players disclosing or revealing their self-talk associated with participation in a game or match. Students may identify how sports coverage focuses more on players' external physical actions than on having players share their self-talk about their internal, emotional perceptions. They could also note how their self-talk contributes to their development as players over time (Bloome, Newell, Hirvela, & Lin, 2020). They may find that if professional athletes do share their self-talk, they may frame their self-talk more in terms of aligning their performance to the overall team's success.

Use of "Insider Language" Constituting Relations

Students also described the use of unique "insider language" (Madsen et al., 2016) that includes uses of metaphors associated with labels or categories for describing team members based on their unique perceptions (Caballero, 2012). In an interview, Josh (2017) noted that on his hockey team, an outsider "starts trying to talk, trying to explain hockey, and they'll be, 'What do those words mean?' [*sic*]. It's not like a dictionary for it, but they just have to be around it to pick up on little things."

Students noted how they employed certain "insider language" categories for describing specific roles they assumed on their teams for identifying how embodied actions and emotions function to enact intimate, human bonds. Tanya (2017) describes how members of her cross-country team assume roles of

> "mother ducks," who always know what's going on, what to say, and where to be. Everyone always asks them questions; the "social butterflies" can always put a smile on everyone's face. They help us to forget about the pain and make eight miles seem like four, and the "hugger" loves to give hugs and not only gives them to some but to everybody on the team, making everyone feel more a part of the team.

William (2017) noted how members of his hockey team

> have different terms that we all know the meaning behind, while outside groups don't know what they mean. For example, there are official hockey terms: five-hole, the area between the legs of a goalie, typically an area to aim when shooting; icing, when the hockey puck is shot from a player's own team's end to the other team's end of the ice; hat-trick, when a player scores three goals in a single game. Along with official terms used in hockey, there are also slang words involved: timber, a hockey stick; twig, also a hockey stick; goon, a player that only tries to check people; bisquit, a hockey puck. This unique language sets us apart from other groups, while keeping us close as a group. These words and phrases may be simple and unimportant, but they help us be adhesive to each other.

These students' use of "insider language" as languaging associated with enacting close, intimate relations between individual team members involves descriptions of emotions not often expressed by professional players who employ languaging to promote their team itself as a media brand.

Teachers could have students compare their languaging as "insider talk" (Madsen et al., 2016), shaping their performance in a game or match with reporters', commentators', or players' use of "insider talk." While they may find that both groups employ instances of "insider talk" language and categories, they may note differences in the *purposes* for the use of "insider talk." Adolescents may employ "insider talk" more for portraying the unique languaging of embodied actions and emotions, as did Tanya (2017) in describing the roles of "mother ducks," "social butterflies," and "huggers." In contrast, commentators and reporters employ descriptors to dramatize players' roles as *super-stars, All-Pro, Super-bowl winner, Hall-of-Famer*, etc., portraying their identities within the context of media contextualization of professional athletes.

These students' writing about their languaging actions portraying their participation in sports focuses on their personal, subjective experiences of enacting relations with players and coaches in ways that differ from the use of languaging actions in media coverage of professional sports.

SUMMARY AND IMPLICATIONS

This chapter examined how commercial media coverage of sports as languaging constituting relations reflects discourses of corporate, commercial agendas that highlight a focus on the team itself as the primary unit of analysis, as opposed to unique or problematic aspects of individual players. This focus on the team itself as a brand represents the need for sports leagues/organizations to use languaging to frame their team as an appealing brand to attract fans, something that sports broadcasters and writers only reify through their commentary.

Portraying teams as a brand is evident in commentary or reporting that highlights team standings or reputation for promotional purposes. This branding marginalizes individual players' unique deviations from their team's overall image. It minimizes players' challenges to the league's or organization's branding efforts, as represented in the NFL's attempt to manufacture their own biased media event to undermine Kaepernick's claims of the NFL's collusion to prevent him from playing in the NFL.

Given that players, commenters, and writers are aware of this overall focus on the team itself, in their media interviews, as "media identities," players use languaging that focuses on the team as opposed to their unique contributions. Outside the context of interview commentary about specific games or matches, they may also engage in self-branding practices related to product endorsements.

In contrast to this use of languaging, adolescents used their writing to portray and reflect on their languaging actions describing embodied actions and emotions, self-talk, and "insider language" for enacting personal, intimate roles and relations with other team members. Their writing included portrayals of coping with unique challenges and issues associated with languaging of racist perceptions and self-doubt that are less likely to be addressed in commercial sports commentary and reporting given how they used languaging for enacting relations with others.

Understanding the role of languaging in enacting relations brings into more significant relief how players construct and negotiate identities individually, as well as collectively, whether in the context of extracurricular or commercial sports. These media representations have several implications for critical literacy education. For teaching CML associated with sports coverage, teachers can draw on students' writing or talk to contrast their perceptions of sports with media sports coverage and commentary that reflects certain corporate and commercial discourses. While such analysis may not result in an either-or comparison, students could engage in CML analysis of how their own languaging entails a more authentic, complex portrayal of their experience when contrasted with media broadcasting or reports about players and their relations with teams. (For CML and curriculum resources on Richard's Teaching Media Literacy website: https://tinyurl.com/ydythcl3 (Beach, 2020)).

Students could also engage in media ethnography studies of their peers' or family members' responses to the use of languaging in media broadcasts of sports.[1]

Students could have players describe their responses to use of specific commentary in terms of their level of engagement in a game or match as well as their perceptions of commentators' motives or agendas in using certain languaging. For example, the use of hyperbolic language is used at times to describe a team or player. They could also determine the degree to which participants adopted a critical stance on commentators' languaging, leading to explanations regarding adopting or not adopting a critical stance.

Perhaps most importantly, examining the mediatization of professional athletes exposes the commercial/corporate interests and agendas embedded in mainstream narratives about sport. Students can compare their portrayals of sports with media representations of sports driven by these commercial/corporate discourses as neutral, apolitical, and postracial (Lee et al., 2018). They may then recognize, as evident in the treatment of Kaepernick, how media coverage can undermine the unique, human, and justice-driven purposes and goals of engagement in sports. At a time when many institutions and individuals are reckoning with the widespread effects of deeply seeded racism, deepening students' understanding of languaging actions can promote the development of critical and humanizing literacies among the athletes who will shape narratives of sport in the years to come.

NOTE

1. For further resources on conducting media ethnography studies on Richard's Teaching Media Literacy website: https://tinyurl.com/y8ezft2a or his *Teaching Literature or Adolescents* (Beach, Appleman, Fecho, & Simon, 2020) website: https://tinyurl.com/y7sdd4eh.

REFERENCES

Bakhtin, M. M. (1984). *Problems of Dostoevsky's Poetics: Theory and History of Literature* (C. Emerson, Ed. & Trans.). Minneapolis, MN: University of Minnesota Press.

Bakhtin, M. M. (1993). *Towards a Philosophy of the Act* (V. Liapunov, Trans.). Austin, TX: University of Texas Press.

Beach, R. (2020). Teaching Media Literacy website. Author. Retrieved from https://tinyurl.com/ydythcl3.

Beach, R., Appleman, D., Fecho, B., & Simon, R. (2020). *Teaching Literature to Adolescents* (4th ed). New York, NY: Routledge.

Beach, R. & Aukerman, M. (2019). Portraying and enacting trust through writing in a high school classroom. In R. Beach & D. Bloome (Eds.), *Languaging Relations for Transforming Literacy and Language Arts Instruction* (pp. 49–68). New York, NY: Routledge.

Beach, R., & Beauchemin, F. (2019). *Teaching Language as Action in the ELA Classroom*. New York, NY: Routledge.

Beach, R., & Bloome, D. (Eds.). (2019). *Languaging Relations for Transforming Literacy and Language Arts Instruction*. New York, NY: Routledge.

Beaton, A. (2020, September 11). The NFL protests with Colin Kaepernick, who's still unsigned. *Wall Street Journal (Online)*. Retrieved from https://tinyurl.com/y32awtq2.

Bertau, M. C. (2014). Exploring language as the "in-between". *Theory & Psychology*, 24(4), 524–541.

Birkner, T., & Nolleke, D. (2016). Soccer players and their media-related behavior: A contribution on the mediatization of sports. *Communication & Sport*, 4(4), 367–384.

Bloome, D., Newell, G., Hirvela, A., & Lin, T-J. (2020). *Dialogic Literary Argumentation in High School Language Arts Classrooms: A Social Perspective for Teaching, Learning, and Reading Literature*. New York, NY: Routledge.

Branch, R. (2020, January 22). 49ers' Raheem Mostert navigates big offers, media storm after overnight fame. *San Francisco Chronicle*, B1, B4. Retrieved from https://tinyurl.com/y5cbvpn5.

Buber, M. (2000). *I and thou*. (R.G. Smith, Trans.). New York, NY: Scribners.

Caballero, R. (2012). The role of metaphor in tennis reports and forums. *Text & Talk*, 32(6). 703–726.

Cosh, S., & Tully, P. J. (2014). "All I have to do is pass": A discursive analysis of student-athletes' talk about prioritizing sport to the detriment of education to overcome stressors encountered in combining elite sport and tertiary education. *Psychology of Sport and Exercise, 15*(2), 180–189.

Di Paolo, E., Cuffari, E. C., & De Jaegher, H. (2018). *Linguistic Bodies: The Continuity between Life and Language.* Cambridge, MA: The MIT Press.

Desmarais, F., & Bruce, T. (2010). The power of stereotypes: Anchoring images through language in live sports broadcasts. *Journal of Language and Social Psychology, 29*(3), 338–362.

Drucker, S. J. (2008). The mediated sports hero. In S. J. Drucker & G. Gumpert (Eds.), *Heroes in a Global World* (pp. 415–432). Cresskill, NJ: Hampton Press.

Eccles, D. W. (2010). The coordination of labour in sport teams. *International Review of Sport and Exercise Psychology, 3*, 154–170.

File, K. A. (2015). The strategic enactment of a media identity by professional team sports players. *Discourse & Communication, 9*(4), 441–464.

Fuller, L. K. (Ed.). (2006). *Sport, Rhetoric, and Gender: Historical Perspectives and Media Representations.* New York, NY: Palgrave Macmillan.

Gee, J. P. (2014). *An Introduction to Discourse Analysis: Theory and Methods.* New York, NY: Routledge.

Gergen, K. J. (2011). *Relational being: Beyond Self and Community.* New York, NY: Oxford University Press.

Gordon, C. (2003). Aligning as a team: Forms of conjoined participation in (stepfamily) interaction. *Research on Language and Social Interaction, 36*(4), 395–431. doi: 10.1207/S15327973RLSI3604_40.

Gregory, A. (2020, June 2). Colin Kaepernick was right, and pro athletes won't stand down. *Time Magazine (Online).* Retrieved from https://tinyurl.com/y2zahp5r.

Grossen, M., & Orvig, A. S. (2011). Dialogism and dialogicality in the study of the self. *Culture & Psychology, 17*(4), 491–509.

Gunther, A. C., & Storey, J. D. (2003). The influence of presumed influence. *Journal of Communication, 53*, 199–215. doi:10.1111/j.1460-2466.2003.tb02586.x.

Jeff. (2017). Refuse to lose. (unpublished writing).

Josh. (2017). Sticks and stones. (unpublished writing).

Hallmark, J. R. (2006). We don't glow, we sweat: The even changing commentary about women's athletics. In L. K. Fuller (Ed.), *Sport, Rhetoric, and Gender: Historical Perspectives and Media Representations* (pp. 159–168). New York, NY: Palgrave Macmillan.

Hatzigeorgiadis, A., Zourbanos, N., Galanis, E., & Theodorakis, Y. (2011). Self-talk and sports performance: A meta-analysis. *Perspectives on Psychological Science, 6*(4), 348–356.

Holt, N. L., Tink, L. N., Mandigo, J. L., & Fox, K. R. (2008). Do youth learn life skills through their involvement in high school sport? A case study. *Canadian Journal of Education/Revue canadienne de l'éducation, 31*(2), 281–304.

Hwang, S., Machida, M., & Choi, Y. (2017). The effect of peer interaction on sport-confidence and achievement goal orientation in youth sport. *Social Behavior and Personality, 45*(6), 1007–1018.

Jensen, T. W. (2014). Emotion in languaging: Languaging as affective, adaptive, and flexible behavior in social interaction. *Frontiers in Psychology, 5.* doi:10.3389/fpsyg.2014.00720.

Kawahara, M. (2020, January 20). 49ers' Kyle Shanahan explains how Super Bowl loss with Falcons keeps him "humble." *San Francisco Chronicle*. Retrieved from https://tinyurl.com/v4qqpcz.

Kennedy, M. (2019, February 19). Colin Kaepernick reaches deal with the NFL to settle collusion allegations. *National Public Radio*. Retrieved from https://tinyurl.com/y2wzypns.

Kent, R. (2014). Learning from athletes' writing: Creating activity journals. *English Journal, 104*(1), 68–74.

Killion, A. (2020a, January 18). 49ers' defining characteristic? They're just so easy to like. *San Francisco Chronicle*, C4. Retrieved from https://tinyurl.com/y67n3bbj.

Killion, A. (2020b, January 20). 49ers vs. Chiefs: A fresh, exciting, L-I-V-E Super Bowl matchup. *San Francisco Chronicle*, C4. Retrieved from https://tinyurl.com/y5xm452a.

Killion, A. (2020c, January 27). 49ers' Katie Sowers is a refreshing addition to a tired showcase. *San Francisco Chronicle*, B1, B4. Retrieved from https://tinyurl.com/unfuwxc.

Kyselo, M. (2014). The body social: An enactive approach to the self. *Frontiers in Psychology*, 5. doi:10.3389/fpsyg.2014.00986.

Lakoff, G., & Johnson, M. (2011). Metaphors we live by. In J. O'Brien (Ed.), *The Production of Reality: Essays and Readings on Social Interaction* (5th ed., pp. 124–134). Los Angeles, CA: Sage.

Lamb, M. S. (2014). Writing: An athletic performance. *English Journal, 104*(1), 62–67.

Lampard, F. (2006). *Totally Frank*. London, UK: HarperSport.

Lee, M., Kim, D., Williams, A. S., & Pedersen, P. M. (2016). Investigating the role of sports commentary: An analysis of media-consumption behavior and programmatic quality and satisfaction. *Journal of Sports Media, 11*(1), 145–167.

Lee, S., Bernstein, M. B., Etzel, E. F., Gearity, B. T., & Kuklick, C. R. (2018). Student-athletes' experiences with racial microaggressions in sport: A Foucauldian discourse analysis. *The Qualitative Report, 23*(5), 1016–1043. Retrieved from https://nsuworks.nova.edu/tqr/vol23/iss5/1.

Linell, P. (2009). *Rethinking Language, Mind and World Dialogically: Interactional and Contextual Theories of Human Sense-Making*. Charlotte, NC: Information Age Publishing.

Lockhart, J. (2020, May 30). Now is the moment to sign Colin Kaepernick. [Video]. *CNN*. Retrieved from https://tinyurl.com/ycuwa8x4.

Lucas, P., & Fleming, J. (2012). Reflection in sport and recreation cooperative education: Journals or blogs? *Asia-Pacific Journal of Cooperative Education, 13*(1), 55–64.

Madsen, L. M., Karrebaek, M. S., & Moller, J. S. (Eds.). (2016). *Everyday Languaging*. Berlin, Germany: Mouton De Gruyter.

McCallister, L., & Mahone, J. (2012). Youth, appearance, and emotion: Commentator framing of the 2009 Softball College World Series. *Journal of Sports Media, 7*(2), 75–93.

McLaren, C. D., & Spink, K. S. (2018). Team member communication and perceived cohesion in youth soccer. *Communication & Sport*, *6*(1), 111–125.

Meân, L. J., & K. Halone, K. K. (2010). Sport, language, and culture: Issues and intersections. *Journal of Language and Social Psychology*, *29*(3), 253–260.

Merullo, J., Yeh, L., Handler, A., Grissom, A., O'Connor, B., & Iyyer, M. (2019). Investigating sports commentator bias within a large corpus of American football broadcasts. [Bog post]. Retrieved from arXiv.org>cs>arXiv:1909.03343.

Michelle. (2017). Double technical. (unpublished writing).

Mitchell. (2017). My test (unpublished writing).

Montgomery, B. (2020, June 5). NFL admits not listening to players protesting racial injustice, proclaims "Black Lives Matter" "we were wrong." [Blog post]. Retrieved from https://tinyurl.com/ycey9j27.

Musto, M., Cooky, C., & Messner, M. A. (2017). "From fizzle to sizzle!" Televised sports news and the production of gender-bland sexism. *Gender & Society*, *31*(5). doi: 10.1177/0891243217726056.

Naula-Rodríguez, A. E. (2018). The language of teammates and coaches in action perspectives on urban girls' volleyball and basketball teams. In I. P. Renga & C. Benedetti (Eds.), *Sports and K-12 Education: Insights for Teachers, Coaches, and School Leaders* (pp. 89–100). Lanham, MD: Rowman & Littlefield Publishers.

Ozturk, O. T., Ozbey, S., & Camliyer, H. (2015). Impact of sport-related games on high school students' communication skills. *Physical Culture and Sport: Studies and Research*, *67*(1), 53–63.

Parsons, C. (2014). The redemptive power of sports in the writing classroom. *English Journal*, *104*(1), 13–18.

Paulsen, J. (2020, January 28). Subtle or not, sexist bias pervades treatment of female basketball leaders. *Minneapolis StarTribune*, D1, D4. Retrieved from https://tinyurl.com/vgx5ahv.

Rada, J. A., & Wulfemeyer, K. T. (2005). Color-coded: Racial descriptors in television coverage of intercollegiate sports. *Journal of Broadcasting & Electronic Media*, *49*(1), 65–86.

Rosenblatt, L. (1939/1996). *Literature as Eexploration* (5th ed.). New York, NY: The Modern Language Association.

Rosen, J. (2019, December 15). Who's better at image management: Colin Kaepernick or the NFL?. *The New York Times Magazine*, p. 15.

Santos, R., Duarte, R., Davids, K., & Teoldo, I. (2018). Interpersonal coordination in soccer: Interpreting literature to enhance the representativeness of task design, from dyads to teams. *Frontiers in Psychology*, 9, 1–6. doi:10.3389/fpsyg.2018.02550.

Schafer, L. (2020, July 9). How major league teams can still make money in front of empty stands. *Minneapolis StarTribune*, D1, D4. Retrieved from https://tinyurl.com/y3r94v6x.

Schultz, B., Sheffer, M. L., & Towery, N. (2018). Sometimes it's what you don't say: College football announcers and their use of in-game stereotypes. *Journal of Sports Media*, *13*(2), 19–37.

Schwartz, D., & Vogan, T. (2017). The Players' Tribune: Self-branding and boundary work in digital sports media. *Journal of Sports Media*, *12*(1), 45–63.

Smith, L. R., Myrick, J. G., & Gantz, W. (2019). A test of the relationship between sexist television commentary and enjoyment of women's sports: Impacts on emotions, attitudes, and viewing intentions. *Communication Research Reports*, *36*(5), 449–460.

Tanya. (2017). sXCy and aTRACKtive runners. (unpublished writing).

The Players' Tribune. (2014). Retrieved from https://www.theplayerstribune.com/en-us.

Tovares, A. V. (2010). Managing the voices: Athlete self-talk as a dialogic process. *Journal of Language and Social Psychology*, *29*(3), 261–277.

William. (2017). The hockey hooligans. (Unpublished writing).

Chapter 8

Performance, Style, and Substance

The Female Athlete

Crystal L. Beach and Katie Shepherd Dredger

PERFORMANCE, STYLE, AND SUBSTANCE:
THE FEMALE ATHLETE

The female athlete garners attention in mainstream and social media, in and out of playing arenas. Teachers can develop readers' critical literacies and incorporate real-world issues by examining the writing style of sports commentary, social media, and other written and spoken words that surround female athletes. Sports and sports media weave through our society, and youth today are consuming more of these messages than they may have before screens were as ubiquitous as they now are (Anderson & Jiang, 2018).

Often considered a male pursuit, participation in sports and consumption of sports media have increased exponentially since the passing of Title IX (Blumenthal, 2005). Girls and women in classrooms and on extracurricular sports teams have worked to define their style on and off the court, and the commentary disseminated around this can be examined and disrupted. Choices in athletic gear, hairstyles, advocacy wear, and off-the-court style have been described and analyzed by media analysts and have been defended by athletes themselves (Cooky & Antunovic, 2020). Readers can be encouraged to deduce bias and to disrupt this language use, calling out text that objectifies, sexualizes, or censures. Furthermore, teachers can show mentor texts written by athletes that have called out and disrupted confining narratives.

This chapter seeks to demonstrate ways readers can employ a critical media literacy (CML) lens in recognizing the ways that journalists and social media creators view female athletic style. In this interpretation, Rose's (2016) theoretical stance is employed, that this interpretation "is for understanding visual images as embedded in the social world and only comprehensible when that embedding is taken into account" (p. xxii). Inequality exists in the way that media attends to style versus substance for females. Yet, there are many examples of ways that athletes and advocates help to shape narratives that focus instead on what the athletic body *can do* instead of how it looks, and ways that athletic style can be artistic, can make statements, and can increase performance as well.

THE GAZE

Historically, men have held the power in media production; therefore, the default viewer has been men. Merrill, Bryant, Dolan, and Chang (2015) define the male gaze as "the imagined or literal presence of . . . male audience and [its effect] is found across a wide swath of modern media content" (p. 40) and suggest that the traditional patriarchal structure of Western society and the social capital that is attributed to appealing to the male is difficult to shake, especially in sport and sports media. The stereotyping of men as superior to women and the demeaning of female representation continues to be pervasive for myriad reasons that speak to the ways that those in power maintain that power. This default position is damaging in so much as it perpetuates the status quo and causes harm to individuals as well as society as a whole. In addition to the sexualization that occurs in media, character traits for female athletes have been found in sports media that perpetuate "obedience, acting inconspicuously and being a good wife/mother" (Brandt & Carstens, 2005, p. 233). The male gaze, even when cast benevolently, has been shown to hinder self-efficacy, reduce self-esteem, and undermine female performance (Nezlek, Krohn, Wilson, & Maruskin, 2015). In contrast, a 2008 study found that when women watch women compete in sports broadcasts, they felt more positive and dominant (Angelini, 2008).

Closely linked to objectification theory (Frederickson & Roberts, 1997), the male gaze blurs the line of ownership of one's body, especially when that body is feminine. The gaze owns, the gaze chooses when to fall, and what is seen is taken as pleasure or disgust for the viewer, instead of seeing the human behind the aesthetically pleasing object. As an example, roller derby skaters have suggested attracting the gaze to disrupt, enacting sexualities that both tempt and terrify the male gaze (Gieseler, 2014). This, and more traditional sexualization, can become objectification and can be negatively internalized by athletes. This objectification is damaging to female athletes because their performance and attention to physicality can suffer in the face of the conflicting desire to please the viewer in power. Evans (2006) found that the "need to focus on image rather than strength" (p. 557) is one of the reasons that some girls choose not to participate in athletics. They feel the pressure to look good but also to excel physically. It is no surprise that beauty and style are part of clothing and gear, when the male gaze is internalized for an athlete looking to strike a balance between what looks good and what improves performance. In a recent video released by ESPN, female athletes perform to a voice-over that states the following:

> What I am doing here is not for you . . . not for your assessment or your arousal . . . I am not worried about getting too big or too strong . . . my effort, my ambition, my desire, for me. For every woman, every girl who dares to see herself as something more than a body to be rated, a score to be kept . . . . (ESPN staff, 2020)

The powerful message is for male audiences and for female athletes supporting the notion that clothing, performance, and gear are for comfort and performance, not for aesthetics.

FUNCTION OVER FORM

Athletic gear is designed to improve the performance of the athlete by making an athlete stronger, faster, more flexible, more protected, or physically supported. Unfortunately, the reality is that for many young women, their athletic wear draws more negative attention based on their bodies' appearance than their male counterparts (Rossingh, 2018a, 2018b). Negative attention detracts from the athletic competition and, at times, can be used to control or to shame (CBSDFW, 2018; Downey, 2018; McLaughlin, 2018; White, 2019). Positive attention drawn by the male gaze can be equally damaging, pulling attention from the physicality of a sport to the objectification of the female body (Daniels & Wartena, 2011). While most female athletes learn to manage this attention, shifting the focus from the female body as ornamental and passive to performing and active seems to be a constant battle in the arena of sports media.

When media is used to sexualize athletes, male athletes report negative effects on perceived athleticism, while performance images increased viewers' esteem (Daniels & Wartena, 2011). The female body is not for someone else's aesthetic or physical pleasure, and objectifying images can be countered and replaced with images of performance and prowess. Girls and women can be reminded of the personal gratification that comes from knowing what one's body can do, and male viewers can be educated in the damaging effects of media images that sexualize and exploit. While on the one hand, choice in clothing for movement, performance, and comfort is personal, the ways that these choices are exploited in the media can be discussed.

For example, McKelle's (2015) article offers an effective mentor text on pushing back against attention to athletic leggings as everyday wear. While many women love the way that an athletic legging can transition comfortably and easily from work to an afternoon workout, McKelle argues that style choices are personal and, for her, leggings help her confidence and productivity. Physically, she finds leggings appropriate for her needs, and even challenges the notion that she is being immodest or sexual. A clothing item is not inherently sexual. Hence, the way that media discuss clothing and depict clothing can educate viewers. This ambiguity became clear in a 2019 Peloton bike commercial where a woman is dressed in a workout top and leggings, ready to work on her physicality, and some viewers question the male gaze as to her "true" motivations (Carras, 2019). The viewer wonders whether the athlete is exercising to feel good for herself or to look good for others, specifically her partner. And if the viewer believes she is exercising to make her partner happy versus working on her own physical health, then the attention turns away from a woman who independently wants to work on her physicality and instead focuses only on the male gaze's desires—which then begs the question, "Could a woman receive workout equipment as a gift and really want to use it on her own accord?" These contradicting analyses suggest that the male gaze always is prioritized over what the female desire could be. As the actress in the advertisement points out, her body language (i.e., facial expression) sparked the controversial advertisement (Carras, 2019); however, the reality is this is yet another example where the male gaze controls women's clothing and bodies—focusing on sexuality over physicality—and has been accepted by society.

PHYSICALITY OVER SEXUALITY

When female athletes are sexualized and the focus is on their attire and not the incredible things that their bodies can do, a barrier is created against many young women who want to focus on crafting their athletic skills to perform at high levels in their respective sport(s). When female athletes are glammed up, young women realize that they often become the center of the male gaze and that can be destructive because the attention is not on their athletic abilities but instead on sexualized ideas of what they should and should not be wearing. Consumers of media need to critically think about the messages and policies in place, such as if a girl is unable to practice in a slim fitting tank top or a sports bra, then young men should not be able to walk out of football or basketball practice without a shirt on (Capone, 2018).

When female athletes are told to cover up when they are wearing, for example, spandex shorts, there is a double standard conveyed when their male peers are not told to cover up when they wear spandex, such as football pants, wrestling singlets, or compression shorts. Youth today see this inequality and are using writing skills to challenge such situations, as evidenced by their ubiquitous social media use (Anderson & Jiang, 2018). The oppressive nature of enforcing unequal dress codes can have damaging effects on female athletes. They may be in a mental state where they are focusing on wellness and experiencing the joy of competing and are then reminded that how they feel is less important than how they look.

Many female runners will tell stories of being catcalled or fat-shamed when they are running outside (Hamilton, 2017). These types of behaviors need to be understood as a way to control and shame women for focusing on their bodies. At the extreme, misogyny kills. The same survey that documented harassment also reflected violence against women running alone (Hamilton, 2017). It's incredibly frustrating when female athletes working toward self-betterment are reminded how they look or are distracted by fear for their safety. An athlete wants to focus on speed, strength, and endurance, but a rude onlooker can remind her that society cares about appearance. In stark contradiction, the athlete may be building strength, but fear of attack reminds her of her vulnerability.

Power is enacted in a reminder of the possibility of being raped or otherwise victimized when engaging in athletic pursuits, particularly alone. Rape culture is the insidious way that survivors are blamed for assault and the varied ways that assault is normalized, particularly for women (WAVAW, 2019). Women Against Violence Against Women (WAVAW, 2019) publications are used to educate people that rape culture is enacted in statements that remind runners, for example, to avoid wearing their hair in a ponytail. Mikkelson (2011) calls this advice "codswallop" (p.1) in a refutation text.

There is no evidence that a hairstyle has ever contributed to assault, and yet hairstyles have been policed by social media users and even referees when the style has no bearing on the physicality of the athletic endeavor. Yet policing of hairstyles is not just for perceived safety but also has been a part of people's desire to have athletes conform to aesthetic norms. For example, Simone Biles was famously hair-shamed after her Olympic gold medal performance and again years later, as she performed as an honorary guest with the Texas Titans (Jamison, 2017). Megan Rapinoe's purple hair has been analyzed on social media, giving the athlete a chance to be a model for personal style and athletic prowess (Rearick, 2019). While women know that hair alone does not have magical powers, commentators concluded that Serena William's act of putting her hair in a bun spurred her semifinal win at Wimbledon (Yahoo Sports Staff, 2019).

Today's athletes are rapidly challenging norms and creating their own performative narratives on and off their competitive spaces. These norms are "grounded in antiquated notions of how women, and specifically female athletes, should present themselves—strong but not too strong, athletic yet feminine" (McCann, 2019, p. 4). Choices for athletes are personal, and "may be a way for them to stand out or promote their personal brand" (McCann, 2019, p. 16). In this way, hair and makeup are a personal choice, and the media attention that comes from the choice may serve a powerful, individual purpose.

MEDIA'S INFLUENCE IS POWERFUL

Female athletes, even in their teens, have agency to use social media to air indignation and to draw attention to sexist norms perpetuated in schools. When schools post quotes on the walls above lockers that read, "The more you act like a lady, the more he will act like a gentleman" (Downey, 2018), students can go to their own social media accounts to call out such norms. These norms perpetuate a culture that does not value and identify women and young women for their athletic purposes. Instead, it perpetuates rape culture in that it suggests that males react to female dress and behavior and that girls are responsible for boys' behavior.

This quote was challenged quickly through individual social media accounts by the young people that went to school there. The local media response helped to critically highlight the ill-advised wall decoration (Downey, 2018). While this is something that happened in the school, the exciting part about it is that a student used social media to call out the school and the message that it was sending. The student argued that it is not a girl's job to act a certain way in order to get attention from the male gaze or to control male behavior. Students challenged this message in their school and used media to garner attention to help them change this quote (Downey, 2018).

Media continue to show how women's bodies are consistently policed whether from classrooms with dress codes or on the athletic fields for high schools or looking ahead into the professional realm. Time after time, female athletes have faced punitive action by what they have or have not worn instead of having the focus on their admirable athletic traits. For example, Alize Cornet, in the 2018 U.S. Open found herself faced with a situation where she was penalized for removing her shirt on the court (Rossingh, 2018b). The issue was that she was changing into a drier outfit, something that male tennis players often do as well directly on the court. However, tennis officials felt that she was not showing appropriate sportsmanship for changing her attire in an open area. Media response generally brought sympathy to Cornet and attention to a double standard (Rossingh, 2018b).

Cornet was in a sports bra and focused on being the best athlete she could be. In order to do that, she needed a drier shirt to get rid of the sweat and focus on the highest level of her sport, the U.S. Open. Yet, what's really frustrating is that officials only cared about what it looked like—a woman undressing on the court. Part of the tragedy that she will never get back from this situation is that wherever her mind was at the moment focused on her best game, she was taken out of that spot and reminded about the way her body looked and how her body was policed. Whether it broke her concentration or infuriated her, viewers will never know, nor will they see what her game might have been that day without the umpire bringing attention to her clothing instead of what her highly trained body was going to do that day during competition.

This is an example of when hired and trained umpires act as clothing police instead of guiding athletes as to the correct way to perform a sport. It is less surprising when rude misogyny can be anonymous. Tayla Harris, Australian soccer player, took on a sexualizing and abusive comment on her own Twitter feed, using media to draw attention to the ways that internet trolls take a toll on female athletes. She called commenters "animals" and posted herself kicking a soccer ball with a powerful leg with the caption, "This is a picture of me at work" (Tayla Harris, 2019). The athlete had scored her first goal, and the picture posted on the Australian Football League's Facebook page was sexualized to the point that photo was taken down (Lewis, 2019). The Australian prime minister recognized that trolls target women and called them "cowardly grubs" (Lewis, 2019, p. 3). While it is refreshing when strong athletes push back and are supported by those in power, there are still policies in place that feed misogyny, specifically social media companies' refusal to police what some call free speech. And these policies only continue to penalize and oppress female athletes.

PENALIZING IS A FORM OF OPPRESSION

Fortunately, while media has brought about a lot of attention to these issues of inequity in attention to style over substance, a real problem of punitive action that has judged female athletes remains. Issues of penalization for clothing choices are still happening for female athletes whether young and amateur or seasoned and professional. Dress codes create stigma when they are not equally devised and applied to both male and female students.

Recently in the media there was a situation where women were told to cover their sports bras while training (Capone, 2018). Students went to media sources because they were running on the track at their school at Rowan University, and the football coach complained that they should have to put a shirt on because their sports bras were distracting to the football players (Capone,

2018). Furthermore, the coaches then proceeded to tell the women that they couldn't use the track around the football field during football practice, they had to run elsewhere.

In addition, when young women violated their school's dress code by wearing athletic shorts and were forced to repeat after the teacher, who would tell them to say, "I will not wear athletic shorts" (CBSDFW, 2018), it sends the message to our young women that their time is better spent being coached in conformity to a standard than on their athletic craft. It is hard to imagine a group of boys being treated the same way. Specifically, this detention situation was where female students were sent to a particular room for detention because they violated the dress code. This is a school that told girls that they could not wear athletic shorts to school, and in a punitive way, they had to be reprimanded about the dress code in detention.

These policing and punitive efforts are continuously documented by media, as shown by a Catholic mother's op-ed asking the female students on Notre Dame's campus to stop wearing leggings because it made it hard for men to not look at their bodies (White, 2019). Here, the male gaze, ironically enacted by a college man's mother, once again normalizes the notion that women, policed even by other women, should not wear clothing that distracts men. The male gaze thus controls what women can and cannot do.

The upside is that through media/social media, many created an "uprising" of tweets, their own op-ed responses, demonstrations, and memes, to push back on the control of their choice to wear athletic wear, specifically leggings. However, once again, "In general this existential interrogation of the soul of a garment (because, really, that's what it is) centers on women, women's bodies and the general discomfort with seeing too much of them, or believing you are" (Friedman, 2019, p. 7). Sometimes the policing is based on silencing of voices. When members of the WNBA wore black T-shirts with messages bringing attention to the Black Lives Matter (BLM) movement, the league fined the teams $5,000 and the players $500 each for uniform violations (Cooky & Antunovic, 2020). A CML lens helps us identify interrogations (Rose, 2016) and why policing and punitive efforts are really put into place.

What's important about these situations that needs to be emphasized are the ways in which students used media to challenge such issues. As previously discussed, for example, the quote on the high school wall was replaced with a quote by Malala (Yousafzai, 2013), thus, the high school heard and responded to this concern (Downey, 2018). In another day and time, the school might have told the students to not worry about the quote, but in this case, a change was made. The detention video also was changed after students went to media saying, "We know this isn't fair; we shouldn't be punished for wearing clothes that are comfortable and that we can learn in. Our job is not to distract boys, but our job is to learn" (CBSDFW, 2018). Unfortunately, this same negative energy and disparity across genders still pervades female athletics regarding equipment and opportunity.

ALL GEAR IS NOT THE SAME

According to League Apps (2018), girls who are constantly asked to practice with castoff equipment and subpar fields are more likely to leave the game. Girls, their parents, and advocates can, in today's connected world, recognize how often this happens, how inequitable it is, and how damaging leaving a sport can be for athletes. Inequities that seem small or isolated can be addressed in a larger arena with digital media. Specifically, the issue for young female athletes is that girls and women are less likely to continue in their athletic pursuits when using gear that is not as good as what the boys have. Silva (2018) at the Squash and Education Alliance explained that unequal access, including clothing and equipment, hinder girls' performance. And when performance is hindered, then female athlete participation decreases, which also can cause a decrease in young female athletes' mental, emotional, and physical health (Olmsted, 2016).

When considering form and function, consumers must acknowledge the color of sports equipment marketed to young girls. It doesn't need to be pink any more than a ballpoint pen should be pink and advertised to women, especially when the pink equipment may be less expensive and of lower quality (Mullins, 2015). Ellen DeGeneres used her media platform to draw attention to the silly notion that regular "stuff," like pens and chips, are for men, while ladies need something else after companies like Bic and Doritos chose to market pink pens and quieter snack chips (*The Ellen DeGeneres Show*, 2018).

When DeGeneres uses her media platform to question marketing to females, one can begin to consider pink ball gloves in the toy section at the local retail shop. It's not that the color isn't appealing to girls; it's that the equipment is often inferior to the brown leather glove sold nearby. This marketing technique only highlights differences, and girls notice the inequity that many studies have shown young female athletes notice as early as ten to thirteen years of age and even younger (League Apps, 2018). The girls may not prefer pink equipment; they just want to play the sport like boys do and don't want to have lesser equipment focused on gender. Mullins (2015) questions pink equipment and suggests that "words, actions, and attitudes can be scrutinized for subtle potential to limit females' activity levels, as can gender traditions during role modeling, supporting, and reinforcing children's physical activity" (p. 34).

Lesser equipment and unequal opportunity hurts participation and achievement. It's not to be taken lightly the fact that the prime field space goes in most high schools to young men. Girls may be asked to go home and come back when they can get court, gym, or field time, and girls' games may be moved to accommodate a rained-out boys' game or playoff game. However, high school girls are learning to speak out when these situations occur. For example, if one looks at the quality of the football field, some schools' fields can't even be used except by the football team so that the grass is in good condition for their games while girls' soccer is played in mud.

Miss Representation, a brand that began as a film documentary about biased media portrayals of women, now has morphed into the media brand The Representation Project (2019), which calls out sexism in media and advertising with social media pages and the hashtags #NotBuyingIt and #MediaWeLike. Media outlets such as this have become places of activism, where female athletes and allies can use the knowledge that others are critical of objectification to call out offending media. When mainstream broadcasts such as the Super Bowl reach girls, they can be rightly confused. Kaskan and Ho (2016) report pervasive media bias that includes assumption of inferiority, objectification, and restrictive gender roles. Based on Sue's (2010) taxonomy (classified as assumption of inferiority, objectification, restrictive gender roles), these slights, characterized as microaggressions, remain subtle and are often invisible, and yet they hurt athletes. Yes, now, women are sports reporters and are more than objects in the commercials, but The Representation Project (2019) reminds readers that society can do better to avoid the microaggressions people might not recognize at first glance.

Tweens are especially vulnerable to media that objectifies. There is intense pressure for ten- to twelve-year-olds to display sexualized behavior (Ontario Teachers' Federation, 2013). Puberty is a challenging time for athletes, especially for females. Instead of focusing on style choices (i.e., ruffles and bows) and on changing bodies, coaches and allies should focus on the substance of their athlete's developing athleticism and not their style choices. While all teens face challenges in different developmental stages, one obvious difference about puberty for men and boys is that it's a steady increase in strength and speed. However, girls don't develop in the same way. Girls hit plateaus that can make them slow down or can affect their agility as their bodies change, but this doesn't need to be an end to their growth in sport (Kowal-Connelly, 2016).

With these physical development differences in mind, student athletes may need to give themselves time to physically develop instead of pushing to extremes during puberty, which also means their coaches need to understand these differences, too. However, it doesn't mean that they quit. If the coaches acknowledge and understand these changes, then they will help the athletes through it. Thus, coaches' training needs to emphasize this difference. Additionally, teens may come to practice in clothes that are too tight as they navigate through growth spurts, especially those with financial difficulties. And yes, some young athletes may be performing a sexualized image to fit in and be "cool." Nonetheless, patience should prevail over censure in these developmentally appropriate practices to further ensure that female athletes have the support they need to become the future game changers in their sport(s).

THE GAME CHANGERS

Called the best athlete of her time (Cayleff, 1995; TDM2000 International, 2017), there was Babe Didrikson Zaharias, who paved so much of the way for today's female athletes; she is one of the athletes that so many women respect as they stand upon her shoulders today. One of her famous quotes where she was talking about golf was, "You gotta loosen your girdle and let 'er fly!" (TDM2000 International, 2017). This metaphorical quote inspires today. The message reminds athletes to forget the conventions of the clothing that are expected of women and pay attention to what the body can do.

Another female athlete who has also faced a lot of criticism over her outfits includes the amazing Serena Williams, who has consistently been in the headlines for turning heads with her "striking outfit[s]" (Rossingh, 2018a). Once again because Serena, who is arguably one of the best athletes of all time, has a certain print (ESPN News Service, 2019), a catsuit (McLaughlin, 2018), or ruffles on her outfit (Erdman, 2018), people may think that she solely wants attention with her clothing instead of pointing to the real focus of her domination in the sport of tennis and how she uses her platform to bring attention to issues that impact women of all backgrounds, which includes their clothing. She is the only athlete to win titles in four different decades and held the #1 title for 186 consecutive weeks (ESPN Stats & Information, 2020). Serena is a spokesperson for issues of bias in sports and in medicine, famously calling out an umpire who showed implicit bias and her medical team who ignored her dangerously declining health while delivering her child. She is also a fashionista (Ford, 2019). For her, personal style is just that, personal. Fans of Serena know that her performance and her style are individual and reflect the person that she wants to perform to the public eye or what she physically needs to play her best game. Her work, her style, and her performances also reflect her belief that her family has been a change-agent of the sport, she says, "not because we were welcomed, but because we wouldn't stop winning" (Stevens, 2019).

Serena's persistence despite obstacles is motivating for others following her. For example, after having been diagnosed with blood clots which necessitated a need to wear spandex for her health, she was still policed (Hohman,

2019). And the bigger picture here is that no one can ignore Serena Williams and the policing of her body without critically thinking of the intersectionality of women, specifically women of color, and the way that she is being policed in that way as well (Crenshaw, 1991). Black women's emotions (Afoko, 2018) and bodies (McLaughlin, 2018) have often been at the center of discriminatory and oppressive critiques, so conversations surrounding athletic wear cannot exclude conversations concerning race, too.

Major League Baseball announced in May 2020 that Rachel Balkovec was named as the first female hitting coach and will start next season with the Yankees. While she is quoted as recognizing and naming discrimination that she has felt, she nodded to women role models and isn't described as the trailblazer that she is (Lindsley, 2020). In addition, while one thinks of the National Football League (NFL) as the most hypermasculine, male-only sports environment there is, several trailblazers are helping to open people's eyes to the possibility of breaking down perceived barriers. For example, the San Francisco 49er's offensive assistant coach, Katie Bowers, quickly became known as she was the first female and openly gay person to coach in the Super Bowl. Bowers's journey to success, however, has been filled with a few detours as she could have been an assistant basketball coach early on but was turned down due to her sexual orientation (Walker, 2020). Nevertheless, her hard work and determination opened up doors for her that she would not have expected within the NFL.

The athletes of the WBNA have also used style, in the form of black T-shirts with hashtags and Martin Luther King Jr. quotes to bring attention to the BLM movement. This movement spanned across players and teams and showed greater solidarity than the NBA's protests did (Blades, 2016; Zirin, 2018). The USWNT soccer team also used clothing to make statements, coming onto the field with names of influential women on their jerseys, such as Ruth Bader Ginsburg, Sojourner Truth, Malala Yousafzai, Doris Burke, and Audre Lorde. Megan Rapinoe (2017) explained in an interview with the Arizona Republic,

> Honestly, I feel like we are a walking protest. The fact that we're women professional athletes says that in and of itself. We've been feeling the inequality; we've been struggling with pay equality . . . or sexism in sports. So, I think when social issues have come up, or you know kneeling or what the WNBA did last summer with wearing black shirts, I feel like every time something like that comes up it just strikes home for us. . . . I think our existence in professional sports is almost a protest in and of itself sometimes in the very sexist society that we live in. (p.3)

Once again, critically considering the intersectionality of women is important when one looks at the critiques and reports surrounding Bowers.

However, she said it best: "The more we can create an environment that welcomes all types of people, no matter their race, gender, sexual orientation, religion, the more we can help ease the pain and burden that many carry every day" (Nuyen, 2020, p. 6). This inclusive environment can be easily destroyed when critical consumption of media is skipped, and consumers do not consider how intricate these connections are. Yet Bowers is up for the challenge of being a game changer as she said, "I am willing and happy to be a trailblazer because I know that other women, other young girls, are watching this and maybe their path seems a little clearer now" (Wagoner, 2020, p. 23). With this point in mind, when it comes to gender, race, sexuality, or any other descriptors, females have, are, and will continue to find success in athletics at any level as they break barriers and push people's understanding of what they can do.

TAKING SMALL STEPS FORWARD

Over the years, there has been a shift in media when it comes to respecting female athletes and empowering young women, such as through the new Nike advertisements including "Because of Them We Can" (Jones, 2018), showing young Serena as a child on the courts ultimately making her way to one of the top athletic events in her career; "Dream Crazier" (Nike, 2019a), showcasing a variety of women pursuing their athletic dreams despite negative critiques for them being passionate, dedicated, or dominate in their respective sport; "Dream with Us" (Nike, 2019b), highlighting a myriad of sports with young female athletes following in the footsteps of adult female athletes and leaders; and "Dream Further" (Nike, 2019c), highlighting a young soccer player bouncing all over the world with different clubs and walking in the shoes of the players and coaches she looks up to in the sport.

In addition, young athletes of both genders are starting to see opportunities in the media where the focus is on what they are able to do as athletes dedicated to their sport(s). For example, boys are wearing U.S. women soccer jerseys, citing the speed and tenacity of the players as inspirational (Tate, 2019). These examples show that strong, athletic women can be role models for all despite their gender if given the chance to be visible for kids to see.

Rose (2016) states,

> Visual imagery is never innocent; it is always constructed through various practices, technologies, and knowledges. A critical approach to visual images is therefore needed: one that thinks about the agency of the image, considers the social practices and effects of its social circulation and viewing, and reflects

on the specificity of that viewing by various audiences, including the academic critic. (p. 23)

Though female athletes are gaining some agency through these media campaigns that are being revealed today, a critical lens is still required to acknowledge the many ways in which powerful messages are being disseminated, consumed, and (re)produced. Text and images, whether they reinforce or contradict stereotypes, affect not only the audience but also social role identities (Angelini, 2008). Thus, it is imperative that athletes of all ages, but especially female athletes, have exposure to powerful role models that exemplify ways to mediate conflicting social demands with individual ownership of performance, style, and substance.

In the 2019 NCAA Women's Basketball Tournament, Notre Dame's head coach, Muffet McGraw, said, "We don't have enough female role models. We don't have enough visible women and leaders. We don't have enough women in power" (espnW, 2019). While she is talking about the role of women in high-ranking positions in sports leadership, we believe that this can also be applied to the notion of performance, style, and substance with regards to sports media.

When media presents leaders such as Serena Williams who is consistently chastised for her style choices, one must wonder how this portrayal creates or disrupts opportunities for future female athletic leaders. Furthermore, performance, style, and substance go beyond athletes to all people in the public eye who may be style-shamed for their lipstick, hair, or body shape where there are fewer women role models with different body types than in positions of power and stardom. Yet with a CML lens, a lens that champions female athletes as performance machines versus performers, the gaze is headed in a better direction both on and off the athletic playing courts, fields, tracks, and all of the places that female athletes compete.

REFERENCES

Afoko, C. (2018, September 10). Serena Williams's treatment shows how hard it is to be a Black woman at work. *The Guardian*. Retrieved from https://www.theguard ian.com/commentisfree/2018/sep/10/serena-williams-black-woman-work-tennis-d iscrimination.

Anderson, M., & Jiang, J. (2018). Teens, social media, & technology 2018. *Pew Research Center*. Retrieved from https://www.pewresearch.org/internet/2018/05/ 31/teens-social-media-technology-2018/.

Angelini, J. R. (2008). How did the sport make you feel? Looking at the three dimensions of emotion through a gendered lens. *Sex Roles, 58*(1–2), 127–135.

Blades, L. A. (2016, October 17). WNBA players protest for Black Lives Matter despite league punishments. *Teen Vogue*. Retrieved from https://www.teenvogue .com/story/wnba-players-protest-black-lives-matter.

Blumenthal, K. (2005). *Let Me Play: The Story of Title IX: The Law that Changed the Future of Girls in America*. New York, NY: Atheneum Books for Young Readers.

Brandt, M., & Carstens, A. (2005). The discourse of the male gaze: A critical analysis of the feature section 'The beauty of sport' in SA *Sports Illustrated*. *Southern African Linguistics and Applied Language Studies, 23*(3), 233–243.

Capone, G. (2018, November 8). A recent sports bra suspension at Rowan University has gotten female athletes outraged. *The Odyssey*. Retrieved from https://www.the odysseyonline.com/sports-bra-suspension.

Carras, C. (2019, December). Peloton actress blames her face for viral ad controversy. *The Chicago Tribune*. Retrieved from https://www.chicagotribune.com/ente rtainment/ct-ent-peloton-ad-controversy-response-20191213-gxdjj3gyzrbo3gvwg fmvor2tza-story.html.

Cayleff, S. E. (1995). *Babe: The Life and Legend of Babe Didrikson Zaharias*. Chicago, IL: University of Illinois Press.

CBSDFW. [CBSDFW]. (2018, August 17). North Texas school receives backlash about video showcasing dress code [Video File]. Retrieved from https://www.you tube.com/watch?v=1X2Y77ruPEw#action=share.

Cooky, C., & Antunovic, D. (2020). "This isn't just about us": Articulations of feminism in media narratives of athlete activism. *Communication and Sport. 8*(4–5), 692–711. doi: 10.1177/2167479519896360.

Crenshaw, K., (1991). Mapping the margins: Intersectionality, identity politics, and violence against women of color. *Stanford Law Review, 43*(6), 1241.

Daniels, E. A., & Wartena, H. (2011). Athlete or sex symbol: What boys think of media representation of female athletes. *Sex Roles,* (65), 566–579.

Downey, M. (2018, August 21). Schools must stop putting girls and their bodies on trial. *AJC*. Retrieved from https://www.myajc.com/blog/get-schooled/schools-mu st-stop-putting-girls-and-their-bodies-trial/tuS9RbCbxnLOiySx4pks8O/.

Erdman, S. L. (2018, August 28). Serena Williams wearing black ruffled tutu wins U.S. Open match. *AJC*. Retrieved from https://www.ajc.com/entertainment/serena-will iams-wearing-black-ruffled-tutu-wins-open-match/4D18ZW9syE791LX5TV4HXO/.

ESPN Stats & Information. (2020, March 27). Did you know? The best Serena Williams stats. Retrieved from https://www.espn.com/tennis/story/_/id/29281944/te nnis-failing-renew-fan-base-serena-williams-coach-mouratoglou.

ESPN News Service. (2019, May 27). Serena's outfit, game make statement in Paris. *ESPN*. Retrieved from https://www.espn.com/tennis/story/_/ id/26832437/serena-o utfit-game-make-statement-paris.

ESPN staff. (2020, June 17). Serena Williams, Sabrina Ionescu, Katelyn Ohashi highlight espnW's celebration of Title IX and women's sports. *espnW*. Retrieved from https://www.espn.com/espnw/story/_/id/29326140/undefined.

espnW. (2019, April 4). Muffet McGraw calls for more women in positions of power [Video file]. *espnW*. Retrieved from https://www.facebook.com/espnW/videos/ 379430782661216/

Evans, B. (2006). 'I'd feel ashamed': Girls' bodies and sports participation. *Gender, Place & Culture, 13*(5), 547–561.

Ford, A. C. (2019, Jan 10). Serena Williams: The power of unapologetic greatness. *Allure.* Retrieved from https://www.allure.com/story/serena-williams-unapologetic -greatness-cover-interview-2019.

Frederickson, B. L., & Roberts, T. A. (1997). Objectification theory: Toward understanding women's lived experiences and mental health risks. *Psychology of Women Quarterly, 21,* 173–206.

Friedman, V. (2019, April 1). It's possible leggings are the future. Deal with it. *The New York Times.* Retrieved from https://www.nytimes.com/2019/04/01/fashion/le ggings-notre-dame-controversy.html.

Gieseler, C. (2014). Derby drag: Parodying sexualities in the sport of roller derby. *Sexualities, 17*(5–6), 758–776.

Hamilton, M. (2017, August 8). Running while female. *Runners World.* Retrieved from https://www.runnersworld.com/training/a18848270/running-while-female/.

Hohman, M. (2019, January 17). Serena Williams still worried about blood clots as she competes in Australia: "It's very scary." *People Magazine.* Retrieved from https://people.com/sports/serena-williams-still-worried-blood-clots-deep-vein-th rombosis-australian-open/.

Jamison, S. E. (2017, December 13). People are shaming Simone Biles for her hair . . . Again. *Ebony.* Retrieved from https://www.ebony.com/life/people-shaming -simone-biles-hair/

Jones, E. [Because of Them We Can by Eunique Jones]. (2018, August 27). *Serena Williams- U.S. Open* [Video file]. Retrieved from https://www.facebook.com/ becauseofthemwecan/videos/2216228831784158.

Kaskan, E. R., & Ho, I. K. (2016). Microaggressions and female athletes. *Sex Roles, 74,* 275–287.

Kowal-Connelly, S. (2016, April). Effects of puberty on sports performance: What parents need to know. *Healthy Children.* Retrieved from https://www.healthychildr en.org/English/healthy-living/sports/Pages/Teens-and-Sports.aspx.

League Apps. (2018, June 19). Eight barriers that stop girls from playing sports— And an Olympian's advice on how to break through [Blog post]. *League Apps.* Retrieved from https://blog.leagueapps.com/encourage-female-players /# .W9BwXu-pv8Y.mailto.

Lewis, A. (2019, March 21). Tayla Harris: How "repulsive" social media comments sparked outrage in Australia. *CNN.* Retrieved from https://www.cnn.com/2019/03 /20/sport/tayla-harris-photo-aflw-trolls-australia-spt-int/index.html.

Lindsley, A. (2020, May 6). LSU grad becomes first female MLB hitting coach. *NBC12.* Retrieved from https://www.nbc12.com/2020/05/07/lsu-grad-becomes- first-female-mlb-hitting-coach/

McCann, A. (2019, June 20). World cup players say muscles and makeup mix just fine, thanks. *New York Times.* Retrieved from https://www.nytimes.com/2019/06 /20/style/world-cup-women-hair-gender.html.

McKelle, E. (2015, March 19). 9 things women who wear leggings as pants are tired of hearing. *Bustle.* Retrieved from https://www.bustle.com/articles/70012-9-things -women-who-wear-leggings-as-pants-are-tired-of-hearing.

McLaughlin, E. C. (2018, August 27). Why Serena Williams' catsuit ban matters, and what it says about us. *CNN.* Retrieved from https://www.cnn.com/2018/08/27/tenn is/serena-williams-catsuit-ban-racism-misogyny/index.html.

Merrill, K., Bryant, A., Dolan, E., & Chang, S. (2015). The male gaze and online sports punditry: Reactions to the Ines Sainz controversy on the sports blogosphere. *Journal of Sport and Social Issues, 39*(1), 40–60.

Mikkelson, D. (2011, July 5). Rape prevention advice. *Snopes.* Retrieved from https:/ /www.snopes.com/fact-check/assaulted-tale-aka-this-bird-wont-fly/

Mullins, N. M. (2015). Insidious influence of gender socialization on females' physical activity: Rethink pink. *Physical Educator, 72*(1), 20–43.

Nezlek, J. B., Krohn, W., Wilson, D., & Maruskin, L. (2015). Gender differences in reactions to the sexualization of athletes. *The Journal of Social Psychology, 155*(1), 1–11.

Nike. [Nike]. (2019a, Feb. 24). *Dream crazier* [Video file]. Retrieved from https://ww w.youtube.com/watch?v=whpJ19RJ4JY.

Nike. [Nike]. (2019b, May 12). *Dream with us* [Video file]. Retrieved from https:// www.youtube.com/watch?v=IHcWPVbDArU.

Nike. [Nike]. (2019c, June 1). *Dream further* [Video file]. Retrieved from https://ww w.youtube.com/watch?v=hOVkEHADCg4.

Nuyen, S. (2020, January 21). 49ers' coach Katie Sowers will make history as the first woman and openly gay coach at the Super Bowl. *WUSA9.* Retrieved from https:// www.wusa9.com /article/ news/nation-world/49ers-coach-katie-sowers-will-ma ke-history-as-the-first-woman-and-openly-gay-coach-at-the-super-bowl/507-84 5cf4d1-d1da-4137-8a76-75acd27348a2.

Olmsted, M. (2016, January 8). How sports help decrease the risk of teen substance abuse. *Women's Sports Foundation.* Retrieved from https://www.womenssp ortsfoundation.org/health/how-sports-help-decrease-the-risk-of-teen-substance -abuse/.

Ontario Teachers' Federation. (2013). Sexism and violence against girls and women. *Safe@School.* Retrieved from https://www.safeatschool.ca/plm/equ ity-and-inclusion/understanding-sexism-racism-and-homophobia/sexism-and-vio lence.

Rapinoe, M. (2017). Moore: U.S. soccer star Megan Rapinoe says female athletes are 'walking protest. *AZ Central.* Retrieved from https://www.azcentral.com/stor y/sports/soccer/2017/10/24/moore-us-soccer-megan-rapinoe-womens-pro-athletes -protest/797253001/

Rearick, L. (2019, July 8). How to get Megan Rapinoe's 2019 World Cup winning purple hair. *Teen Vogue.* Retrieved from https://www.teenvogue.com/ story /styl ists-ways-to-get-megan-rapinoe-inspired-purple-hair.

Rose, G. (2016). *Visual Methodologies: An Introduction to the Interpretation of Visual Materials* (4th ed.). London, UK: Sage.

188   *Crystal L. Beach and Katie Shepherd Dredger*

Rossingh, D. (2018a, August 28). Serena Williams turns heads with striking outfit at US Open. *CNN*. Retrieved from https://www.cnn.com/2018/08/28/sport/serena-w illiams-us-open-outfit-tennis-spt-intl/index.html.
Rossingh, D. (2018b, August 30). Alize Cornet: US Open embroiled in sexism controversy. *NN*. Retrieved from https://www.cnn.com/2018/08/29/tennis /us- open-alize-cornet-sexism-row/index.html.
Silva, B. (2018). Best practice guides: Supporting female athletes. *Squash Education Alliance*. Retrieved from https://squashandeducation.org/wp-content/uploads/ 2018/07/Best-Practices-Female-Athletes.pdf.
Stevens, H. (2019, July 10). Column: Put this Serena Williams quote on all the motivational posters. The world needs to hear it. *The Chicago Tribune*. Retrieved from https://www.chicagotribune.com/columns/heidi-stevens/ct-heidi-stevens-wedne sday-serena-williams-harpers-bazaar-0710-20190710-oxs3res7yzgkxf7c3l6v bume6e-story.html.
Sue, D. W. (2010). *Microaggressions in Everyday Life: Race, Gender, and Sexual Orientation*. Hoboken, NJ: Wiley.
Tate, A.S. (2019, June 24). Among US women's soccer's jersey-wearing fans? Young boys. *Today*. Retrieved from https://www.today.com/parents/boys -wear -u-s-women-s-Soccer-world-cup-jerseys-t156959.
Tayla Harris [Tayla Harris]. (2019, March 20). [Twitter moment, account since deleted]. *Twitter*.
TDM2000 International. (2017, October 5). Babe Didrikson Zaharias. Retrieved from https://www.sportvalues.eu/dz/.
The Ellen Show. [TheEllenShow]. (2018, February 7). *Ellen won't stay quiet about lady Doritos* [Video file]. Retrieved from https://www.youtube.com/watch?v=RnO AzmZQd_c.
The Representation Project. (2019). #NotBuyingIt. Retrieved from http://therepre sentationproject.org/the-movement/notbuyinglt/.
Wagoner, N. (2020, January 28). 49ers' Katie Sowers calls becoming first woman to coach at Super Bowl 'surreal.' *ESPN*. Retrieved from https://www.espn.com/nfl/ story/_/id/28580558/49ers-katie-sowers-calls-becoming-first-woman-coach-super -bowl-surreal.
Walker, T. (2020, January 30). Katie Sowers blazes trail as first woman, and openly gay, coach in Super Bowl. *CBC*. Retrieved from https://www.cbc.ca/sports/foot ball/nfl/katie-bowers-first-female-gay-coach-super-bowl-1.5446914.
WAVAW Rape Crisis Center. (2013). What is rape culture? *WAVAW*. Retrieved from https://www.wavaw.ca/what-is-rape-culture/
White, M. (2019, March 25). The legging problem [Letter to the editor]. *The Observer*. Retrieved from https://ndsmcobserver.com/2019/03/the-legging-prob lem/
Yahoo Sports Staff. (2019, July 10). It's a thing: Serena Williams photo sparks strange theory at Wimbledon. *Yahoo Sports*. Retrieved from https://sports.yahoo .com/wimbledon-serena-williams-hair-strange-theory-093110343.htm.

Yousafzai, M., & Lamb, C. (2013). *I am Malala: The Girl Who Stood up for Education and was shot by the Taliban*. New York, NY: Little, Brown, and Company.

Zirin, D. (2018, May 21). Uncovering the hidden resistance history of Black women athletes. *The Nation*. Retrieved from https://www.thenation.com/article/uncovering-the-hidden-resistance-history-of-black-women-athletes/.

Chapter 9

Booth, Sidelines, or Studio

How Place Defines Women Sports Broadcasters on Television

Cathy Leogrande

Ask a sports fan to name ten sports broadcasters. From Bob Costas to Chris Berman, the list will likely include men of all ages who have covered a variety of sports from the Kentucky Derby to the Olympics. Women such as Linda Cohn or Lesley Visser who have broadcast that same assortment of sports for high-profile outlets such as CBS and ESPN will most likely be left off the list or added as an afterthought. Women sports broadcasters began to break barriers over fifty years ago, yet they continue to be a small percentage of the journalists seen on the screen at sporting events (Eli, 2016). Women are also likely to be marginalized in terms of the roles they are given. Thirty second sound bites from the sidelines or segments in the studio highlight show remind us that women are still not regarded as equal to their male counterparts.

This text explores the ways that the place in which women do their job as televised sports journalists informs how they are perceived (DiCaro, 2016). Women sports broadcasters are more numerous in certain spaces, such as sidelines, that by default limit the style and substance of their reporting as well as their appearance (Deford, 2011). Place also determines the tone and style of their interaction with both their sources, such as players and coaches, and colleagues in other places. Some places, such as in the broadcast booth calling games, seem to imbue inhabitants with more credibility and status; yet, these are generally places in which fewer women are seen and heard (Arnold, Chen, & Hey, 2015). The use of critical media literacy (CML) concepts as a lens through which to interrogate aspects of place that define messages and messengers provides an opportunity to reframe gender inequity, persistent stereotypes, and media impact on beliefs and values.

WHY MEDIA MATTERS

This chapter provides details about the three places most often occupied by women in sports broadcasting: studio host, sideline reporter, or team member in the booth. Examination of these places through CML analysis allows viewers to question how roles in each place maintain and subvert the dominance of male sports broadcasters. Several bodies of research inform this analysis of the literal place of women in sports broadcasts.

Sports and sports reporting are part of popular culture media texts. Without critical examination, viewers may fall into functional consumption of messages, in which they grasp the basic meaning of media texts at the literal level, but do not turn a critical eye toward the deeper values and ideas. In contrast, a critical consumer applies media literacy concepts and seeks to analyze aspects such as format and language (Lin, Li, Deng, & Lee, 2013). CML practices ensure that audiences understand that no media message is neutral and expose the underlying values and beliefs of the authors, which often serve to shape societal and cultural views (Garland & Mayer, 2012). In the case of women sports broadcasters, places where they *are* and where they *are not* can create beliefs that women are less able to analyze and communicate about sporting events and individuals than men (Hardin & Shain, 2006). CML practices also move the viewer to syntheses, in which individuals integrate their own views and reconstruct new and different meaning and even counternarratives (Gainer, 2010; Vasquez, Janks, & Comber, 2019). When consumers see women sports broadcasters in new spaces and roles, they may revise their beliefs and begin to rethink the credibility and skills of these females doing traditionally male work well. CML also includes evaluation through which viewers "question, criticize and challenge the credibility of media contents" (Lin et al., 2013, p. 164). Consumers can become critical of network decisions to exclude competent and experienced women sports broadcasters from specific jobs and challenge the accepted norms of older white men maintaining their status as play-by-play announcers in booths. These skills help guide critical thinking abilities and empower audiences with healthy skepticism about the media messages they see and the values they impart (Hobbs & Jensen, 2009; Jolls & Wilson, 2014).

Close examination of popular culture texts helps individuals understand the power of the messages they consume and the relationship between the format of a message and the information it presents. Individuals must understand and accept that complex literacy transactions occur every time they engage with popular culture texts (Gainer, 2010). If consumers take for granted the assumptions that are embedded in the messages they watch, they may unwittingly accept prejudices, such as racism, sexism, and ageism, and reproduce hegemonic values. This analysis causes viewers to rethink their past practices and acceptance of status quo. Some warn that CML practices may produce cynics incapable of enjoying any media. Gainer (2007) presents strategies that allow individuals to critically analyze popular culture texts without "squashing the pleasure" (p. 109). Redmond (2012) describes critical enjoyment as the process by which her students not only analyzed media but also expressed their feelings about the analysis process and insights while finding ways to continue to take pleasure in and appreciate the material.

Media may impact individuals' actions as well as thoughts. Popular culture is seen as a component of social learning theory, which asserts that one of the ways people learn to behave based on beliefs is observation (Seelow, 2017). Individuals watch others and imitate their behaviors, especially if they aspire to those positions or roles. Television can be a powerful model that impacts the collective social group as well as the individual. In sports, there are limited and dynamic images and sound bites. Choices about what to say and show are made quickly, and these choices implicitly shape values and limit variation in perspectives (Fortuna, 2015). The places where women sportscasters are seen impact the substance of their work. How each place supports existing gender norms or provides impetus for change is worthy of examination. In many cases, members of cultural groups embrace shared perceptions about "the way things are and assumptions about the way they ought to be" (Seelow, 2017, p. 6). These assumptions may seem factual but are actually part of particular ideologies. These ideologies may be reinforced or possibly reformed through rhetorical messages. These persuasive messages are carefully designed to confirm or challenge a "taken-for-granted belief or behavior about what is 'appropriate' or 'inappropriate,' 'desirable' or 'undesirable,' 'good' or 'bad'" (Seelow, p. 6). Televised sports form mediated popular culture texts which generally work to maintain hegemonic masculinity, a cultural ideal of manhood that is understood by both men and women (Jewkes et al., 2015).

CML is a way to reflect on the pleasures derived from mass media and popular culture and as a way to deconstruct the values and implicit impact (Kellner & Share, 2005). Individuals learn to examine more deeply the subtle effects of television viewing. As Kellner (1995) describes how the media have "colonized culture" and become "the primary distribution and dissemination of culture" (p.35). He states that "the mass media of communication have supplanted previous methods of culture like the book or spoken work, that we live in a world in which media dominate leisure and culture" (p. 35). By using CML practices, individuals can recognize that dominant groups are represented as a powerful majority, that messages become normalized and that people seldom question the construction of the representations (Behrman, 2006). Sports reporting "holds tremendous power to mold people's outlooks, actions and beliefs" (Fortuna, 2015, p. 83).

Several CML concepts and corresponding questions are used to inter-rogate places where women sports broadcasters are seen (Kellner & Share, 2019). First, *social construction* means that individuals and groups of people make very specific choices to create media texts. In the case of women sports broadcasters, this is almost exclusively men in positions of leadership, whether at local stations or large media companies. Second, *politics of representation* asks consumers to consider how media messages privilege or omit particular points of view or groups. The examples that follow show a tension between changing stereotypes and maintaining the dominant power hierarchy. On one hand, hiring women in traditionally male spaces on camera appears to break with existing norms. However, women sports broadcasters are marginalized in terms of limits placed on them by the places they inhabit; these spaces can actually reinforce exist-ing hierarchies. Finally, *production*, much like social construction, explores creative choices and the underlying goal for the texts, including camera shot selection, background, wardrobe, and other features of broadcasts. These contribute to the perception of women sports broadcasters as sex objects and "window dressing" in order to sell the product to the viewing public (Arnold et al., 2015; Markovits & Albertson, 2012). CML concepts help demonstrate the power of spaces in sports broadcasting and the correspond-ing messages that are conveyed.

This chapter explores the three most visible places in which women sports broadcasters are most often seen and heard: studio shows, sidelines at games, and announcing booths. Topics explored are how and why women are selected to occupy these positions, constraints, and ancillary components (such as appearance and content of their reports), and audience perception (including issues of credibility and skill). Questions include how what view-ers see and hear impacts what they think and feel, what they believe, and how they act in the larger society (Gainer, 2010). Viewers must learn to interro-gate choices that are made to include and exclude talented and knowledgeable women sports journalists from certain spaces and what impact that has on cultural values, beliefs, and actions.

HAVE A SEAT: THE STUDIO HOST

When network sports television began airing in the mid-to-late 1940s, it was a medium totally dominated by men. The very idea of a woman being included to even talk about sports on television was considered ludicrous at the time. There were only a few women print sports reporters and on radio sports broadcasts (Halper, 2014).

The Pioneers

Several women broke barriers early on and covered sports in the media in television (Grubb & Billiot, 2010; Hardin & Shain, 2005; Kuiper, 2015). One was Jane Chastain. She began on a local news station in Atlanta. Billed as "Coach Friday," she appeared in a coach's uniform and a miniskirt to make predictions about upcoming games (Ryan, 2001). She should have been the perfect woman to crash the glass ceiling after her twelve years of experience and proven competence in sports broadcasting. She was the first woman to work for a large network (CBS) and actually did play-by-play analysis. Although Chastain reported from the field, sideline, locker room, booth, and studio, that would be the last time one female reporter was afforded diverse roles open to their male counterparts. CBS didn't quite know what to do with her. Chastain recalls,

> They thought I was too glamorous. . . . They made me tie my hair in a bun and take off my makeup. When I'd cover football, the producers would tell me to talk about what the women in the stands were wearing or how cute a player was. They wanted me to interview cheerleaders. I said, "I don't know how to do that. I've been doing sports for 10 years." (Ryan, 2001, para. 14)

Chastain was not the problem. CBS kept changing their mind and changing her. It was clear that the experiment was a failure for both parties and her contract was not renewed. As she tells it, "I was told, 'You're not the person we hired.' After everything they'd changed about me, of course I wasn't!" (Ryan, 2001, para. 17). Although Lesley Visser called her, "our Jackie Robinson" (Ryan, 2001, para. 4), few sports fans know her name or story.

Phyllis George, a former Miss America with no prior experience in sports or broadcasting, was hired for the very public spot as cohost on *The NFL Today* pregame show (Markovits & Albertson, 2012). She was followed by Jayne Kennedy, the first African American woman to host a network sports broadcast as well as appear on the cover of *Playboy* (Mead, 2010). This uncomfortable mix of competence and credibility with appearance and sexuality was part of the role of women sports broadcasters from the beginning. Lesley Visser and Gayle Gardner talk about enduring discrimination in those early years while establishing themselves as skilled professionals (de la Cretaz, 2018; Mead, 2010). The perception was that women sports broadcasters were dumb but pretty accessories to the men who had the real knowledge.

CML: Men in Charge

Sociocultural aspects of CML examine the construction how ideology and social values are embedded in media, and why (Chen, Wu, & Wang, 2011).

In the earliest days of women sports broadcasters, sports media were constructed by men executives and producers. Men like Bob Wussler, who made the decision to hire Chastain, later bowed to pressure and removed these women when mail and telephone calls ran heavily against them (Bhandari, 2019). Men hired women for vague reasons and did not really have a clear plan for integrating them into existing broadcast situations, setting them up to fail. Women in studios sometimes reinforced existing perceptions that females were only there as a novelty. The production of sports shows with women may have been a ploy to gain male viewers at a time when no one believed there were women sports fans tuning in to the broadcasts. The purpose was vague and not necessarily positive.

With regard to politics of representation, women on early studio shows were seen as an add on to the men who were doing the real job of reporting (Kuiper, 2015). Men were still the main sources of content, and the few women on televised media were more set decoration than credible journalists. The prevailing perception was that they did not need communication skills because they just read words others had written or smiled and joked with male cohosts. Place had become a limitation rather than an opening. Few skilled female sports broadcasters were hired, and women that were included in broadcasts did more at times to construct concepts of inept females who were only included to add beauty not substance to broadcasts (Kuiper, 2015).

Welcome to Bristol: Cable Sports Channels Bring Changes

The advent of ESPN as a cable home for twenty-four-hour sports reporting in 1979 offered more opportunities for on-air broadcasters. Rhonda Glenn became the first female anchor for *SportsCenter*, ESPN's main studio show (Zumoff & Negin, 2017). Like Chastain, Glenn and her successor, Gayle Gardner, have been forgotten when naming pioneers of sports broadcasting, further indicating the limits of their impact despite being on ESPN (Kuiper, 2015). More women began to appear here and there on studio shows. Women found more opportunities behind the desk where the work is not always seen as *real* reporting. Places began to define women sports broadcasters' roles as *lesser than* by virtue of the nature of that type of reporting (Grubb & Billiott, 2010).

Although lists of top ESPN anchors from the last forty years rarely include women, Linda Cohn is always mentioned (Farred, 2000; Yoder, 2016). Avi Wolfman-Arent (2011) wrote, "Cohn is Bristol's rock, an uncommonly reliable voice in the tumultuous waters of ESPN" (Linda Cohn section, para. 1). Her longevity has helped normalize the position. Current ESPN sports broadcaster Diana Russini referred to the power of normalizing the position. She said, "Linda is the first female to make hosting 'SportsCenter' no big deal for a woman" (Jacobs, 2016, para. 15). Cohn has lasted, hosting her 5000th show in 2016, roughly 8 percent of over 60,000 at that time (Keeley, 2016). Robin Roberts became the first African American female *SportsCenter* host in 1990 (Furdyk, 2020). Wolfman-Arent (2011) wrote of Roberts, "Never as entertaining as some of her more carnival-esque colleagues, she was nonetheless the most immediately likable anchor on the network . . . viewers clearly connected with her warm, composed manner of speech" (Robin Roberts section, para. 1). Other women behind a desk at ESPN included Hannah Storm and Lesley Visser (Grubb & Billiott, 2010; Mead, 2010).

Women hosts were often "complimented" for their staid, perhaps bland, reporting style. Contrast that with male "characters" on those same lists, like Kenny Mayne with "acerbic wit" and Charlie Steiner who "could play straight man or satirist with equal aplomb" (Lee, 2012; Wolfman-Arent, 2011). Would this type of praise be given to a woman? Using CML questions, one can ask who hired these women and who made decisions to assign them to certain *SportsCenter* time slots (often early morning hours with low viewership) with certain particular cohosts. Were these women meant to appear second-best? Was their role to quietly introduce highlights while their male counterparts established outrageous and memorable personalities while also doing the same job? Since *SportsCenter* was the flagship program at the self-proclaimed "Worldwide Leader in Sports," it provided powerful messages about the degree to which women were allowed to enter this sacred ground (Butterworth, 2005). Without clear purposes, male executives often made production choices that did little to advance perceptions or reality. Representation alone did not necessarily change audience views of women in sports broadcasting, since their role was seemingly less than that of their male colleagues.

The Studio Show Evolves

Burgeoning sports coverage meant more and different studio shows: personality-based (where a group, generally including journalists, analysts, and former players) discuss a wide spectrum of sports and issues; specific shows devoted to one sport (such as football); or a highlight show with updated scores and plays and feature stories (Harden, & Shain, 2005). This type of studio host is a role that brings benefits and challenges for women. Hosts become a friend invited into viewers' homes to discuss current games, players, and events. Different types of shows are framed around different types of hosts.

Some men, like Stephen A. Smith and Max Kellerman, get their own show because of shock appeal (What will he say next?). It is rare for a woman to have a personality that executives find worthy to be the focus of a show, like Tony Kornheiser and Michael Wilbon on *Pardon the Interruption*. Many male broadcasters bring expertise from a long career in print journalism or radio. Since fewer women sports journalists find careers in those fields, there is a smaller pool of candidates able to make the jump to the studio (Harden, Genovese, & Yu, 2009; Harden & Shain, 2006). Women may have expertise that allows them to be part of a group show, but not to have a main role. In 2016, the panel on *Around the Horn* was comprised of four female reporters for the first time after episode 3,000 (Bumpus, 2018). Men took to Twitter to express their ire. Tweets included, 'What the hell is this? The View? . . . c'mon man this is like listening to hens in a hen house, stop it now please'; 'U know how ya mom tell you something over and over again that's what first take felt like today lol'; and '4 ladies on first take. About 3 too many' (Payne, 2016). The all-women panel has not been done again.

Attempts at change can backfire and possibly make things worse. Jemele Hill joined Michael Smith as one of the first African American sportscaster duos to be given a high-profile show at ESPN driven by their personalities and chemistry. On *His & Hers*, they brought original content and other entertainment-related material (like spoofs of *Empire* and *Anchorman*) along with sports and were very successful (Saponara, 2017). ESPN tapped them as hosts for *SC6*, a reinvention of *SportsCenter*, at a peak time slot (Penrice, 2017). What had worked on *His & Hers* was a disaster on the new show. ESPN did not quite know what they wanted *SC6* to be; the new show became something that wasn't *His & Hers* and certainly wasn't what *SportsCenter* fans wanted. James Andrew Miller (2018) wrote, "Executives believed the pair could be the answer to declining viewership. But what had worked on other shows proved too great a departure for *SportsCenter* viewers, who wanted more highlights and less opining" (para. 6). Hill and Smith were blamed rather than the executives who conceived and shaped the show.

At the same time, Hill became embroiled in controversy with her tweets about Dallas Cowboys owner, Jerry Jones, and President Trump. She was suspended by ESPN and Trump responded with a tweet: "With Jemele Hill at the mike, it is no wonder ESPN ratings have 'tanked,' in fact, tanked so badly it is the talk of the industry!" (Bogage, Bieler, & Boren, 2017; Miller, 2018). The network found itself in the midst of accusations that it had an ultraprogressive liberal agenda. In this time of crisis and decreasing subscribers, *SC6* and Hill became targets. Critics dubbed it "*WokeCenter*"; the pair faced external criticism and lack of support from traditionalists at the network (Guthrie, 2018). Hill was a lightning rod that personified for some all that was "wrong" with ESPN (Harrison, Pegoraro, Romney, & Hull, 2019; Mudrick, Burton, & Lin, 2016). She returned to print journalism as a reporter for *The Atlantic*. Sadly, her gender served as a cautionary tale to some male executives who used it to maintain quiet compliant woman on shows.

CML: How Smart Is Too Smart?

Using CML questions to examine women in studio shows can help expose concerns despite more women on air. The increase in the number of female sports broadcasters hides problems and limits of structure and discourse. Women find it difficult, almost impossible, to attain full legitimacy when male executives are conflicted over the expectations of their role. In describing reporting versus commentary, Markovits and Albertson (2012) describe the "quandary" of male station managers, who can fill quotas with females who read stories written by someone else but do not upset the viewership with real analysis (p. 167). In some ways, by achieving visibility on a highlights show like *SportsCenter*, women may have to accept the limits of quick stories without depth and analysis. Social construction and production questions address the dilemmas surrounding these positions. If the viewership is primarily male, are women sports broadcasters hired because of physical appearance to increase ratings? These male viewers seem threatened by competent women who know sports and are not afraid to express opinions like Jemele Hill.

If these attractive women do not know sports, they may be scorned as just another pretty face, merely hired to provide evidence that a network is addressing a perceived gap in representation (Sheffer & Schultz, 2007). The lower the expectations, the greater likelihood of success; a bland but competent and attractive woman behind a desk, smiling and laughing with a male cohost as she reads simple scores, will not upset male viewers. As Markovits and Albertson (2012) stated, "In narratives that are deemed male, women are to operate as objects of male attention but not as propagators of the narrative itself" (p. 188). For women, competence is questioned because of their gender. There is always a group who feels they do not belong behind that desk. This may cause women studio hosts to be more cautious and less spontaneous, which could result in a perception as stiff and uncertain, qualities that can diminish their effectiveness (Markovits & Albertson, 2012; Serazio, 2019a).

In recent years, there has been a slight shift. Some women, like Rachel Nichols and Laura Rutledge, withstood the discrimination they faced to gain more prominent roles in studio shows (Hofheimer, 2020; Knight, 2017). Rather than window dressing or add-ons, these women have claimed their place and demonstrate credibility and competence, not merely representation without substance (Harden et al., 2009). Sports remains an area in which toxic masculinity is often celebrated just by reporting events that inherently reinforce those values (Kellner & Share, 2019). Critical literacy questions of purpose, representation, and choices are worth posing when watching studio sports shows. Male and female audiences should ask whose voice is heard, when and where, and whose is silenced and why?

CLOSE TO THE ACTION: SIDELINE REPORTING

Women sports broadcasters are highly visible on the sidelines at games. Their on-air work generally consists of brief lines to fill in during time-outs or commercials or asking a difficult question to a coach at halftime or after a game. The sideline reporter has to respond immediately to what is happening and be able to report quickly as well as get coaches and athletes to respond to questions in the heat of competition. These positions are both prominent and marginalized. This section raises issues around the ways this role supports and demeans women sports broadcasters and proposes this as another area in which CML analysis can reveal deeper problems.

The Role of the Sideline Reporter

The sideline reporter became a job on ABC in 1974. From the beginning it was never meant to be serious reporting as the first sideline reporter Jim Lampley stated, "It was someone with nice hair and a bright smile, delivering 24 seconds of cheerful inanities into a microphone . . . the job was very explicitly about, to borrow Christine Brennan's phrase, playing to the frat house" (Craggs, 2009). Many female reporters found sidelines to be one of the few places from which they could talk about sports on air (Coventry, 2004). Pam Oliver and Suzy Kolber have both spent years covering games in all types of weather and venues, and gained reputations as credible journalists (Gordon, 2014). However, this has also been a space where it seems women are assigned because of their looks more than competence (Maney, 2017).

Problems on the Sidelines

The sidelines remain a controversial place, especially for women. Frank Deford (2011) described ridiculous expectations on the women who do these jobs: "But the irony is that most sideline reporters—whatever sport, whichever gender—really have done their homework and really do know their stuff. Most of them are terribly overqualified for the assignment of being a human scroll." There remains a lack of journalistic credibility associated with the position. Players and coaches have treated women sideline reporters with unprofessional behavior that borders on harassment. There have been spontaneous and inappropriate incidents, most famously when an intoxicated Joe Namath asking to kiss Suzy Kolber (Complex, 2012). Josh Robertson (2012) wrote an article entitled "The 25 Hottest Sideline Reporters Right Now," described of ESPN's Wendy Nix, thirty-eight, as "a bit older for a sideline gal, but she's still a lovely woman. Her years of experience give her an edge both in football knowledge and working the coaches. After all, they're getting a little old to be chasing twenty-somethings" (Wendy Nix section, para. 1). The literal and figurative position of sideline reporter carries implicit messages that perpetuate a belief that women sports broadcasters are inferior to their male counterparts in the booth and not deserving of professional respect (Mudrick & Lin, 2017).

"Sideline Barbie" Changes the Game?

Rather than improving, current trends further reinforce the stereotype of the pretty but simple sideline reporters in nice outfits without much to add to the broadcast. Erin Andrews was dubbed "Sideline Barbie" when she first appeared on television (Guthrie, 2013). In a YouTube video (The Hollywood Reporter, 2013), she and Charissa Thompson appear on the Fox set in extremely tight short dresses and high heels. The rolling text in the video states, "They're fun, they're beautiful AND they sing! But most important they report on sports!" Andrews and Thompson lip-synch to a song and toss around a football. The optics of the video are the opposite of the kind of professional demeanor these women espouse in the interview. Fox was accused of ageism when Andrews, twenty-six, replaced longtime sideline reporter Pam Oliver (Henderson, 2014). Oliver, a twenty-year veteran, was fifty-three, well-respected, and one of few longtime African American female sports broadcasters Jeff Pearlman praised Oliver: "She knows how to interview and doesn't merely ask fluff nonsense. She's quick on the fly, researches the hell out of games, has a long and storied history of asking the right question at the right moment" (as cited in Boren, 2014, para. 6). He lamented the move to sideline reporters that are less skilled but more attractive. He called them, "eye candy for the Neanderthals who need eye candy" (as cited in Boren, 2014, para. 6). Fox reversed the decision a few months later and brought Oliver back for two more years, but people felt it was done to mitigate the backlash (Deitsch, 2015).

Gender inequity on the sidelines is obvious and troubling. Dan Bernstein (2014) went right to the heart of the issue:

> Fox pays Tony Siragusa to stand in the end zone and talk about local food, tell us that the fans are loud or that the field is increasingly slippery in a rainstorm, providing all the insight of a beef sandwich. He's not a woman, so he's not part of the conversation. The rules don't apply to him. (para. 10)

Ann Doyle (2013) wrote about instances of inappropriate comments by men on the appearance of female colleagues. She said there is a "proliferation of busty, blonde, tightly clad, female microphone holders masquerading these days as sports reporters—laughing off the inevitable leers and degrading 'pranks'" as part of the reason men feel perfectly able to act in this manner (Entertainers or Reporters section, para. 1). One wonders if the women are acting and dressing to meet expectations of the job as defined by those who hired them.

Fan Frustration

Michelle Ruiz (2019) expressed her frustration as a fan watching "highly skilled women sports journalists . . . relegated to reporting from the sidelines while men occupy the top jobs of calling the games, providing color commentary, and analyzing the action in-studio" (para. 1). She wonders what it will take for a woman to earn a coveted seat in the commentator's chair or on a studio show. Women like Allison Williams and Laura Rutledge have demonstrated expertise and skill over their tenure at ESPN, but that is still not enough to promote them to the roles with greater responsibility and visibility. Women are the majority of sideline reporters, despite the fact an estimated one in three men's basketball fans and viewers are female (Ruiz, 2019). The structure of the broadcast diminishes these women. As Ruiz sees it, when the camera cuts away from the important action and comments of the male broadcasters to the women on the sidelines for a few quick seconds, it suggests to viewers that "they are not worthy or qualified for the top, most forward-facing jobs in the game, no matter how many years they've logged" (Ruiz, 2019, para. 4). The position is "largely off to the side, just out of bounds" (O'Shaughnessy, 2017, para. 8). Frank Deford (2011) summed up the problematic result: "And so, the sideliners are delegated to freeze down on the tundra while the male play-by-play announcer and his hefty old gridiron warrior expert babble on comfortably up in the heated booth." The sidelines continue to be a dead end rather than a door to other opportunities.

No Good Answer to Why

The sideline reporter's job is highly visible but without the respect or responsibility attached to other members of the broadcast team at the same events (Farhi, 2009). The actual place defines the work. How the sideline reporter is able to add to the broadcast depends greatly on the players and coaches, conditions, and broadcast team. Reporting is a function of the nature and pace of the interaction. This is an area ripe for analysis of both visual and audio "text." What makes a good sideline reporter? Can one be seen as competent if there is no time to ask thoughtful questions or access to those who would provide the kind of intel that would add to the viewer's enjoyment and appreciation of the game and the sport? Unlike the studio host with a planned production, the sideline reporter is at the mercy of a consonantly changing event, weather conditions, mobile equipment, player injuries, and coaches trying to win a game, not answer questions. At best the reporter does not look or sound ridiculous and perhaps gets a response that makes for a good sound bite. The team in the booth then gets unlimited time to analyze and extend the topic while the sideline reporter waits for another opportunity to jump in during a break in the action.

CML helps examine the dynamics of this role. The role is constructed to be ancillary, not critical to the broadcast or game analysis. At the surface, it seems like a job that does not require skill or expertise. How difficult can it be to ask a quick question or make a short comment before saying "And now back to you" as the "real" broadcasters take over the important work? It is difficult to communicate a depth of knowledge about a sport in the thirty-second on-air hits that must be approved by a (usually male) producer before being aired (O'Shaughnessy, 2017). The requirements of the job, brief often innocuous sound bites, may exacerbate the perception that these women are not knowledgeable about the game. It is important to ask how this position became one primarily filled by women and why it seems to be without advancement. What is the purpose of the sideline reporter? Is it essential to the broadcast? The stereotype of the pretty reporter dressed in her attractive outfits standing silent for much of the game is not one that changes perceptions about female sports reporters' credibility. The motives and objectives behind the staffing and lack of willingness to advance from the position are unclear. Without information from executives who make decisions about hiring sideline reporters, viewers are left to wonder: Who gets to do what job? Who decides? What qualifications are the basis for these decisions? What purpose does the female sideline reporter fill? What values are being passed on and strengthened by keeping these competent women on the fringes of the work? Why are women still literally on the sidelines after decades, despite an increase in broadcast outlets and qualified candidates? These CML-based questions help expose the sexism that continues in sports broadcasting.

THE BROADCAST BOOTH: DOES IT HAVE A GLASS FLOOR?

The last hurdle for women sportscasters is to be part of the team that actually calls and analyzes the game in real time. With so many games in various sports, there should be more positions than ever for women. The reality is this is the last arena that women have to fight to enter (de la Cretaz, 2018). Over forty years after Jane Chastain made play-by-play one more accomplishment, the number of women who do the same is woefully small.

The Boys in the Booth

The baseball broadcast booth is a small space, usually with two or three people in it. Games are slow and require people who can carry on an entertaining, relevant conversation. Some believe it is easier for a pair or trio of men to keep discussions going. They feel a female would make them more self-conscious and their talk would be stilted and boring. Others feel that since estimates claim 45 percent of all baseball fans are women, it would be a welcome change for them, and everyone, to bring a different perspective (Strupp, 2015). This raises the question of the actual job of those in the booth. Are they entertainers or journalists, or a combination of both? Answers to that type of role-defining question might reshape the job and open up the booth to women.

In the past, a few women found their way to the booth. Mary Shane, Betty Caywood, and Pam Boucher announced Major League Baseball (MLB) games in the 1960s and 1970s (ESPN, 2018). Gayle Gardner became the first woman to do play-by-play on television in 1993 followed by Suzyn Waldman in 1995. She has been a familiar voice on Yankee radio broadcasts since then and was the first woman to call a World Series game on the radio in 2009 (Albanese, 2019; de la Cretaz, 2018). Within the last few years, there has been some progress. Jessica Mendoza became the first female baseball analyst on ESPN for the Sunday night baseball game (Glanville, 2017). It was not a planned decision; Curt Schilling was fired for inappropriate remarks on Twitter (Sandomir, 2015). No matter how the door opened, it did. Mendoza is a regular in the booth and it is reporter Buster Olney who is on the sidelines. Mendoza is a role model for a generation of young women who aspire to sports broadcasting. She is also a link to the type of backlash most female sportscasters experience (Glasspiegel, 2015). Glanville (2017) quoted from negative tweets: "She doesn't belong in the booth with men discussing a game she knows nothing about. It's like watching a game with a girlfriend," and "Jessica Mendoza is that annoying sister your mom makes you bring everywhere." One tweet addressed her race, despite the fact Mendoza was born in America and does not broadcast in Spanish: "I just changed the channel to ESPN2 so I could stop listening to Jessica Mendoza. BTW I don't understand Spanish." One tweet reinforced the double standard: "I hate hearing men commentating softball, and I hate hearing women commentating baseball." Mendoza endured these comments and more with both skills and persistence.

Colorado Rockies' announcer, Jenny Cavnar, became the first woman to perform televised play-by-play for an MLB game (Axson, 2018). Cavnar worked in MLB for twelve years before she got this chance, primarily in pre- and postgame shows. Some men, like broadcaster and former pitcher Dallas

Braden, have become more vocal in their support, countering the negative reactions Braden went to the foundation of what should matter—competence. Before Cavnar's first game, Braden stated, "By the third inning after all of the pleasantries have been exchanged, you will forget who is on the microphone, you will be learning about the game of baseball, you will be enjoying the stories being told to you" (as cited in Bieler, 2018, para. 10). While Cavnar had her detractors, she also heard from parents who let their little girls stay up late and listen (Rahimi, 2018).

Calling the Games in Other Sports

Play-by-play announcer or analyst in other sports remains one of the last spaces to open up for women. Doris Burke is the first female in a full-time regular game analyst role in the NBA (Gregory, 2018). Burke has earned many accolades and awards, but also had negative reactions. Even renowned sports journalist, Bill Simmons (who later said he regretted his words), said in 2008, "She's doing a fine job, but does it make me a sexist that I can't listen to Doris Burke analyze NBA playoff games without thinking, 'Woman talking woman talking woman talking woman talking . . .' the entire time?" (as cited in Remnick, 2019, para. 7). She gave up trying to look like one of the guys by wearing blazers, found her own style, and gained respect of players and coaches, usually the most critical audience (D'Arcangelo, 2017; Gregory, 2018). She grew to fit herself to "the place" and became her own person, a celebrity in her own right. Jeff Van Gundy nicknamed her "the LeBron James of sportscasters" and Drake wore a T-shirt with her photo (Deitsch, 2019; Gregory, 2018). However, Burke's success has not opened doors for other women (Macur, 2017). Women such as Stephanie Ready, Kara Lawson, and Sarah Kustok have been elevated to analyst roles with individual teams, but they are few in number among the list of NBA analysts (O'Shaughnessy, 2017; Weitzman, 2017).

Football saw the first crack in the established order when Amazon Prime Video broadcast Thursday Night Football with the first all-women duo calling the games (Bonesteel, 2018). Well-respected sports journalists Hannah Storm and Andrea Kremer were hired, signaling that this effort is meant to succeed. The games are broadcast through a premium streaming service, not traditional networks. Calls for similar moves on mainstream platforms have gone unanswered (Wilder, 2019). Amazon Prime may be the kind of new "place" in which women sports broadcasters can multiply and thrive.

CML: Booth as the Last Fortress

The sports broadcast booth appears to be a sacred space guarded by men against an invasion of aspiring female announcers. CML questions the nature of that space, the work of calling a live game, and why it remains a male-dominated position. When creating broadcasts, choices are made to include certain groups and individuals and exclude others (Kellner & Share, 2019). Production of the text shapes the broadcast by who gets to say what where. While plausible reasons are given by those in charge, these choices generally reproduce the dominant hegemonic male culture associated with sports broadcasting. Markovits and Albertson (2012) state that culture assumes all men know sports and all women do not. When women attempt to break this norm, "the norm breakers are punished by the very group whom they are trying to join via the very act of norm breaking" (p. 178). This is especially true of women announcing games. Women are viewed favorably in supporting roles, but with suspicion when trying to advance (Scheiber, 2018). Female sideline reporters maintain gender roles; women in the booth make men uncomfortable, even hostile.

Women announcers are often criticized about their voice, something that seems to uncover blatant sexism. Since the role of play-by-play broadcaster was created and staffed by white men, audiences expect that norm when they watch or listen to a game. When a woman enters that arena, she can expect to receive negative feedback. The sexism is often hidden within coded phrases: "It's not that I have a problem with a woman calling the game, it's just that her voice is so annoying/shrill/grating/insert sexist adjective here" (de la Cretaz, 2018). This gender-specific and intangible part of a woman's physical identity allows male audience members to avoid addressing skill and representation and making it a production issue out of the women's control. Julie DiCaro (2017), who works primarily in sports radio, wrote that the safest bet in sports is men complaining about a woman's voice. She said, "I've been told my voice is too high, too low, too young-sounding, too Chicago-sounding, too harsh, too soft, and 'just generally obnoxious'" (para. 17). However, when she had bronchitis, some men called in to the show to compliment her on her sexy voice. Andrea Kremer said, "'Hating the sound of her voice' is code for 'I hate that there was a woman announcing football'" (DiCaro, 2017, para. 7). The response to female broadcasters' voices is not new. Sports are commonly perceived to be an arena for men, of men, and by men. Disruption to the existing social construction of sports announcers brings discomfort. Pioneers break rules, and do not easily fit in (Glanville, 2017).

Women in the booth are often criticized for not having knowledge about the sport that comes from playing the game. This supposed rationale is hypocritical. Doug Glanville (2017) said, "Comments can be made that dismiss Mendoza for 'never having played,' yet in the same breath recognize that Vin Scully and countless other men who never played pro baseball are regarded as among the greatest announcers ever" (para. 17). He reminded fans, "Having been a player is not a requirement for great commentary. And neither is

being a man" (para. 27). Gender-related issues are more than merely questions of representation; they are "the luxury of a biased duality" (Glanville,
2017, para. 16). Men are allowed "to be both competent and likable, cutthroat
and inspiring, inappropriate and employable, equal but better. The 'benefits'
of these dichotomies and contradictions are rarely granted to women" (Glanville, 2017, para. 16). The unfortunate truth is that any of those women who
rise to the challenge will find themselves working in spaces where "a segment
of men will harass, denigrate and question her place" (Glanville, 2017, para.
20). New formats, such as streaming services, may offer counternarratives,
but the struggle continues.

WHERE WOMEN ARE DEFINES WHO WOMEN ARE

This CML examination of places in which women sports broadcasters find
themselves supports the power of visual texts as a factor in credibility and
perception of competence (Gunther, Kautz, & Roth, 2011). Sports have provided opportunities for women but places where those opportunities exist
relegate women to limited roles that reinforce the idea that they are less competent than their male colleagues (Markovits & Albertson, 2012). It is possible that more women in executive and production positions will help change
what viewers see and hear, and that will help change beliefs and values.

Public discussion of the treatment of women spirts journalists may help
bring about change. Julie DiCaro and Sarah Spain spotlighted sexist treatment on social media with their video #MoreThanMean (Just Not Sports,
2016; Mettler, 2016). Men read horrific tweets these women receive, including threats of violence and death, merely for doing their job. Humor may also
be a catalyst for change. ESPN (2019, 2020) videos show well-known female
sports broadcasters as part of a "secret society," complete with a mantra
("Praise be to Doris," said in unison in front of a giant photo of Doris Burke),
and tips on how to take something men love and ruin it (wear a turtleneck).
These spotlights on the harassment women sports journalists still face may
be a step toward change.

Place as Opportunity or Limit?

Television is a visual medium; therefore, dress and appearance become a
much-discussed aspect of the work across studio, sidelines, and booth. These
three places require and allow very different types of visuals for women
broadcasters. How and why women get and keep specific jobs in sports
broadcasting is impacted by factors beyond ability, including physical appearance and fashion (Davis & Krawczyk, 2010). From hairstyles and jewelry to

clothing that is considered too dowdy, women broadcasters discuss heightened awareness of their appearance in addition to their performance. What can and should be worn standing in front of screen or sitting behind a desk in a studio is different from what is appropriate on the sideline. Image is a concern for females despite the fact they work with older, overweight men who would not necessarily be considered attractive, and few of their male counterparts have the same cosmetic and fashion scrutiny (Grubb & Billiot, 2010). Ageism is another factor in who is on the air and where. Although fans can recount how much they continue to enjoy beloved male announcers over seventy, it is impossible to find a comparable comment about an older woman sports broadcaster. Studies have shown that physical appearance impacts perceived credibility (Gunther et al., 2011; Houston, 2008). How one looks determines to some extent whether or not one's words are believed or valued.

Where we see women sportscasters is as important as how we see and hear them. Different places in sports reporting carry expectations, because the work and purpose for being there are diverse. Lack of women executives in broadcasting who make hiring decisions is a factor and contribute to institutional and structural discrimination (Farhi, 2014; Serazio, 2019a; Serazio, 2019b). The perceptions that male fans will not accept or tolerate women announcers is used as an excuse (by male executives) to limit participation due to fiscal impact. Advertising targets are mostly men; no one seems to consider women fans as potential new markets. Women with strong skills may lose the position in the booth or studio to former coaches or players who are assumed to have knowledge and analysis merely based on their playing experience. That is another implicit way to limit women; since playing opportunities in the main televised sports are not usually open to women as easily, they cannot bring playing experience from the field to the booth. Changing this practice of business as usual will not be easy, but Glanville (2017) notes the impact: "Sports, on and off the field, should set an example for fairness, decency and humanity for all of our children, not just the legacy of boys already in the boys club."

Will Representation and Production Mean Real Change?

Type the words "women sportscasters" into a search engine and the results include "60 Sexiest Female Sports Reporters," "Top 15 Hottest Women Of ESPN," and other comparable links. Enter the words "men sportscasters" and the results include "sports announcers," giving the impression that all announcers are male. Despite the progress and talented women who can be found on set and at games, stereotypes persist. Markovits and Albertson (2012) asked, "What does looking good have to do with being a respected sportscaster?", and they described the ambivalence of the "babe" factor (p. 189). Some women come to an unhappy acceptance that appearance is one route into the sports crew of a news station and a path that may ultimately lead to their desired career in a ruthless and competitive business.

As long as mostly male executives buy into the belief that physically attractive women are best placed in studios or sidelines, women sports broadcasters will continue to be seen as less skilled and valued than their male counterparts. Even smart and capable females will be forced to work within existing norms while attempting to break new ground. Factors that support change include more women fans demanding different products on their television than what they see now, females in decision-making positions in both the leadership of leagues and teams as well as networks and media producers, and the growth of digital platforms that allow more variety and less overhead. The numbers of viewers of traditional sports media (such as print newspapers and cable channels like ESPN) is decreasing as sports enthusiasts cut cords, cancel subscriptions, and look elsewhere for information (Guthrie, 2018).

Perhaps women can find different outlets to add their voice to analysis and discussions of sports and athletes. New media spaces such as blogs, podcasts, and independent websites like The Undefeated and The Athletic may be the perfect places in which women sports broadcasters can find their stages. Until then, CML skills help viewers analyze and closely examine media texts in order to challenge the myth that sports media is neutral and objective (Kellner & Share, 2019). Who reports sports and from what spaces matter. CML skills can help uncover how the places in which women find themselves impact and perpetuate societal beliefs and values. That can be a beginning of change, when women sports broadcasters working in certain spaces is no longer a novelty worthy of a headline, but merely business as usual.

REFERENCES

Albanese, L. (2019, March 30). Pioneering Yankees broadcaster Suzyn Waldman has had to deal with sexism and abuse throughout her career. *Newsday*. Retrieved from https://www.newsday.com/sports/baseball/yankees/yankees-suzyn-waldman-1.29148226.

Arnold, T., Chen, S., & Hey, W. (2015). The rise of women sportscasters: A struggle from sideline to centerfield. *Missouri Journal of Health, Physical Education, Recreation & Dance, 25*, 36–43.

Axson, S. (2018, May 18). Meet the Rockies' barrier-breaking play-by-play announcer: Jenny Cavnar. *Sports Illustrated*. Retrieved from https://www.si.com/mlb/2018/05/18/jenny-cavnar-colorado-rockies.

Behrman, E. H. (2006). Teaching about language, power, and text: A review of classroom practices that support critical literacy. *Journal of Adolescent & Adult Literacy, 49*(6), 490–498.

Bernstein, D. (2014, July 15). Erin Andrews over Pam Oliver raises questions. *CBS Chicago*. Retrieved from https://chicago.cbslocal.com/2014/07/15/bernstein-erin-andrews-over-pam-oliver-raises-questions/.

Bhandari, L. (2019, August 21). Meet Jane Chastain: First woman to provide colour commentary for an NFL game. *NFL Girl UK*. Retrieved from http://www.nflgirluk.com/2019/08/21/meet-jane-chastain-first-woman-to-provide-colour-commentary-for-an-nfl-game/.

Bieler, D. (2018, April 24). "Fire up the fountains!": Woman does TV play-by-play of MLB game for first time in 25 years. *Washington Post*. Retrieved from https://www.washingtonpost.com/news/early-lead/wp/2018/04/24/fire-up-the-fountains-woman-does-tv-play-by-play-of-mlb-game-for-first-time-in-25-years/.

Bogage, J., Bieler, D., & Boren, C. (2017, October 10). Trump blasts ESPN's Jemele Hill after her suspension for tweet about Cowboys owner Jerry Jones. *Washington Post*. Retrieved from https://www.washingtonpost.com/news/early-lead/wp/2017/10/09/jemele-hill-suspended-two-weeks-by-espn-after-tweet-about-cowboys-owner-jerry-jones/.

Bonesteel, M. (2018, September 25). Andrea Kremer, Hannah Storm to partner in NFL's first all-woman broadcast booth for Amazon Prime. *Washington Post*. Retrieved from https://www.washingtonpost.com/sports/2018/09/25/andrea-kremer-hannah-storm-will-call-thursday-night-football-games-amazon-prime/.

Boren, C. (2014, July 15). Why FOX replaced Pam Oliver with Erin Andrews. *Washington Post*. Retrieved from https://www.washingtonpost.com/news/early-lead/wp/2014/07/15/why-fox-replaced-pam-oliver-with-erin-andrews/.

Bumpus, D. A. (2018, January 3). Women made sports media history in 2017, but obstacles in the industry persist. *Fansided*. Retrieved from https://fansided.com/2018/01/03/women-sports-media-history-2017-obstacles-remain/.

Butterworth, M. (2005). "This is SportsCenter": 25 years with the worldwide leader in sports: A review. *Aethlon: The Journal of Sport Literature, 22*(2), 157–158.

Chen, D. T., Wu, J., & Wang, Y. M. (2011). Unpacking new media literacy. *Journal of Systemics, Cybernetics, and Informatics, 9*(2), 84–89.

Complex. (2012, May 14). The 20 most awkward moments in female sports reporting. *Complex*. Retrieved from https://www.complex.com/sports/2012/05/the-most-awkward-female-sports-reporter-moment/what-the-fuck-was-that.

Coventry, B. T. (2004). On the sidelines: Sex and racial segregation in television sports broadcasting. *Sociology of Sport Journal, 21*(3), 322–341.

Craggs, T. (2009, July 28). The first sideline reporter: "All of this was just nonsense." *Deadspin*. Retrieved from https://deadspin.com/the-first-sideline-reporter-all-of-this-was-just-nons-5323838.

D'Arcangelo, L. (2017, August 9). How Doris Burke became the best damn basketball broadcaster there is. *Deadspin*. Retrieved from https://deadspin.com/how-doris-burke-became-the-best-damn-basketball-broadca-1797546866.

Davis, C. D., & Krawczyk, J. (2010). Female sportscaster credibility: Has appearance taken precedence? *Journal of Sports Media, 5*(2), 1–34.

Deford, F. (2011, September 21). *No respect for the women on the sidelines* [Radio broadcast transcript]. National Public Radio Morning Edition. Retrieved from https

://www.npr.org/2011/09/21/140591732/no-respect-for-the-women-on-the-sidelin
es.

Deitsch, R. (2015, March 9). Pam Oliver returning to NFL sidelines for two more
years with Fox. *Sports Illustrated*. Retrieved from https://www.si.com/more-sports
/2015/03/09/pam-oliver-fox-sports-nfl-sideline-reporters-erin-andrews.

Deitsch, R. (2019, May 28). Media circus: Doris Burke on her future and making
history; plus, others discuss Burke's influence. *The Athletic*. Retrieved from https:/
/theathletic.com/996790/2019/05/28/media-circus-doris-burke-on-her-future-and-
making-history-plus-others-discuss-burkes-influence/.

de la Cretaz, B. (2018, October 10). Where are all the women in play-by-play broadcasting? *The Ringer*. Retrieved from https://www.theringer.com/2018/10/11/179
63320/women-play-by-play-broadcasting-andrea-kremer-hannah-storm-amazon
-nfl.

DiCaro, J. (2016, April 30). Women in sports media face unrelenting sexism in challenges to their expertise and opinions. *Women's Media Center*. Retrieved from
https://www.womensmediacenter.com/speech-project/women-in-sports-media
-face-unrelenting-sexism-in-challenges-to-their-expertise-and-opinions.

DiCaro, J. (2017, September 18). Safest bet in sports: Men complaining about a
female announcer's voice. *New York Times*. Retrieved from https://www.nytimes.
com/2017/09/18/sports/nfl-beth-mowins-julie-dicaro.html.

Doyle, A. (2013, January 21). It's time for sports broadcasting to stop relegating
women to sideline eye candy. *Forbes*. Retrieved from https://www.forbes.com
/sites/annedoyle/2013/01/21/its-time-for-sports-broadcasting-to-stop-relegating
-women-to-sideline-eye-candy/#5276c7bc3fc9.

Eli, S. H. (2016). Those women have all the headaches: Inside the world of sports
broadcasting. (Master's thesis). Retrieved from https://scholarworks.bgsu.edu/
hmsls_mastersprojects/10.

ESPN. (2018, April 25). Jenny Cavnar breaks barriers, calls televised play-by-play.
ESPN. Retrieved from https://www.espn.com/mlb/story/_/id/23298426/jenny-cavn
ar-calling-play-play-monday-rockies-broadcast.

ESPN. [ESPN]. (2019, November 21). *Katie Nolan joins secret society of women in
sports media* [Video file]. Retrieved from https://www.youtube.com/watch?v=BuN
RvHt8t1Y.

ESPN. [ESPN]. (2020, March 5). *Inside the exclusive clubhouse for the women in
sports media.* [Video file]. Retrieved from https://www.youtube.com/watch?v
=oY0dIjVS_ho.

Farhi, P. (2009, January 31). TV's female sports reporters are stuck on the sidelines.
Washington Post. Retrieved from https://www.washingtonpost.com/wp-dyn/co
ntent/article/2009/01/30/AR2009013004045.html.

Farhi, P. (2014, August 7). Pundits drive the sports news industry, but women's
opinions are almost totally absent. *Washington Post*. Retrieved from https://ww
w.washingtonpost.com/wp-dyn/content/article/2009/01/30/AR2009013004045
.html.

Farred, G. (2000). Cool as the other side of the pillow: How ESPN's *SportsCenter* has
changed television sports talk. *Journal of Sport and Social Issues, 24*(2), 96–117.

Fortuna, C. (2015). Digital media literacy in a sports, popular culture, and literature course. *Journal of Media Literacy Education, 6*(3), 81–89.

Furdyk, B. (2020, February 20). The untold story of Robin Roberts. *The List.* Retrieved from https://www.thelist.com/189627/the-untold-truth-of-robin-roberts/.

Gainer, J. (2007). Social critique and pleasure: Critical media literacy with popular culture texts. *Language Arts, 85*(2), 106–111.

Gainer, J. (2010). Critical media literacy in middle school: Exploring the politics of representation. *Journal of Adolescent & Adult Literacy, 53*(5), 364–373.

Garland, K., & Mayer, M. (2012). Traditional language arts viewed through a media lens: Helping secondary students develop critical literacy with media literacy education. *Counterpoints, 425,* 207–222. Retrieved from www.jstor.org/stable/42981799.

Glanville, D. (2017, July 29). Who gets to call the game? *New York Times.* Retrieved from https://www.nytimes.com/2017/07/29/opinion/sunday/jessica-mendoza-baseball-espn.html.

Glasspiegel, R. (2015, October 7). Here's the Twitter rant about ESPN's Jessica Mendoza that got an Atlanta radio host suspended. *The Big Lead.* Retrieved from https://thebiglead.com/2015/10/07/mike-bell-jessica-mendoza-twitter-suspended/.

Gordon, A. (2014, July 17). The plight of the sideline reporter. *Sports on Earth.* Retrieved from http://www.sportsonearth.com/article/84942428/female-sideline-reporters-erin-andrews-pam-oliver-held-back-by-biases-restrictions.

Gregory, S. (2018, November 15). NBA Analyst Doris Burke is blazing a trail in sportscasting. *TIME.* Retrieved from https://time.com/5455510/doris-burke-basketball-sportscasting/.

Grubb, M. V., & Billiot, T. (2010). Women sportscasters: Navigating a masculine domain. *Journal of Gender Studies, 19*(1), 87–93.

Gunther, A., Kautz, D., & Roth, A. (2011). The credibility of female sports broadcasters: The perception of gender in a male-dominated profession. *Human Communication, 14*(2), 71–84.

Guthrie, M. (2013, August 14). Female sports reporters Erin Andrews and Hannah Storm on rampant sexism and fashion faux pas. *The Hollywood Reporter.* Retrieved from https://www.hollywoodreporter.com/news/erin-andrews-hannah-storm-rampant-604915.

Guthrie, M. (2018, June 20). ESPN's internal political divide: Bristol traditions vs. "woke" reformers. *The Hollywood Reporter.* Retrieved from https://www.hollywoodreporter.com/features/espns-internal-political-divide-bristol-tradition-woke-reformers-1121634.

Halper, D. (2014). *Invisible Stars: A Social History of Women in American Broadcasting* (2nd ed.). New York, NY: Routledge.

Harden, M., & Shain, S. (2005). Female sports journalists: Are we there yet? 'No' *Newspaper Research Journal, 26*(4), 22–35.

Harden, M., & Shain, S. (2006). "Feeling much smaller than you know you are": The fragmented professional identity of female sports journalists. *Critical Studies in Media Communication, 23*(4), 322–338.

Harden, M., Genovese, J., & Yu, N. (2009). Privileged to be on camera: Sports broadcasters assess the role of social identity in the profession. *Electronic News, 3*(2), 80–93.

Harrison, G., Pegoraro, A., Romney, M., & Hull, K. (2019). The "Angry Black Woman": How race, gender, and American politics influenced user discourse surrounding the Jemele Hill controversy. *Howard Journal of Communications, 31*(2), 137–149.

Henderson, N. M. (2014, July 15). Did Fox's NFL sideline reporter Pam Oliver get demoted because she's too old for TV? *Washington Post*. Retrieved from https ://www.washingtonpost.com/blogs/she-the-people/wp/2014/07/15/did-foxs-nfl-s ideline-reporter-pam-oliver-get-demoted-because-shes-too-old-for-tv/.

Hobbs, R., & Jensen, A. (2009). The past, present, and future of media literacy education. *Journal of Media Literacy Education, 1*(1), 1–11.

Hofheimer, B. (2020, June 30). ESPN to relaunch *NFL Live* in August with new host Laura Rutledge and analysts Marcus Spears, Dan Orlovsky, Mina Kimes and Keyshawn Johnson. *ESPN Press Room*. Retrieved from https://espnpressroom.com /us/press-releases/2020/06/espn-to-relaunch-nfl-live-in-august-with-new-host-lau ra-rutledge-and-analysts-marcus-spears-dan-orlovsky-mina-kimes-and-keyshawn -johnson/.

Houston, W. (2008, December 19). Looks first, knowledge later. *The Globe and Mail*. Retrieved from https://www.theglobeandmail.com/sports/looks-first-knowledge -later/article20391253/.

Jacobs, J. (2016, February 19). Lead story (teller) on "SportsCenter" is Linda Cohn. *Hartford Courant*. Retrieved from https://www.courant.com/sports/hc-jacobs-col-linda-cohn-0218-20160217-column.html.

Jewkes, R., Morrell, R., Hearn, J., Lundqvist, E., Blackbeard, D., Lindegger, . . . Gottzén, L. (2015). Hegemonic masculinity: Combining theory and practice in gender interventions. *Culture, Health & Sexuality, 17*(sup2), 112–127.

Jolls, T., & Wilson, C. (2014). The core concepts: Fundamental to media literacy yesterday, today and tomorrow. *Journal of Media Literacy Education, 6*(2), 68–78.

Just Not Sports. [Just Not Sports]. (2016). #MoreThanMean - Women in sports 'face' harassment [Video file]. Retrieved from https://www.youtube.com/watch?v=9tU -D-m2JY8.

Keeley, S. (2016, January 29). Linda Cohn set to anchor record 5,000th *SportsCenter* on February 21. *Awful Announcing*. Retrieved from https://awfulannouncing.com /2016/linda-cohn-set-to-anchor-record-5000th-sportscenter-on-february-21.html

Kellner, D. (1995). *Media Culture: Cultural Studies, Identity and Politics between the Modern and the Post-modern*. New York, NY: Routledge.

Kellner, D. & Share, J. (2005). Toward critical media literacy: Core concepts, debates, organizations, and policy. *Discourse: Studies in the Cultural Politics of Education, 26*(3), 369–386.

Kellner, D. & Share, J. (2019). *The Critical Media Literacy Guide: Engaging Media and Transforming Education*. Boston, MA: Brill Sense.

Knight, M. (2017, June 5). Rachel Nichols is one of the sports world's few female voices—But that's not why she's a game-changer. It's because she's not afraid to ask the tough questions. *Marie Claire.* Retrieved from https://www.marieclaire.c om/culture/interviews/a27458/rachel-nichols-espn-the-jump-show/.

Kuiper, B. (2015). Women and sportscasting: A different kind of ballgame. *Pro Rege, 44*(1), 18–28.

Lee, A. (2012, May 16). 25 greatest SportsCenter anchors in ESPN history. *Bleacher Report.* Retrieved from https://bleacherreport.com/articles/1184115-25-greatest -sportscenter-anchors-in-espn-history.

Lin, T. B., Li, J. Y., Deng, F., & Lee, L. (2013). Understanding new media literacy: An explorative theoretical framework. *Educational Technology & Society 16*(4), 160–170.

Macur, J. (2017, March 10). Another woman at the March Madness mike? That only took 2 decades. *New York Times.* Retrieved from https://www.nytimes.com/2017 /03/10/sports/ncaabasketball/another-woman-at-the-march-madness-mike-that-onl y-took-2-decades.html.

Maney, B. (2017, February 2). Gender quality in sports reporting is still a Hail Mary. *Mediafile.* Retrieved from http://www.mediafiledc.com/gender-equality-sports- broadcasting-still-hail-mary/.

Markovits, A. S., & Albertson, E. (2012). Sportista I: Professional women in the con- tested space of sports media. In A. S. Markovits & E. Albertson (Eds.), *Sportista: Female Fandom in the United States* (pp. 167–200). Philadelphia PA: Temple University Press.

Mead, D. (2010, August 21). Twelve women who pioneered the era of female sports broadcasters. *Bleacher Report.* Retrieved from https://bleacherreport.com /articles/440556-twelve-women-who-pioneered-the-era-of-female-sports-broad casters.

Mettler, K. (2016, April 28). The disgustingly obscene "everyday" harassment of sports media women: A lesson for men. *Washington Post.* Retrieved from https ://www.washingtonpost.com/news/morning-mix/wp/2016/04/28/morethanmean-a -graphic-lesson-for-men-in-the-everyday-harassment-of-women-in-sports-media/.

Miller, J. A. (2018, October 1). Jemele Hill waves goodbye to ESPN and hello to "places where discomfort is OK." *The Hollywood Reporter.* Retrieved from https ://www.hollywoodreporter.com/news/jemele-hill-interview-leaving-espn-joining -atlantic-1148171.

Mudrick, M., & Lin, C. A. (2017). Looking on from the sideline: Perceived role congruity of women sports journalists. *Journal of Sports Media, 12*(2), 79–101.

Mudrick, M., Burton, L., & Lin, C. A. (2016). Pervasively offside: An examination of sexism, stereotypes, and sportscaster credibility. *Communication and Sport, 5*(6), 669–688. doi: 10.1177/2167479516670642.

O'Shaughnessy, H. (2017, June 9). Breaking into the booth. *The Ringer.* Retrieved from https://www.theringer.com/2017/6/9/16038476/nba-announcing-doris-burke -rosalyn-gold-onwude-f1080dfa68c4.

Payne, M. (2016, June 29). Cavemen on Twitter pout about all-female panel on ESPN's "First Take." *Washington Post.* Retrieved from https://www.washingt

onpost.com/news/early-lead/wp/2016/06/29/cavemen-on-twitter-pout-about-all-female-panel-on-espns-first-take/.

Penrice, R. R. (2017, February 6). Jemele Hill and Michael Smith are taking over *SportsCenter*, and somewhere, Stuart Scott is smiling. *The Root*. Retrieved from https://www.theroot.com/jemele-hill-and-michael-smith-are-taking-over-sport scen-1792022949?rev=1486398677767.

Rahimi, L. (2018, May 1). Baseball Night conversation: Play-by-play announcer Jenny Cavnar. *NBC Sports*. Retrieved from https://www.nbcsports.com/chicago/c ubs/baseball-night-conversation-play-play-announcer-jenny-cavnar.

Redmond, T. (2012). The pedagogy of critical enjoyment: Teaching and reaching the hearts and minds of adolescent learners through media literacy education. *Journal of Media Literacy Education, 4*(2), 106–120.

Remnick, D. (2019, June 13). In praise of Doris Burke, basketball's best TV analyst. *New Yorker*. Retrieved from https://www.newyorker.com/culture/cultural-co mment/in-praise-of-doris-burke-basketballs-best-tv-analyst.

Robertson, J. (2012, December 12). The 25 hottest sideline reporters right now. *Complex*. Retrieved from https://www.complex.com/sports/2012/12/the-25-hottest -sideline-reporters-right-now/.

Ruiz, M. (2019, March 16). The real March Madness: Why are women always on the sidelines of sports reporting? *Vogue*. Retrieved from https://www.vogue.com/art icle/march-madness-women-sideline-reporters.

Ryan, J. (2001, January 16). A woman's place. *Village Voice*. Retrieved from https://www.villagevoice.com/2001/01/16/a-womans-place/.

Sandomir, R. (2015, August 27). Jessica Mendoza to replace Curt Schilling for ESPN broadcast. *New York Times*. Retrieved from https://www.nytimes.com/2015/08/28/ sports/baseball/jessica-mendoza-to-replace-curt-schilling-for-espn-broadcast.html.

Scheiber, N. (2018, April 28). Doris Burke has game. *New York Times*. Retrieved from https://www.nytimes.com/2018/04/28/business/doris-burke-nba.html.

Sheffer, M. L., & Schultz, B. (2007). Double standard: Why women have trouble getting jobs in local television sports. *Journal of Sports Media, 2*(1), 79–104.

Seelow, D. (2017). *The Rhetorical Power of Popular Culture: Considering Mediated Texts* (3rd ed.). Thousand Oaks, CA: Sage.

Serazio, M. (2019a, June 13). Female sports journalists still face rampant sexism on the job. *The Conversation*. Retrieved from https://theconversation.com/i-still-get-tweets-to-go-back-in-the-kitchen-the-enduring-power-of-sexism-in-sports-media -116795.

Serazio, M. (2019b). *The Power of Sports: Media and Spectacle in American Culture*. New York, NY: New York University Press.

Strupp, J. (2015, September 1). Trailblazing female sports journalists want an end to the TV booth mancave. *Media Matters for America*. Retrieved from https://www .mediamatters.org/new-york-times/trailblazing-female-sports-journalists-want-end -tv-booth-mancave.

The Hollywood Reporter. [The Hollywood Reporter]. (2013, August 14). Fox Sports' Erin Andrews, Charissa Thompson cut loose [Video file]. Retrieved from https:// www.youtube.com/watch?v=Xw8o8UFDsVU.

Vasquez, V. M., Janks, H., & Comber, B. (2019). Critical literacy as a way of being and doing. *Language Arts, 96*(5), 300–311.

Weitzman, Y. (2017, December 22). Let's normalize this: Meet Sarah Kustok, the NBA's first solo female analyst. *Bleacher Report*. Retrieved from https://bleache rreport.com/articles/2749476-meet-sarah-kustok-the-nbas-1st-full-time-female-col or-commentator.

Wilder, C. (2019, March 13). Hire women as announcers in NFL booths. *Sports Illustrated*. Retrieved from https://www.si.com/media/2019/03/13/female-nfl-com mentators-hire-women-announcers-broadcast-booth.

Wolfman-Arent, A. (2011, August 13). Ranking the 10 best anchors in *SportsCenter* history. *Bleacher Report*. Retrieved from https://bleacherreport.com/articles/8041 72-ranking-the-10-best-anchors-in-sportscenter-history.

Yoder, M. (2016, February 18). The top 25 *SportsCenter* anchors of all-time. *Awful Announcing*. Retrieved from https://awfulannouncing.com/2016/the-top-25-sports center-anchors-of-all-time.html.

Zumoff, M., & Negin, M. (2017). *Total Sportscasting: Performance, Production, and Career Development*. New York, NY: Routledge.

Index

9/11, 27, 34, 35, 39

Abdul-Rauf, Mahmoud, 5
ableism, 95, 98, 109, 114, 122
advertising, 19, 28, 37–38, 130, 147,
    149, 152, 155, 157, 174, 179–80,
    183, 208
ageism, 192, 201, 208
Ali, Muhammad, 5, 17
Andrews, Erin, 201
audience, 2, 9–11, 16, 21, 28, 40–51,
    63–67, 71, 73–75, 77–78, 80–81, 84,
    86–89, 99–100, 116–17, 142, 145,
    147–51, 153–54, 156, 172–73, 184,
    192, 194, 197, 199, 205–6

Balboa, Rocky, 49
baseball, 1, 27–49, 54, 72, 76, 92, 136,
    149, 157, 182, 184, 202
basketball, 5, 54–55, 59, 61, 65, 72, 92,
    111, 130, 153–54, 159, 169, 174,
    182, 184, 202
bias, 2, 7, 9–11, 17, 19, 21, 28, 30, 51,
    87, 113, 153, 156, 164, 171, 180,
    181, 207
Black Lives Matter (BLM), 149, 178,
    182
Boldin, Anquan, 19–20
Bowers, Katie, 182–83

Brown, Michael, 6
Burke, Doris, 182, 205–7
Bush, George W., 34–35

Carlos, John, 5–6
Castile, Philandro, 6
Cavnar, Jenny, 204–5
CBS, 65, 173, 191, 195
Chastain, Jane, 195–96, 203
cinematic techniques, 50–51, 54, 58, 72,
    99, 106, 118, 150–51
Civil War, 27
coach, 1–2, 18, 49–67, 72, 95, 102, 111,
    149–51, 153, 154, 159, 160, 164,
    177, 178, 180, 182–84, 191, 195,
    200, 202, 205, 208
Coffee, Glen, 14
Cohn, Linda, 191, 196–97
color commentary, 151–53, 202
counternarratives, 2, 10, 12, 13, 20, 127,
    133–37, 139, 192, 207
critical consumer, 71, 73, 77, 192
critical lens, 84, 184
critical literacy pedagogy (CLP),
    7–9
critical media literacy (CML), 1–2,
    7–13, 17, 19–22, 27–30, 32, 34–35,
    38–40, 50–51, 54, 63, 70–71, 85–87,
    89–90, 126, 139, 150–51, 165, 171,

About the Contributors

Crystal L. Beach, PhD, is a high school ELA teacher and basketball coach in the Appalachian Mountains of Northeast Georgia. As a former D1 athlete, she understands the importance of positive female athletic role models for young women. Her scholarly research focuses on literacies, identity, multimodalities, and popular culture.

Richard Beach, PhD, is professor emeritus of Literacy Education, University of Minnesota. His research focuses on adolescents' use of language to enact relations with others. He is coauthor of *Teaching Language as Action in the ELA Classroom* (http://languaging.pbworks.com) and *Teaching Climate Change to Adolescents: Reading, Writing, and Making a Difference* (http://climatechangeela.pbworks.com).

Alan Brown, PhD, is associate professor of English Education and Bryant/Groves Faculty Fellow in the Department of Education at Wake Forest University. He teaches and researches topics at the intersections of sports culture, contemporary literacies, arts and movement, educational leadership, English methods, and young adult literature.

Limarys Caraballo, PhD, is associate professor of Urban and English Education at CUNY Queens College and Graduate Center. She cofounded and codirects Cyphers for Justice, a youth-engaged research program that supports intergenerational participatory inquiry. Her research reframes deficit discourses about minoritized youth by amplifying their multiple voices, literacies, and identities.

Katie Shepherd Dredger, PhD, is associate professor and the academic unit head for the Middle, Secondary, and Mathematics Education Department in the College of Education at James Madison University in Harrisonburg, VA. A former secondary English teacher and coach, she examines intersections of theory and practice in today's classrooms.

Mark A. Fabrizi, PhD (University of Hull, U.K.), is an associate professor of Secondary English Education at Eastern Connecticut State University and an eighteen-year veteran high school English teacher. He has edited two scholarly texts examining the development of critical literacy skills through fantasy literature (Sense Pub) and horror (Brill Pub).

Katherin Garland, PhD, is assistant professor of Education at Santa Fe College. Her research is centered on preservice and practicing teachers' uses of media literacy education and critical media literacy pedagogy. To this end, her publications are focused on theory-to-practice methods for preparing students to be critical media readers.

Cathy Leogrande, PhD, is a teacher education professor at Le Moyne College, a Jesuit college in Syracuse, New York. Her teaching and research focus is on media literacy and popular culture to provide K-12 teachers skills to teach all students in inclusive classrooms and address issues of race, class, gender, and disability.

Mark A. Lewis, PhD, has over twenty-five publications, including multiple book chapters and in scholarly journals such as *English Education*, *Middle Grades Research Journal*, *Study & Scrutiny*, *Journal of Literacy Research*, and *Reading Research Quarterly*. He is also a coauthor of *Rethinking the "Adolescent" in Adolescent Literacy* (NCTE Press).

Cynthia Martin is an instructor in the School of Writing, Rhetoric and Technical Communication at James Madison University, where she teaches courses in introduction to writing and rhetoric, professional editing, document design, and digital writing and rhetoric. Her research interests include the rhetoric of disease and digital writing pedagogy.

Ewa McGrail, PhD, is associate professor of Language and Literacy at Georgia State University. She examines literacy, digital writing, and new media composition; copyright and the media; and disability representation in the media and popular culture. Her research also explores young adult literature that features diversity and inclusion.

J. Patrick McGrail, PhD, is associate professor and department head of Communication at Jacksonville State University. He teaches news, media literacy, and video and film studies. Dr. McGrail has also worked as an actor and director. He has research programs in copyright, media literacy, and disability representation in the media.

Alicja Rieger, PhD, is professor of Special Education at Valdosta State University. Her scholarship focuses on inclusion, humor in families that have a member with a disability, as well as second language acquisition and culturally responsive teaching. Most recently, she has been honored with VSU's Presidential Excellence Award in Research.

Luke Rodesiler, PhD, is associate professor of Education and Coordinator of Secondary Education in the School of Education at Purdue University Fort Wayne. His scholarly interests include the critical study of sports and society in the English language arts classroom, nontraditional forms of teacher professional development, and media literacy education.

Brian Sheehy is the History Department Coordinator at North Andover High School in North Andover, MA, where he teaches AP European History, Sports of the Past, and Sports in American Culture. He is the winner of the 2020 Organization of American Historians, Mary K. Bonsteel Tachau Teacher of the Year Award and the winner of the Williams College: Olmstead Secondary Teacher of the Year Award.

www.ingramcontent.com/pod-product-compliance
Lightning Source LLC
Chambersburg PA
CBHW050643280326

41932CB00015B/2759